Catholic Apologetics: Witnessing to and Defending the Faith

Fr. Peter Samuel Kucer, MSA

En Route Books and Media, LLC
5705 Rhodes Avenue
St. Louis, MO 63109

Cover credit: TJ Burdick

Copyright © 2018 Peter Samuel Kucer

All rights reserved.

ISBN-10:0-9994704-6-9
ISBN-13: 978-0-9994704-6-6

Library of Congress Control Number: 2017956391

DEDICATION

In memory of my mother, Roberta Kucer, who instilled in me a love of study and a love of her people, the chosen people.

In addition, I dedicate this book to the members of my community, the Missionaries of the Holy Apostles.

ACKNOWLEDGMENTS

I would particularly like to acknowledge Fr. Isaac Martinez, MSA, former General of the Missionaries of the Holy Apostles, who gave me permission to publish.

I would also like to acknowledge Bishop Christian Rodembourg, MSA, who as the first Missionary of the Holy Apostles to be ordained a bishop brought our charism into a deeper ecclesial dimension.

Special thanks also to Dr. Sebastian Mahfood, OP, president of En Route Books and Media, for publishing this work.

CONTENTS

Chapter One: Effective Apologetics..................1
Prayers for the Apologist......................................1
Qualities of an Apologist 4
Practical Steps in Doing Apologetics Well 8
Evangelization Tips 14
Knowing Why Potential Converts are not Catholic...26
Excuses for not Evangelizing............................. 27
Quiz 1 29
Additional Activities and Resources 30

Chapter Two: Arguing Effectively..................33
Terms, Propositions and Arguments 34
Faith and Reason..35
Scripture, History and Non-Rational Arguments 45
Quiz 2 55
Additional Activities and Resources 56

Chapter Three: God's Existence..................... 59
Five Ways of Aquinas 60

Additional Ways from the Physical World 67
Contingency, the Kalam argument, the World as an Interacting Whole 68
Miracles 69
Ways from the Human Person 73
Human Intelligence and the True 73
Sense of Morality and the Good 76
Desire for the Infinite 77
Pascal's Wager 78
Quiz 3 81
Additional Activities and Resources 82

Chapter Four: Objections of Atheists 85
Evil 85
Athiestic non-God Standards of Goodness 86
The "Unjust" Distribution of Evil 92
Atheistic World View 98
Miracles 102
Atheism and Foolishness 105
Compassion for Atheists 107
Quiz 4 112
Additional Activities and Resources 113

Chapter Five: Faith and Science 115
The Galileo Affair 115
The Scientific Method 121
Evolution 124
Modern Physics: Gravity and a Multi-Universe 128
Chance 133
Human Intelligence, Animal Intelligence and Computer Intelligence 141

Quiz 5.. 146
Additional Activities and Resources 147

Chapter Six: Divinity and Resurrection of Christ 151
Who Christ Identified Himself As..................... 151
Reasonableness of Christ's Claim to Divinity ..155
Christ's Resurrection.. 160
Quiz 6 165
Additional Activities and Resources 166

Chapter Seven: *Sola Scriptura*, *Traditio*, Magisterium... 169
Definition of *Sola Scriptura*............................. 169
Catholic Response to *Sola Scriptura* 171
Sola Scriptura is Unhistorical..........................176
Sola Scriptura is Unbiblical 181
Sola Scriptura is Unworkable 185
Protestants do not in Practice or Follow *Sola Scriptura*...187
The Catholic Church's Historical Relationship to Scripture... 189
Quiz 7..191
Additional Activities and Resources 191

Chapter Eight: The Eucharist 195
Catholic Eucharistic Belief 196
Protestant Objections to Catholic Eucharistic Theology...204
Quiz 8 214
Additional Activities and Resources 216

Chapter Nine: The Papacy 219
　Objections to the Papacy 219
　Objection 1: Peter Was Never A Pope 219
　Objection 2: The Original Greek New Testament Language Indicates that Jesus Did Not Build His Church on Peter as a Rock 221
　Objection 3 – That Jesus Called Peter "Satan" in Matthew 16:23 Indicates that Jesus Never Intended to Make Peter the First Pope 223
　Objection 4 – Peter's False Teaching That Paul Rebuked Him for in Galatians 2:11-14 Indicate That Neither Peter Nor His Supposed Successors Are Infallible 224
　Objection 5 – According to Scripture, Peter Did Not Pass Down His Authority to Anyone Else - Apostolic Succession, Therefore, Is a False Teaching 227
　Objection 6 Since the Roman Numerals of the Pope's Official Latin Title of *Vicarious Filii Dei* Adds Up to 666, the Pope Is the Anti-Christ .. 230
　Objection 7 According to Revelations 17:9 The Whore Of Babylon Is Situated on Seven Hills - Since Rome Has Seven Hills, The Catholic Church Is the Whore of Babylon 230
　Objection 8 Since Scripture Does Not Ever State That Peter Ever in Rome He Could Not Have Been the First Bishop of Rome 231
　Objection 9 The Modern Papacy is Invalid Since It Directly Contradicts the Simple Life of Peter 232
　Objection 10 The Papacy was Invented During Medieval Times 232

Objection 11 Early Christians Only Saw Rome as First Among Equals 233
Objection 12 The Numerous Bad Popes Is Proof that the Papacy was Never Intended by Christ 234
Objection 13 Papal Infallibility is False Since Not Only Did Popes Live Bad Lives but They Also Taught Falsehood 234
Objection 14 The Action of Pope Liberius (352-366) Signing an Arian Creed Contradicts Papal Infallibility 237
Objection 15 The Action of Pope Vigilius (r. 537-555) Approving the Monophysite Heresy Directly Contradicts Papal Infallibility.......................... 238
Objection 16 Pope Gregory the Great's Rejection of the Title Universal Bishop is Proof that the Early Church Did Not See the Recognize the Papacy as Having Juridical Authority Over Other Bishops... 239
Objection 17 The Condemnation of Pope Honorius (r. 625-638) as a Heretic by the Third Council of Constantinople (680-681) Indicates that Popes are not Infallible 240
Objection 18 If the Papacy was Instituted by Christ as a Principle of Ecclesial Unity, Then Why During the Middle Ages Did Three Men Claim to be Popes?... 241
Objection 19 Pope Joan, Who Gave Birth to a Child as Pope Before, Being Killed by an Angry Mob Further Discredits the Papacy 242
Objection 20 The Papal Condemnation of Galileo Discredits the Infallibility of the Papacy 244

Objection 21 During the Crusades Popes Encouraged the Murdered Millions of Innocent, Peaceful Muslims 244
Objection 22 Acting as a Mere Worldly Leader, in Pride Pope Alexander VI Divided up the New World Between Portugal and Spain 245
Objection 23 Proof of Papal Depravity is Their Long-Standing Support of Slavery 247
Objection 24 Pope Sixtus IV Began and Oversaw the Spanish Inquisition Under Which Thousands of Muslims and Jewish People Were Tortured and Murdered 249
Objection 25 Pope Sixtus V Ordered the Publication of an Error Filled Latin Vulgate Bible 251
Objection 26 Matthew 16 Neither Teaches Papal Succession nor Papal Infallibility and yet Vatican Council I (1870) Refers to This Passage When Defining Papal Infallibility 251
Objection 27 At Vatican Council I the Prominent Bishop Joseph Strossmayer Rejected Papal Infallibility 254
Objection 28 There Hasn't Been a Valid Pope Since Pope Pius XII 254
Objection 29 Appealing to Scripture and to the Fathers of the Church to Defend the Papacy is Anachronistic 255
Objection 30 Because Pope Pius XII Cowardly Refused to Denounce Hitler He is Responsible for the Murder of Millions 256
Quiz 9 261

Additional Activities and Resources 264

Chapter Ten: The Communion of Saints and the Blessed Virgin Mary 265
   Objections to the Communion of Saints 266
   Catholic Devotion to Saints Is Not Idolatrous 268
   Catholic Marian Doctrine 279
    Immaculate Conception 279
    Perpetual Virginity 281
    Mother of God 285
    Assumption 287
   Quiz 10 288
   Additional Activities and Resources 289
    Readings 291
    Audio 291

Chapter Eleven: Mormonism 293
   The Great Apostasy 293
   Eternal Progression 298
   Extra-Biblical Public Revelation 302
   Recent Developments in Mormonism 308
   Quiz 11 312
   Additional Activities and Resources 313
    Readings 313
    Audio 314

Chapter Twelve: Hinduism, Buddhism, Islam 315
   Hinduism 315
   Buddhism 318
   Islam 325
   Quiz 12 336

Additional Activities and Resources.................... 337

Chapter One: Effective Apologetics

Introduction

Before we begin studying what an apologist needs to know, we will reflect on the qualities an apologist needs before, during and after witnessing to the truths of our Catholic faith. We will begin with a selection of prayers that aid in the development of virtues necessary to do apologetics well. This will be followed by sections that describe effective, humble ways of evangelizing. The chapter will conclude with a discussion on why people resist converting and why we resist evangelizing.

Prayers for the Apologist

The following are a selection of prayers that students of apologetics may wish to pray before and after engaging in apologetics.

Grant, O Lord, that none may love Thee less

this day because of me; that never a word or act of mine may turn one soul from Thee; and, ever daring, yet one more grace would I implore, that many souls this day, because of me, may love Thee more. Amen.[1]

Prayer to the Holy Spirit – Attributed to St. Augustine

Breathe into me, Holy Spirit, that my thoughts may all be holy. Move in me, Holy Spirit, that my work, too, may be holy. Attract my heart, Holy Spirit, that I may love only what is holy. Strengthen me, Holy Spirit that I may defend all that is holy. Protect me, Holy Spirit, that I may always be holy.[2]

St. Michael Prayer

Saint Michael the Archangel, defend us in battle. Be our protection against the wickedness and snares of the devil. May God rebuke him, we humbly pray; and do Thou, O Prince of the Heavenly Host - by the Divine Power of God - cast into hell, Satan and all the evil spirits, who roam

---

[1] Patrick Madrid, *A Pocket Guide to Catholic Apologetics* (Huntington: Our Sunday Visitor, 2006), 56.

[2] "Prayer to the Holy Spirit #2 - Prayer of St. Augustine," Catholic Online (accessed December 13, 2014).

throughout the world seeking the ruin of souls.

Prayer attributed to St. Teresa of Avila

Lord, grant that I may always allow myself to be guided by you, always follow your plans, and perfectly accomplish Your Holy Will. Grant that in all things, great and small, today and all the days of my life, I may do whatever you require of me. Help me respond to the slightest prompting of Your Grace, so that I may be your trustworthy instrument for your honor. May Your Will be done in time and in eternity by me, in me, and through me.[3]

Prayer of St. Thomas á Kempis

God, our Father, we are exceedingly frail and indisposed to every virtuous and gallant undertaking. Strengthen our weakness, we beseech you that we may do valiantly in this spiritual war; help us against our own negligence and cowardice, and defend us from the treachery of our unfaithful hearts, for Jesus Christ's sake.[4]

---

[3] Patrick Madrid, *Search and Rescue* (Manchester: Sophia Institute Press, 2001), 160.

[4] Madrid, *Search*, 183.

Prayer of Patience

Oh my God, henceforth I resolve to strive earnestly to be patient and gentle, and not to allow the waters of contradiction to extinguish the fire of that charity that I owe to my neighbor.[5]

The Grail Prayer

Lord Jesus, I give you my hands to do your work. I give you my feet to go your way. I give you my eyes to see as you do. I give you my tongue to speak your words. I give you my mind that you may think in me. I give you my spirit that you may pray in me. I give you my whole self that you may grow in me so that it is you Lord Jesus who live and work and pray in me.[6]

Qualities of an Apologist

St. Paul in his letter to the Galatians identifies Christian qualities. These qualities are essential in order to defend the Catholic faith in a loving manner. The qualities are being loving, joyful, peaceful, patient, kind, generous, faithful, gentle and having self-control. (Galatians 5:22-23) A few opposite qualities that St. Paul enumerates are being envious, jealous and quarrelsome. (Galatians 5:19-

---

[5] Madrid, *Search*, 206.
[6] Madrid, *Search*, 223

21) Simply because we are defending the truths of our faith does not gives us sufficient reason to do so in a quarrelsome, angry manner which might even be tinged by a desire to conquer another individual not for Christ's sake but so that the individual apologist can brag about whom he has brought into the faith. May we not fall for the temptation, as Fr. Eusebe Menard warns us, of doing "God's work with rich, flashy or violent means."[7] If we do fall into this temptation, we will be using anti-gospel means for the good end of defending the faith.

The *Catechism of the Catholic Church* clearly teaches that "A good intention (for example, that of helping one's neighbor) does not make behavior that is intrinsically disordered, such as lying and calumny, good or just. The end does not justify the means. Thus, the condemnation of an innocent person cannot be justified as a legitimate means of saving the nation. On the other hand, an added bad intention (such as vainglory) makes an act evil that, in and of itself, can be good (such as almsgiving)."[8] As applied to apologetics, seeking to bring about the conversion of another for vain self-glorification in order to boast before others, as one may do after shooting a big game animal and mounting the head of the animal on a wall, is disordered. This does not

---

[7] Eusebe M. Menard, *At All Times, In Every Age*, trans. Paul Schwartz (Chicago: Franciscan Herald Press, 1977), 42.

[8] "Catechism of the Catholic Church," Vatican.va, http://www.vatican.va/archive/ccc_css/archive/catechism/p3s1c1a4.htm (accessed April 4, 2016), No. 1753.

mean that displaying pictures of recent converts we helped to bring into the faith is necessarily disordered. It is disordered, and hence sinful, when these public actions become our primary motive for engaging in apologetics.

A saint who was consistently patient and kind when presenting the truths of our faith in order for people to know Jesus Christ was St. Francis de Sales. In a number of his books, the well-known modern-day apologist Patrick Madrid encourages us to learn from St. Francis de Sales in order to be effective apologists. A virtue Madrid, following the example of St. Francis de Sales, consistently teaches his fellow apologists to grow in is patience. With reference to Hebrews 10:36 and Luke 31:19, St. Francis de Sales wrote, "The greatest happiness of any one is, 'to possess his soul;' and the more perfect our patience, the more fully we do so possess our souls."[9] As a patient man, St. Francis de Sales persevered in prayer and in his mission to Protestants living in Calvinistic, Geneva, Switzerland. There, St. Francis de Sales persevered with creativity.

One creative way he evangelized the Calvinists was by writing apologetic tracts, printing them in bulk quantities and distributing them personally or by sliding them under doors. His patient perseverance paid off. By 1622, the year he was born into eternal life, around 60,000 Protestants living in the region that St. Francis de Sales was

---

[9] Francis de Sales, *Introduction to the Devout Life* (Kindle E-Book: Catholic Way Publishing, 2015), 101.

evangelizing had converted to the Catholic Faith.[10] During moments when we are tempted to be impatient with those we are trying to evangelize may we go to the Lord in prayer for apart from Jesus we can do nothing. (John 15:5)

Below is a simple table that contrasts qualities of an effective apologist who defends truth in a loving manner with apologists in whom the truth they are defending is not formed by love. The chart is based on Madrid's vast experience as an apologist.

What an Effective Apologist Is and What an Effective Apologist Is Not

Is	**Is not**
• Faith Filled	• Weak in Faith
• Knowledgeable	• Makes up answers on the spot and hopes for the best.
• Humble Willing to say "I do not know. Allow me time to find the answer,"[11]	• A know it all.
• Prays and Relies on the Holy Spirit	• Preoccupied with his own thoughts.
• Self-Deprecatory Humor[12]	• Mocks others Laughs at others at

---

[10] Patrick Madrid, *On a Mission: Lessons from St. Francis de Sales* (Cincinnati: Servant Books, 2013), 10.

[11] Patrick Madrid, *Envoy for Christ* (Cincinnati: Franciscan Media, 2012), viii.

Laughs at self and with others	their expense
• Argues out of other-centeredness with the goal to win both hearts and minds.[13]	• Argues out of self-centeredness with the goal of simply winning an argument.

Practical Steps in Doing Apologetics Well

In addition to explaining in both his books and his way of practicing apologetics the proper spiritual attitudes we are to live by, Madrid also offers very practical advice to apologists. In his audio "Winning Souls, Not Just Arguments," Madrid gives us six practical steps to follow in order to evangelize well.[14] These steps are enumerated below with commentary on each one.

1. <u>Know Scripture by Chapter and Verse</u>

Apologetics is about helping to remove obstacles that prevent someone from coming to faith. One important way to collaborate with God in this mission of salvation is by knowing Scripture, especially since Protestants focus on Scripture. Catholics know Scripture more than we realize, but often we only know Scripture by its general location and not by its proper address. In contrasting how

---

[12] Patrick Madrid, *Envoy,* ix.

[13] Patrick Madrid, *Envoy,* ix.

[14] Patrick Madrid and Curtis Martin, *Winning Souls Not Just Arguments*, 4 CDs (Patrick Madrid.com).

Protestants know the bible from how Catholics know the bible, Scott Hahn says, "They [Protestants] got the menu. We [Catholics] got the meal."[15] The meal Hahn is referring to is the Holy Sacrifice of the Mass which also is a sacred meal. Within the mass, Catholics repeatedly encounter Scripture.

Since the liturgy as Vatican Council II's document *Sacrosanctum Concilium* states is the source and summit from which and toward "which the activity of the Church is directed,"[16] the liturgy, above all the mass, is the most fitting context or home of Sacred Scripture. Within this liturgical context, Hahn reminds us that although a mail carrier may know all the addresses of houses in a

---

[15] Scott Hahn, *How to Make Sense Out of the Mass*, CD (St. Joseph Communications, 2005).

[16] "Sacrosanctum Concilium," Vatican.va, http://www.vatican.va/archive/hist_councils/ii_vatican_council/documents/vat-ii_const_19631204_sacrosanctum-concilium_en.html (accessed April 5, 2016). "10. Nevertheless the liturgy is the summit toward which the activity of the Church is directed; at the same time it is the font from which all her power flows. For the aim and object of apostolic works is that all who are made sons of God by faith and baptism should come together to praise God in the midst of His Church, to take part in the sacrifice, and to eat the Lord's supper. 14. ... In the restoration and promotion of the sacred liturgy, this full and active participation by all the people is the aim to be considered before all else; for it is the primary and indispensable source from which the faithful are to derive the true Christian spirit; and therefore pastors of souls must zealously strive to achieve it, by means of the necessary instruction, in all their pastoral work."

certain town, he may not really know them if he doesn't know any of them as homes. A child living in one of the homes, which the mail carrier knows the address of, may forget the address of his house but knows his home better than the mail carrier since the child knows it personally.[17] With that said, if we want to help Protestants who place great value in memorizing chapter and verses of Scripture, it is important for us as well to begin memorizing scripture passages. As long as we memorize scripture with the aim of glorifying God and loving our neighbor and not in order to vainly display our knowledge, the time spent in memorizing scripture will also help us to grow spiritually.

2. Know What the Catholic Church Actually Teaches

We need to know the doctrines of our faith in an accurate manner, such as good works in relationship to salvation. Catholicism does not teach that we earn our way to salvation. We hold as Catholics that salvation is not a result of works. Rather, salvation is a gift that we receive, cooperate with and express by good works. St. Paul clearly stresses that salvation is a gift in his Letter to the Ephesians, "For it is by grace you have been saved, through faith – and this is not from yourselves, is the gift of God— not by works, so that no one can boast. For we are God's handiwork, created in Christ Jesus to

---

[17] Scott Hahn, *How to Make Sense Out of the Mass*, CD (St. Joseph Communications, 2005).

do good works, which God prepared in advance for us to do." (NRSV Ephesians 2:8-10)

3. Bring Back the Faith in its Fullness on Catholic College Campuses

According to converts from Evangelicalism to Catholicism, explains Madrid, one of the most common obstacle they encountered when deciding on converting are ignorant Catholics who are not filled with faith. Many Evangelicals also know of countless cases of Catholic youth going to Catholic colleges and while there ceasing to believe. Correlation, of course, does not necessarily indicate causation. However, the correlation just mentioned to which Protestants sometimes direct our attention may indicate some degree of causation.

4. Love Christ

Catholics who are filled with faith and have a deep love for Christ will be more effective instruments in helping people to embrace Catholicism. In reference to a loving friendship with Christ, the Catholic Scripture scholar Brant Pitre points out the New Testament never refers to a personal relationship with Jesus Christ. This is never explicitly mentioned. Instead, Scripture encourages us to develop a spousal relationship with God as the Catechism says, "The entire Christian life bears the mark of the spousal love of Christ and the Church. Already Baptism, the entry into the People of God, is a nuptial mystery; it is so to speak the nuptial bath which precedes the wedding feast, the Eucharist..."[18] (CCC 1617) In other words, Scripture offers us a reality far better than just a personal friendship, which can contain many types. Revelation offers the best personal relationship that is analogously like the intimacy between a husband and a wife. True intimacy of a marriage demands sacrifice in a way that a personal relationship between a teacher and student, or with the mail carrier does not necessarily demand. We have a personal relationship with Jesus Christ but also something much more since we are members of the bride of Christ, the Church who is wedded to Christ as one by His death on the cross.[19]

5. Acknowledge the Virtues of Non-Catholics

Many Protestants manifest a deep faith in Jesus Christ, love Scripture and love truth. It is important for Catholics to acknowledge these stellar qualities within Protestantism since these three common characteristics can provide an excellent foundation for Catholicism to take root.

---

[18] "Catechism of the Catholic Church," Vatican.va, http://www.vatican.va/archive/ENG0015/__P51.HTM (accessed April 5, 2016).
[19] Brant Pitre, *Jesus the Bridegroom: The Divine Love Story in the Bible,* CD 1 of 20 (Catholic Productions).

6. Present our Faith in Christ's Eucharistic Presence While Anticipating that Our Belief in the Eucharist May Be Difficult for Non-Catholics to Accept

In John chapter six, Jesus teaches essential salvific truth to a large group of people. Notice that Jesus does not reject the Jewish objection that Jesus promised to offer his very flesh. He does precisely the opposite. He confirms their objection. In the original Greek, the verb that Jesus uses when saying "whoever eats my flesh" is τρώγων, which literally means to chew, or gnaw upon. This word is used when someone wants to graphically describe the physical activity of eating. The Greek word φάγητε, which John chapter six verse 56 does not use, also means eating but not in the graphic sense as τρώγων. Jesus, therefore, is presented in John's Gospel as wanting his words on eating his flesh to be literally understood. (It is important to keep in mind, though, that the flesh we eat in the Eucharist is the risen flesh of the Lord Jesus.[20]) After hearing

---

[20] "1392 What material food produces in our bodily life, Holy Communion wonderfully achieves in our spiritual life. Communion with the flesh of the risen Christ, a flesh "given life and giving life through the Holy Spirit,"[229] preserves, increases, and renews the life of grace received at Baptism. This growth in Christian life needs the nourishment of Eucharistic Communion, the bread for our pilgrimage until the moment of death, when it will be given to us as viaticum." "Catechism of the Catholic Church," vatican.va, http://www.vatican.va/archive/ccc_css/archive/catechism/p2s2c1a3.htm (accessed April 25, 2016).

Jesus' clarification and agreement that he is indeed referring to his flesh, many of his disciples left him. (John 6:66) In commenting on this passage, Bishop Sheen comments that Christ's Eucharistic presence has been an obstacle for Catholics as well. Disrespectful behavior by Catholics to the Eucharist can indicate those who are on the road to leaving the faith.[21] May our faith in Christ's Eucharistic presence increase even if we witness many people turning away from the faith because of this teaching.

Evangelization Tips

In his *Search and Rescue* book, Madrid, relying on his vast experience as an apologist, details effective methods for evangelizing. Ten of them are listed below.

- Pray Before, During and After Evangelizing[22]

Archbishop Sheen used the example of a mole who once was able to see but no longer does since it has lived underground for so long. Similarly, Sheen explains, when we stop living above ground in the spiritual world that prayer offers to us we will lose our ability to see spiritually. Once we become blind

---

[21] Fulton Sheen, *Vintage Sheen*, Disc 11 of a 13 Disc Set, 16 Meditations (Ramsey, N.J.: Keep the Faith-Latin Mass Magazine).

[22] Patrick Madrid, *Search and Rescue* (Manchester: Sophia Institute Press, 2001), Location 344 of 2422.

to spiritual realities, we no longer recognize people as made in the image and likeness of God and then treat them as objects of use, as John Paul II warns against, and not as persons to be loved even if the lover no longer feels he or she is getting anything in return from the one they are loving.[23]

Dom Chautard in his spiritual classic *The Soul of the Apostolate* warns us from the "heresy of good works".[24] This "heresy" occurs when a Catholic becomes so busy in saving others that he stops praying. Sadly, writes Chautard, "these activistic heretics, for their part, imagine that they are giving greater glory to God in aiming above all at external results."[25] Instead of sacrificing prayer for the apostolate, asserts Chautard, "the life of action ought to flow from the contemplative life, to interpret and extend it, outside oneself, though at the same time being detached from it as little as possible."[26] At a retreat, directed in part by Chautard, a very active man, experienced a profound conversion when he admitted:

---

[23] Fulton Sheen, *Vintage Sheen*, Disc 4 or a13 Disc Set, 16 Meditations (Ramsey, N.J.: Keep the Faith-Latin Mass Magazine).

[24] Dom Jean-Baptiste Chautard, *The Soul of the Apostolate*, trans. A Monk of Our Lady of Gethsemani (Unidentified: Catholic Way Publishing, 2014), 26.

[25] Dom Jean-Baptiste Chautard, *The Soul of the Apostolate*, 26; Cf. Patrick Madrid, *On a Mission: Lessons from St. Francis De Sales* (Cincinnati: Servant Books, 2013), 32.

[26] Dom Jean-Baptiste Chautard, *The Soul of the Apostolate*, 69.

My self-sacrifice is what has ruined me! My nature and temperament make it a joy for me to spend myself, and a pleasure to serve. What with the apparent success of my enterprises, the devil has contrived, for long years, to make everything work together for my deception, stirring me up to furious activity, filling me with disgust for all interior life, and finally leading me over the edge of the abyss.[27]

- Find Common Ground[28]

Pope Francis in his Apostolic Exhortation *Joy of the Gospel* encourages Catholics to evangelize by first being willing to understand where those we are bringing the Good News to come from. Then, we are to affirm in their lives whatever is true and good. In so doing, we are building a bridge that spans from their experiences we affirm as good and true to the proper home of truth, goodness and beauty in the Catholic Church. In describing such an evangelizing community, Pope Francis writes, "An evangelizing community gets involved by word and deed in people's daily lives; it bridges distances, it is willing to abase itself if necessary, and it embraces human life, touching the suffering flesh of Christ in others. Evangelizers thus take on

---

[27] Dom Jean-Baptiste Chautard, *The Soul of the Apostolate*, 92.

[28] Patrick Madrid, *Search and Rescue*, Location 1141 of 2422.

the 'smell of the sheep' and the sheep are willing to hear their voice."[29]

Taking on the smell of the sheep includes, when called upon by God to do so, engaging in ecumenical dialogue. In describing authentic ecumenical dialogue, which begins from a common ground that the various sides agree upon, Madrid pithily states, "Authentic ecumenism (between Christians) is dialogue based on truth that leads to conversion."[30] This phrase of Patrick Madrid succinctly sums up the Church's teaching in St. Pope John Paul II's 1995 ecumenically-minded encyclical *Ut Unum Sint*. According to the encyclical, "The ultimate goal of the ecumenical movement is to re-establish full visible unity among all the baptized."[31]

---

[29] Pope Francis, "Joy of the Gospel," November 24, 2013, w2.vatican.va, http://w2.vatican.va/content/francesco/en/apost_exhortations/documents/papa-francesco_esortazione-ap_20131124_evangelii-gaudium.html (accessed April 10, 2016), 24.

[30] Patrick Madrid, "Prepare the Way Part I Discussions on Catholic Apologetics with Special Guest Patrick Madrid, Hosted by Martha Fernandez – Sardina", YouTube, https://youtu.be/NoxOfILoOEY (accessed April 24, 2016).

[31] John Paul II, *Ut Unum Sint*, 1995, no. 77, The Vatican, http://www.vatican.va/holy_father/john_paul_ii/encyclicals/documents/hf_jp-ii_enc_25051995_ut-unum-sint_en.html (accessed December 30, 2014).

- Appeal to Human Experience[32]

One way to connect with those we are evangelizing is by teaching the Catholic faith in a way that rings true to our shared common experience of life. Jesus repeatedly taught in this manner. One example is found in Luke chapter fourteen. Here, Jesus, before a crowd of people, states:

> For which of you, intending to build a tower, does not first sit down and estimate the cost, to see whether he has enough to complete it? Otherwise, when he has laid a foundation and is not able to finish, all who see it will begin to ridicule him, saying, 'This fellow began to build and was not able to finish.' Or what king, going out to wage war against another king, will not sit down first and consider whether he is able with ten thousand to oppose the one who comes against him with twenty thousand? If he cannot, then, while the other is still far away, he sends a delegation and asks for the terms of peace. So therefore, none of you can become my disciple if you do not give up all your possessions. (NRSV Luke 14: 28-33)

---

[32] Patrick Madrid, *Search and Rescue*, Location 1286 of 2422.

- Listen and Do Not Interrupt[33]

The book of Sirach teaches us, "Do not answer before you listen, and do not interrupt when another is speaking." (NRSV Sirach 11:8) Similarly, Jesus asks us to be as harmless as doves (also translated gentle as doves or innocent as doves). One way to exhibit a dove-like peaceful approach to evangelization is simply by refraining to interrupt while others are speaking. Obviously, there may be exceptions to this rule, but if people perceive we listen to them they are more likely to open up to us and, in the process, be more receptive to the saving truth we hope to give to them.

- Be Respectful and Sensitive[34]

Another tip that Madrid offers that demonstrates his dovelike qualities as an apologist is his sensitivity to former Catholics. He discovered that some former Catholics find the term ex-Catholics offensive but are not as easily offended by the terminology "you were once Catholics."[35] This is a small detail, but love is expressed in details. Jesus told us that our heavenly Father knows every hair on our heads. (Luke 12: 7) Being meek and humble

---

[33] Patrick Madrid, *Search and Rescue*, Location 2315 of 2422.

[34] Patrick Madrid, *Search and Rescue*, Location 722 of 2422.

[35] Patrick Madrid, *Search and Rescue*, Location 2329.

of heart like Jesus is the necessary pre-condition for one to be sensitive to details, such as what names and titles are most conducive in leading someone to the fullness of truth. As explained by Aquinas, in a way evocative of the Greek myth of Icarus, a humble heart prevents us from tending "to high things immoderately," and fortifies our minds "against despair, and urge [them] on to the pursuit of great things according to right reason."[36] Supplementing this definition of humility as a virtue, Madrid points out that the word humility originates from the Latin word *humilitas* which is related to the Latin word *humus* meaning earth. The origin of the word is a reminder of Christ's willingness to be trodden down, beaten, scourged and crucified for the glory of his Heavenly Father and out of love for us.[37]

- Redirect the Conversation[38]

Along with telling us to be as harmless as doves

---

[36] Thomas Aquinas, *Summa Theologica*, newadvent.org, http://www.newadvent.org/summa/3161.htm (accessed April 24, 2016), II-II, Q. 161, art. 1. Response; Patrick Madrid, *On a Mission: Lessons from St. Francis De Sales* (Cincinnati: Servant Books, 2013), 49.

[37] Patrick Madrid, *Meek & Humble of Heart*, MP3 (Patrick Madrid.com). Scriptural passages on humility include the following: Psalm 149:4, Isaiah 57:15, Philippians 2:3-11; Colossians 3:12; Matthew 20:16-28; Matthew 23:12; 1 Corinthians 1: 26-31.

[38] Patrick Madrid, *Search and Rescue*, Location 1205 of 2422.

Jesus also asks us to be wise as serpents (also translated as shrewd, cunning, crafty and prudent). (Matthew 10:16) One way to be wise as serpents is to redirect a conversation away from the topics that those with whom we are talking are comfortable and appear to be well-rehearsed in with pre-made memorized answers. Once the conversation is subtly redirected, the individual is freed from preconceived notions so that they can think critically in the light of the God's truth.

Redirection is similar to a boxer's parry. When parrying a blow, a boxer will step to one side and then, with a very small pop of the palm of his hand, redirect his opponent's punch. Madrid relates a highly effective way where he redirected the argument.[39] While debating with Protestants who were defending the Protestant teaching of *Sola Scriptura*, Madrid wrote on a napkin, "I never said you stole money."[40] Madrid then asked how they would interpret these words. Afterward, Madrid demonstrated to the Protestants that the meaning of the sentence depends on which word is emphasized. For example, by stressing the word "I," the sentence indicates that although I didn't say you stole money someone else said you did. As an exercise, stress different words in the sentence in order to see how the meaning of the sentence changes. The reason why Madrid invited the Protestants to do this exercise was to demonstrate

---

[39] Patrick Madrid, *On a Mission* (Cincinnati: Servant Books, 2013), 55.
[40] Patrick Madrid, *On a Mission*, 59-60.

that without reference to an authority, other than the words on the napkin, how can one know what meaning the author of the words intended?

- Socratic Method[41]

The apologist Trent Horn is well known for his wise, "cunning" ability of subtly directing a conversation by relying on the Socratic method. According to the Socratic method, a teacher does not directly state truth but rather asks questions to students in order that they come to truth by their own reasoning. Horn simplifies the Socratic method by dividing it into three types of questions: gathering, clarifying and challenging questions. Even though it will not always be clear what category a question falls under, remembering these three categories can help in directing people to discover the truth themselves. Ideally, a gathering question draws out information from an individual which later can be used to ask further questions that clarify their position. Once their position is established, including how they define key terms, a challenging question can then be posed to them that will reveal the errors or weaknesses in their thought process. Once they realize that their reasoning is not as strong as they assumed, they will often more readily choose a different line of reasoning that, hopefully, is in more accordance with truth.

---

[41] Patrick Madrid, *Search and Rescue*, Location 1233 of 2422.

Below are examples of various types of questions.

"Why is this question important for you?"
"What does your Church teach on this issue?"
"How do you define that term?"
"What criteria do you use to arrive at your conclusion?"
"What do you mean by that?"
"How do you come to that conclusion?"
"What are the consequences of this conclusion?"
"Which position is more reasonable?"
"What is another way of understanding this topic?"
"Can you verify your position?"

- Let God Work Through You[42]

When John the Baptist was asked if he was the Messiah, he responded, "I am baptizing you in water, but there is one to come who is mightier than I. I am not fit to loosen his sandal strap. He will baptize you in the Holy Spirit and fire." (NAB Luke 3: 16) John the Baptist knew that he was only a sign post pointing to the Messiah. As sign post, and a messenger who prepared the way, he never presented himself as the Messiah but instead reminded his followers that the Christ was coming. Jesus Christ is the message or word taken flesh of

---

[42] Patrick Madrid, *Search and Rescue*, Location 141 of 2422.

which John the Baptist was a preparatory messenger. Similarly, as we evangelize may we always remember that our role is at the service of Christ and not a replacement for Jesus. We are only his messengers. He is the message. He is the living Word spoken by the Father in the Love of the Holy Spirit.

- Radiate Christ's Truth and Love[43]

Father James J. Clarke's comparison of the sun with God's truthful love helps us to understand the importance of witnessing to truth in a loving manner. We know from experience that a sun can give us light, warmth and energy. We also know from experience that the sun also can "blast, wither and crush"[44] that upon which it shines its powerful rays. Like the life affirming aspects of the sun Jesus as the "Light of the World" gives us direction in our lives with moral and theological truth. He does so, however, in a loving manner and not a crushing, blasting manner that causes those who hear his truth to be disheartened and depressed. Presenting truth in an excessively condemnatory manner is the way of Satan, who seduces us by setting us up to failure with warmth without truth. Then, when we fall the devil accuses and condemns us without mercy.

---

[43] Patrick Madrid, *Search and Rescue*, Location 1358.
[44] James J. Clarke, *The Way to God: A Guide for Men*, study guide (Now You Know Media, 2012), 29.

- Be Agents of Reconciliation[45]

By our baptism, we participate in the one priesthood of Jesus Christ. This includes the laity. According to the *Catechism of the Catholic Church*, with reference to *Lumen Gentium*, the laity, "are made sharers in their particular way in the priestly, prophetic, and kingly office of Christ, and have their own part to play in the mission of the whole Christian people in the Church and in the World."[46] In paragraph 1547, the Catechism clarifies that the common priesthood of the laity differs in kind, in other words essentially, from the ministerial priesthood of ordained bishops and priests. Nonetheless, each kind of priesthood participates in the one priesthood of Christ, but in different ways.

A common mission of both is, through Christ, reconciling the world to God. Christ did this as a priest who offers a sacrifice to God and as the sacrifice who is offered to God. Consequently, as the late Archbishop Sheen repeatedly emphasized, we are called not simply to be priests but also to be priest-victims who in union with Christ offer ourselves for the redemption of the world. In reference to the Church as Christ's Mystical Body (1 Cor. 12:12-31; Col. 1:18; 2:18-20; Eph. 1:22-23; 3:19; 4:13), Archbishop Sheen explains that as a doctor

---

[45] Patrick Madrid, *Search and Rescue*, Location 1305.
[46] "Catechism of the Catholic Church," vatican.va, http://www.vatican.va/archive/ccc_css/archive/catechism/p123a9p4.htm (accessed April 21, 2016), no. 897.

can graft skin from one part of the body to the other, in an analogous sense, through sacrifice and prayer we can graft one part of the mystical body to another in order to bring redemption to those members who are spiritually sick. We can do so by praying and sacrificing for others. Archbishop Sheen did this in a heroic manner by asking God to send suffering his way so as to atone and intercede for others.[47]

Knowing Why Potential Converts are not Catholic

In his book *On a Mission*, Madrid wisely cautions us from assuming we know why a person rejects the Catholic faith even if the person tells us his reason. Sometimes, there are deeper reasons that the person is concealing. For example, an anti-Catholic who claims to reject Catholicism on biblical and historical claims, may have been hurt by bad examples set by Catholics and for that reason has rejected the faith. In *Search and Rescue*, Madrid specifies a number of reasons which include the following:

- Disagreement with Catholic Doctrine
- Angry at Catholic Moral Teaching
- Apathy
- Have been scandalized

---

[47] Fulton Sheen, *Vintage Sheen*, 13 Disc Set, 16 Meditations (Ramsey, N.J.: Keep the Faith-Latin Mass Magazine).

- Believe the Church Abandoned Them
- Angry with God
- Misconceptions of the Church
- Prejudicial Against the Church
- Have Genuine Disagreements[48]

Excuses for not Evangelizing

Archbishop Sheen pointed out that in our present age we have lost sign of the sense of mission (being sent) that is a prominent theme in both the Old Testament and in the New Testament. Abram, later re-named Abraham, was told by the Lord to "go forth from your country and your kindred and your father's house to the land that I will show you. I will make of you a great nation, and will bless you, and make your name great, so that you will be a blessing." (Genesis 12: 1-2 NRSV) After Abraham, God sent many others on similar missions that all prepared the way for the revelation of the eternal mission of the Son from the Father in the Love of the Holy Spirit. In the fullness of time (Galatian 4:4), the Son was sent into the world and was born of a woman. Through Jesus in the love of the Holy Spirit, the heavenly Father also calls us to go out on missions. These missions include not knowing exactly what is entailed. Even though many are still being called by the Father to missions, we often reject his invitation

---

[48] Patrick Madrid, *Search and Rescue*, Locations 474, 505, 536, 552, 568, 583, 600, 616, 635.

since we want to decide for ourselves where we will go and what we will do.[49]

Madrid reminds us that in order to be a follower of Jesus we need a missionary spirit that is open to going where one may not want to go and once there, relying on grace, to persevere in evangelization.[50] We will face excuses that come from the evil one, who wants to discourage us, or from our own fallen nature, or from both. Common excuses Madrid identifies include the following. I am afraid. I am the wrong person. I lack the necessary authority. They will ignore me. I am not trained. I will do it later. I do not want to.[51]

Upon committing ourselves to our mission and while in the midst of evangelization we will also face many similar temptations and obstacles. Sometimes, they will be manifested in people who will directly oppose us. In order keep the peace of Christ, especially during these times of difficulty, we ought to pray silently for guidance and for those with whom we are in conversation. Our friendly patience, evident by a smile, often disarms those who want to keep on attacking, but when they do not receive a similar response they may back off and reevaluate their position and assumptions. Later, those we are striving to bring to the fullness

---

[49] Fulton Sheen, *Vintage Sheen*, Disk 5 of a 13 Disc Set, 16 Meditations (Ramsey, N.J.: Keep the Faith-Latin Mass Magazine).

[50] Patrick Madrid, *On a Mission*, 33.

[51] Patrick Madrid, *Search and Rescue*, location 1434-1540.

of truth may talk to someone else and through that person, and not through us, God may bring about their conversion. He after all is the one who causes seeds to grow. We are only His servants on a mission to sow his seeds of truth.[52]

In sowing seeds of truth to those we meet God wants us to approach each person we encounter on an individual basis and not from the standpoint of how many we can bring about to convert. The example of King David's offending God by taking a census may serve as a reminder to us that evangelization is not about self-glorification but is about glorifying God and loving each person in a unique and personal manner. David sinned since, as indicated in Scripture, he took a census in order to be reminded of his own glory and power while forgetting he was a king in order to serve the people and not to rule it over them. (2 Samuel 24; 1 Chronicles 21)

Quiz 1

1. Contrast at least three qualities of an effective apologist with at least three qualities of an ineffective apologist.

2. List the six practical steps identified by Patrick Madrid for doing apologetics well.

---

[52] Patrick Madrid, *Search and Rescue*, location 1645-1796.

3. Choose three of the ten evangelization tips provided by Patrick Madrid. First, name them. Then, reflect upon them in light of your experience or experience of others. In so doing, give specific examples of these tips in practice.

4. Chose three reasons identified by Patrick Madrid that help to explain why people do not want to be Catholic. Then, in light of your experience or experience of others, describe specific examples for each reason.

5. Write on our Catholic calling to mission. Include the following in your response: definition of mission, mission examples from the Old Testament, mission examples from the New Testament, excuses people give to avoid missions, and how to evangelize properly.

Additional Activities and Resources

Respond to the following. Include in your response specific reference to Christ, Scripture, the Catechism of the Catholic Church, the example of a saint and qualities an apologist ought to have. When responding, do so according to the Socratic method of gathering, clarifying and challenging questions.

- Success is the primary goal of apologetics. As long as the apologist is defending the truth it matters little what means the apologist chooses in order to win a debate.

- The only reason people reject the Catholic faith is because they are convinced that Catholic Doctrine is false, a lie.

- I am the wrong person to evangelize. I can't do it.

Readings

Chapters Three through Six from Madrid, Patrick. *Search and Rescue*. Manchester: Sophia Institute Press, 2001.

Introduction from Madrid, Patrick. *Envoy for Christ: 25 Years as a Catholic Apologist*. Cincinnati, OH: Servant Books, 2012.

Chapters One through Five from Madrid, Patrick. *On a Mission: Lessons from St. Francis de Sales*. Cincinnati: Servant Books, 2013.

Fr. Peter Samuel Kucer, MSA

Chapter Two: Arguing Effectively

Introduction

In order to argue effectively in a truthful manner, we need to define our terms carefully, make sure our premises are true, and verify the arguments we use are valid. Being demanding on ourselves in this manner will train us to more readily recognize when someone else in error. Error in reasoning can be reduced to three factors: overly loose definition of terms, false premises and illogical arguments.[53] When it comes to leading people to the truths of faith, it is also important to properly understand the relationship of faith and reason. Once this relationship has been clarified it will be evident that faith is not only aided by logic and reason alone but also by appeals to authority

---

[53] Peter J. Kreeft and Ronald K. Tacelli, *Handbook of Catholic Apologetics* (San Francisco: Ignatius Press, 2009). 139.

and to non-rational arguments that are not necessarily opposed to the logical and rational arguments.

Terms, Propositions and Arguments

The left column of the chart below lists the three acts of the human mind. The right column states how these acts are expressed. Understanding is expressed in the comprehension of terms, such as the term dog signifies a four legged, canid, meat-eating mammal. Terms grasped by understanding can overly be general or be precise. Judging is expressed by determining whether or not a predicate that is claimed of a subject, such as meat-eating with respect to dogs, is in accordance with reality and not simply theory. Conversely, judging can also be expressed by determining whether or not a predicate that is denied of a subject is actually absent from a subject, such as dogs are not cats. If my judgment is in accordance with reality, then the proposition is true. If not, then it is not true. Reasoning is expressed in argumentation by linking together a series of propositions in a logical manner that lead to a conclusion. An example in syllogistic fashion is as follows. All men are mortal. I am a man. Therefore, I am mortal. Reasoning can be logical or illogical, and hence invalid.[54]

---

[54] Peter J. Kreeft and Ronald K. Tacelli, *Handbook of Catholic Apologetics*, 19.

Acts of the Mind	Expressions of the Mind's Acts
1. Apprehending	1. Terms
2. Judging	2. Propositions
3. Reasoning	3. Arguments

The conclusion from the argument that I am mortal is an example of a conclusion that is demonstratively certain since the propositions, or premises, it is based upon are known and experienced as true. Not all arguments, however, are demonstratively certain. Some arguments simply demonstrate that a conclusion is reasonable to hold since it is probably true as indicated by a number of factors that indicate it is likely true. Such arguments range from low probability to high probability. Many arguments concerning the faith are of the latter type of probable argumentation and not the former, logically, demonstratively certain type.[55] Arguments of reason that support the faith only indicate that the faith is reasonable and likely. The gift of theological faith, which we will discuss in the next section, gives us certainty, greater than the certainty modern science offers us, that what we believe is true.

Faith and Reason

According to Aquinas, faith is the mean

---

[55] Peter J. Kreeft and Ronald K. Tacelli, *Handbook of Catholic Apologetics*, 18-19.

between knowledge obtained from scientific inquiry and opinion.[56] This means that faith has something in common with and differs from both certain knowledge obtained from scientific inquiry and opinion. Faith is similar to certain knowledge obtained from "science" while differing from opinion in that what we believe is certain. Faith differs from "science" while being similar to opinion in that like opinion and unlike "science" the object of faith is something that is unseen.[57]

---

[56] Thomas Aquinas, *Summa Theologica,* II-II, Q. 1, Art. 2, http://www.newadvent.org/summa/3001.htm (accessed July 21, 2016). "Faith is a mean between science and opinion. Now the mean is in the same genus as the extremes. Since, then, science and opinion are about propositions, it seems that faith is likewise about propositions; so that its object is something complex."

[57] Thomas Aquinas, *Summa Theologica,* II-II, Q. 1, Art. 5, ad. 2, http://www.newadvent.org/summa/3001.htm (accessed July 21, 2016). "As the Philosopher says (Poster. i), "science and opinion about the same object can certainly be in different men," as we have stated above about science and faith; yet it is possible for one and the same man to have science and faith about the same thing relatively, i.e. in relation to the object, but not in the same respect. For it is possible for the same person, about one and the same object, to know one thing and to think another: and, in like manner, one may know by demonstration the unity of the Godhead, and, by faith, the Trinity. On the other hand, in one and the same man, about the same object, and in the same respect, science is incompatible with either opinion or faith, yet for different reasons. Because science is incompatible with opinion about the same object simply, for the reason that science demands that its object should be deemed impossible to be otherwise, whereas it is essential to opinion, that its object should be deemed

possible to be otherwise. Yet that which is the object of faith, on account of the certainty of faith, is also deemed impossible to be otherwise; and the reason why science and faith cannot be about the same object and in the same respect is because the object of science is something seen whereas the object of faith is the unseen, as stated above."

St. Thomas Aquinas, *Summa Theologica*, II-II, q. 4, art. 1, reply, http://www.newadvent.org/summa/3004.htm (accessed January 6, 2014). In his *Summa Theologica* Aquinas further explains how faith is similar and different from opinion and scientific knowledge. Faith is similar to scientific knowledge in that it is certain. It differs from scientific knowledge and is similar to an opinion in that the one who believes does directly touch, taste, feel or hear what he believes in.

"...In this way faith is distinguished from all other things pertaining to the intellect. For when we describe it as 'evidence,' we distinguish it from opinion, suspicion, and doubt, which do not make the intellect adhere to anything firmly; when we go on to say, 'of things that appear not,' we distinguish it from science and understanding, the object of which is something apparent; and when we say that it is 'the substance of things to be hoped for,' we distinguish the virtue of faith from faith commonly so called, which has no reference to the beatitude we hope for.

Whatever other definitions are given of faith, are explanations of this one given by the Apostle. For when Augustine says (Tract. xl in Joan.: *QQ. Evang.* ii, qu. 39) that 'faith is a virtue whereby we believe what we do not see,' and when Damascene says (*De Fide Orth*. iv, 11) that 'faith is an assent without research,' and when others say that 'faith is that certainty of the mind about absent things which surpasses opinion but falls short of science,' these all amount to the same as the Apostle's words: 'Evidence of things that appear not'; and when Dionysius says (*Div. Nom.* vii) that 'faith is the solid foundation of the believer, establishing him in the truth, and showing forth the truth in him,' comes to the same as "substance of things to be hoped for."

St. Thomas Aquinas: *Quaestiones disputatae de veritate*, q. 14 ("On faith") translator Alfred J. Freddoso. http://www3.nd.edu/~afreddos/translat/aquinas5.htm (accessed January 6, 2014). "Article 2: What is faith?

In Hebrews 11:1 the Apostle says that faith is the substance of things to be hoped for, the argument (argumentum) of things that are not apparent. ...

I REPLY:

One should reply that, according to some people, the Apostle intended by this definition to show not what faith is but rather what faith does.

However, it seems better to reply that this explanation of faith is the most complete definition of it--not in the sense that it is rendered in the form appropriate to a definition, but rather because it adequately touches upon all the things that are required for a definition of faith. For sometimes it is sufficient for even philosophers themselves to touch upon the principles of [given] syllogisms and definitions, and once these principles are had, it is not difficult to reduce them to forms that are in keeping with the doctrine of the art [of logic]....

For by saying 'of things that are not apparent' one distinguishes faith from knowledge (scientia) and understanding (intellectus). Again, by saying 'the argument' one distinguishes faith from (i) opinion (opinio) and doubt (dubitatio), in which the mind is not convinced, i.e., not determined to some one thing, and also from (ii) all habits which are not cognitive. Again, by saying 'the substance of things to be hoped for' one distinguishes [faith in the proper sense] from (i) faith as it is commonly understood (fides communiter accepta), in accord with which we are said either to believe that which we strongly opine or to believe in the testimony of some human being, and also from (ii) prudence

In focusing on faith, Aquinas distinguishes between various objects of faith. The most important object of faith is God who is not comprised of a complex arrangement of propositions. Instead, God is personal. However, on the part of the believer who does not see the object of faith, faith involves "something complex by way of a proposition."[58]

Believing in God requires the intellectual appetite called the will to desire and consent to what is believed, and the intellect to believe. Simply consenting to believe and accepting in the intellect what is believed is not sufficient since the truths of faith are to be formed by charity. The Letter of James warns us, "You believe that God is one; you do well. Even the demons believe-and shudder." (James 2:19 NRSV) Prior to this verse James reminds us that our faith is to be formed by charity. "What good is it, my brothers and sisters, if you say you have faith but do not have works? Can faith save you? If a brother or sister is naked and lacks daily food, and one of you says to them, 'Go in peace; keep warm and eat your fill,' and yet do not supply their bodily needs, what is the good of that? So faith by itself, if it has no works, is dead." (James

---

(prudentia) and the other cognitive habits, which are not ordered toward the things to hope for or which, if they are so ordered, are not such that a proper inception of the things to be hoped for comes to exist in us through them."

[58] Thomas Aquinas, *Summa Theologica*, II-II, Q. 1, Art. 2, new advent.org, http://www.newadvent.org/summa/3001.htm (accessed July 21, 2016).

2:14-17 NRSV)

In order to understand how reason relates to faith, the various acts of reason need to be discussed. Following Aristotle, Aquinas distinguishes between three operations of the intellect: apprehension, judgment and reasoning.[59] In apprehension, the human intellect simply grasps a truth. In order to see why the truth is reasonable, the intellect needs to analyze and judge that which is simply apprehended. This intellectual movement from simple apprehension to discovery by analyz-

---

[59] Thomas Aquinas, *Summa Theologica*, I, Q. 79, Art. 8, newadvent.org, http://www.newadvent.org/summa/1079.htm, "For to understand is simply to apprehend intelligible truth: and to reason is to advance from one thing understood to another, so as to know an intelligible truth. And therefore angels, who according to their nature, possess perfect knowledge of intelligible truth, have no need to advance from one thing to another; but apprehend the truth simply and without mental discussion, as Dionysius says (Div. Nom. vii). But man arrives at the knowledge of intelligible truth by advancing from one thing to another; and therefore he is called rational. Reasoning, therefore, is compared to understanding, as movement is to rest, or acquisition to possession; of which one belongs to the perfect, the other to the imperfect. And since movement always proceeds from something immovable, and ends in something at rest; hence it is that human reasoning, by way of inquiry and discovery, advances from certain things simply understood--namely, the first principles; and, again, by way of judgment returns by analysis to first principles, in the light of which it examines what it has found. Now it is clear that rest and movement are not to be referred to different powers, but to one and the same, even in natural things: since by the same nature a thing is moved towards a certain place."

ing, judging and discerning leads the intellect into reasoning whether what is proposed to the intellect is rational or irrational, logical or illogical. In Aquinas's words:

> For to understand is simply to **apprehend** intelligible truth: and **to reason is to advance from one thing understood to another**, so as to know an intelligible truth. And therefore angels, who according to their nature, possess perfect knowledge of intelligible truth, have no need to advance from one thing to another; but apprehend the truth simply and without mental discussion, as Dionysius says (Div. Nom. vii). But man arrives at the knowledge of intelligible truth by advancing from one thing to another; and therefore he is called rational. Reasoning, therefore, is compared to understanding, as movement is to rest, or acquisition to possession; of which one belongs to the perfect, the other to the imperfect. And since movement always proceeds from something immovable, and ends in something at rest; hence it is that human reasoning, by way of inquiry and discovery, advances from certain things simply understood--namely, the first principles; and, again, **by way of judgment returns by analysis** to first principles, in the light of which it examines what it has found."

An example of the first two steps of this reasoning process is listening, appreciating and apprehending the performance of a musical piece. This may be followed later by examining and analyzing the sheet music and, in the process, discovering the key signature of the piece. An example involving proving is the simply grasp of what water is. This is followed by discovering that every molecule of water is composed of hydrogen and oxygen atoms. Finally, that water has two hydrogen atoms for every oxygen atom may be proven.

	Apprehension (understanding)	Judgment (Discovering)	Reasoning (Proving)
Reason Alone	Water	Every molecule of water has hydrogen and oxygen atoms.	Proving that every water molecule is comprised of one oxygen atom bonded to two hydrogen atoms

Since some aspects of the Catholic faith involve what can be apprehended, seen, judged, and proven there is an overlap between faith and reason. For example, not only is it revealed that the universe is ordered but reason can apprehend and study this order. One example is the periodic table, which orders chemical elements by their number of protons, called the atomic number. In addition, upon examination of documentary and archaeological evidence the human intellect can discover that it is highly reasonable to hold that Jesus existed. Revelation teaches with certainty that Jesus truly lived. That the soul is immaterial, due to its ability to abstract from matter, is a truth that reason can prove and is taught with certainty by revelation.[60] Some truths of faith can only be received by revelation and cannot be discovered by the intellect alone. Examples include: Salvation, Jesus' divinity, and the Trinity. In reference to the three acts of reason Peter Kreeft shows that the reason that is formed by faith first apprehends that God's plan of salvation which in turn leads the believer to discover God's infinite love for us. God's infinite love for us is in a sense proven by God being a community of persons where the Father eternally loves the Son, the Son eternally loves the Father, and the love between the Father and the Son is the Holy Spirit.[61]

A diagram that properly depicts the overlap without identification of faith and reason is on the next page.

---

[60] Peter J. Kreeft and Ronald K. Tacelli, *Handbook of Catholic Apologetics*, loc. 284.

[61] Peter J. Kreeft and Ronald K. Tacelli, *Handbook of Catholic Apologetics*, loc. 284.

The following diagrams depict erroneous concepts of how faith and reason interact. In the first example, faith and reason are understood as completely unrelated. This leads to the notion that there can be two set of truths one for reason and one for faith, which may contradict one another.

Catholicism holds that truth is one, and, consequently, articles of faith do not contradict truths discoverable by reason. In contrast with dualism another false position is to hold that faith and reason are completely identical with one another. This position is, points out Kreeft, a logical possibility but not one that is commonly held.

A related error, called rationalism, maintains that truths of faith can be proven by reason which is greater than what is proposed by faith. The opposite error to rationalism is fideism, that hold that the only way to know anything is by faith.[62]

---

[62] Peter J. Kreeft and Ronald K. Tacelli, *Handbook of Catholic Apologetics*, loc. 291-332.

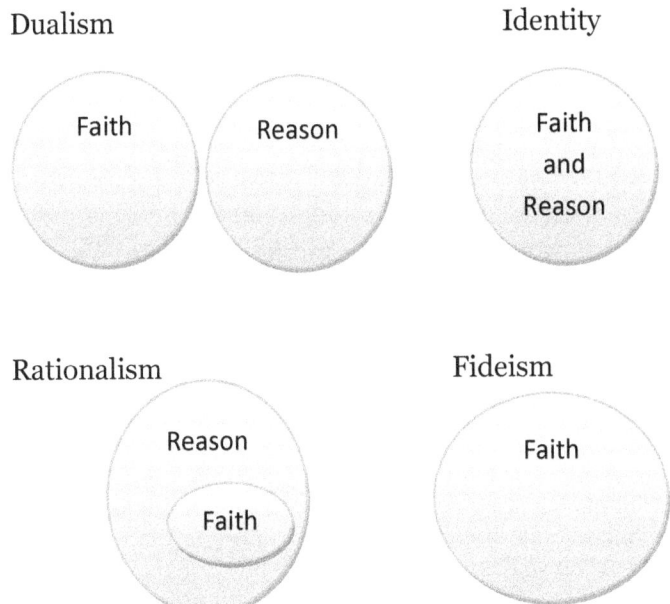

Scripture, History and Non-Rational Arguments

It is debated among theologians to what extent faith partially overlaps with reason. For example, can reason alone prove the immaterially and immortality of the soul or does it need the aid of revelation? Can reason alone prove that the universe has not eternally existed or does it need the aid of revelation?[63] Appealing to authority,

---

[63] Thomas Aquinas, "On the Eternity of the World," legacy.fordham.edu, http://legacy.fordham.edu/halsall/basis/aquinas-eternity.asp (accessed July 23, 2016). "First, we should show that it is not necessary that an agent cause, in this case God, precede in time that which

these questions and others can be answered with certainty, certainty given by faith. The authority referred to is revelation which includes Scripture, Tradition and the Magisterium. These three authorities, as the Vatican document *Dei Verbum* teaches, are not to be understood as standing alone and unrelated to one another. Rather, Vatican

---

he causes, if he should so will. This can be shown in several ways. First, no cause instantaneously producing its effect necessarily precedes the effect in time. God, however, is a cause that produces effects not through motion but instantaneously. Therefore, it is not necessary that he precede his effects in time. The first premise is proved inductively from all instantaneous changes, as, for example, with illumination and other such things. But the premise may be proved by reason as well.

For, at whatever instant a thing exists, at that instant it can begin to act, as is clear in the case of all things that come to be by generation: in the very instant at which there is fire, the fire heats. But in an instantaneous action, the beginning and the end of the action are simultaneous, indeed identical, as is clear in the case of all indivisible things. Hence, at whatever moment an agent instantaneously producing an effect exists, the end of its action can exist as well. The end of the action, however, is simultaneous with the thing made. Therefore, there is no contradiction if we suppose that a cause instantaneously producing an effect does not precede its effect in time. A contradiction does obtain if the cause involved is one that produces its effects through motion, for the beginning of the motion precedes in time the end of the motion. Since people are accustomed to considering the type of cause that produces effects through motion, they do not easily grasp that an agent cause may fail to precede its effect in time, and so, having limited experience, they easily make a false generalization."

Council II instructs, "It is clear, therefore, that sacred tradition, Sacred Scripture and the teaching authority of the Church, in accord with God's most wise design, are so linked and joined together that one cannot stand without the others and that all together and each in its own way under the action of the one Holy Spirit contribute effectively to the salvation of souls."[64]

Revelation given in these three complementary ways that is accepted by believers cooperating with the gift of grace can be supplemented not only by rational arguments but also by non-rational arguments. These non-rational arguments, clarifies Kreeft, are not to be confused with irrational arguments.[65] It is not irrational, contrary to reason, to maintain that something is beautiful. Likewise, it is not irrational to be persuaded by the beauty of the Catholic faith. For example, it is not irrational for one to enter Rome's St. Peter's basilica for the first time and there, standing before Michelangelo's Pieta, accept God's grace given through the beautiful experience evoked by the statue.

In affirming the role of non-rational support of the faith, Benedict XVI asserted that:

> The only really effective apologia (defense)

---

[64] Vatican II, *Dei Verbum*, 1965, chap. 2, no. 10, The Vatican, http://www.vatican.va/archive/hist_councils/ii_vatican_council/documents/vat-ii_const_19651118_dei-verbum_en.html (accessed January 6, 2015).

[65] Peter J. Kreeft and Ronald K. Tacelli, *Handbook of Catholic Apologetics*, loc. 78.

for Christianity comes down to two arguments, namely the *saints* the Church has produced and the *art* which has grown in her womb. Better witness is borne to the Lord by the splendor of holiness and art which have risen in the community of believers than by the clever excuses which apologetics has come up with to justify the dark side which, sadly, are so frequent in the Church's human history.

If the Church is to continue to transform and humanize the world, how can she dispense with beauty in her liturgies (and in all of her life) that beauty which is so closely linked with love and with the radiance of the Resurrection? No. Christians must not be too easily satisfied. They must make their Church into a place where beauty-- and hence truth-- is at home. Without this the world will become the first circle of hell.[66]

The defense of the truth of the faith is to be aided and, often preceded, by goodness and beauty both of which, if properly ordered, inform one another. St. Teresa of Calcutta, responsible for helping to bring about the conversion of many, did so primarily with the witness of her good deeds. She

---

[66] Joseph Ratzinger, *The Ratzinger Report: An Exclusive Interview on the State of the Church*, trans. Salvator Attansio and Graham Harrison (San Francisco: Ignatius Press, 1985) 129-130.

also stood for truth, for example for the rights of the unborn, but her primary witness was through a good, sacrificial life in service to the poorest of the poor. Mother Teresa's evangelical approach in which goodness led the way is evident, as described by Stephen Schwartz, "by her decision to adopt a white and blue sari, or traditional Indian women's covering, as their uniform. The Indian-style dress was intended to minimize the difference between the Missionaries of Charity and those they served. Furthermore, the Missionaries of Charity refrained from proselytizing and pledged simply to demonstrate their love of the people for whom they cared."[67]

Through the witness of the often silent goodness of these sisters, people encountered Christ. The relationship of Christ's very name with goodness was made by early Christians as Benedict XVI, writing as a theologian, explained. For example, the early Church Father Ignatius of Antioch (c. 35-107) identified moral goodness directly with Christ since in Greek the word *chrestos* means good while the word *christos* means *Christ*. Benedict XVI further points out that when Christians are persecuted, "the conspiracy of the *Christos* is a conspiracy of those who are *chrestos*, a conspiracy of goodness. Thus Tertullian... assert[s] that 'the word Christ comes from the word for

---

[67] Stephen Schwartz, "Mother Teresa's World," *First Things* June/July 2016, no. 264 (2016), 18.

goodness.'"[68]

Due to the diversity of roles in the mystical body (1 Corinthians 12), not all are called to follow the example of Mother Teresa's subtle way of evangelizing by her good and relatively silent life. All though, are called by our Christian faith, to be formed by charity. This means that those who are inspired to defend the faith with intelligent argumentation need to be formed by charity, as the first letter of Corinthians chapter thirteen warns:

> If I speak in the tongues of mortals and of angels, but do not have love, I am a noisy gong or a clanging cymbal. And if I have prophetic powers, and understand all mysteries and all knowledge, and if I have all faith, so as to remove mountains, but do not have love, I am nothing. If I give away all my possessions, and if I hand over my body so that I may boast, but do not have love, I gain nothing.
>
> Love is patient; love is kind; love is not envious or boastful or arrogant or rude. It does not insist on its own way; it is not irritable or resentful; it does not rejoice in wrongdoing, but rejoices in the truth. It bears all things, believes all things, hopes all

---

[68] Joseph Cardinal Ratzinger, Heinz Schurmann, and Hans Urs von Balthasar, *Principles of Christian Morality*, trans. Graham Harrison (San Francisco: Ignatius Press, 1986), 60-61.

things, endures all things. (1 Corinthians 13: 1-7 NRSV)

Patrick Madrid in his book *Search and Rescue* identifies the boastfulness, arrogance and rudeness referred to in the above passage with an unfettered "ego." He writes, "Your ego, if uncontrolled, will quickly distort your search-and-rescue mission into a search-and-destroy mission."[69] Essential attributes of an apologist who speak the truth in love are, described Madrid, as follows. A Christian apologist is to be filled with faith, hope and love. The apologist is also to be humble, persevering and patient. A temptation an apologist faces, especially when he is "successful," is to do apologetic work for self-glorification. When this occurs, an apologist begins to approach evangelization and conversions like a trophy seeker in order to display his own power. In contrast, we are to seek not our glory but the glory of God.[70]

In his book *The Splendor of the Church*, the highly influential theologian Henri de Lubac warns us that we can become false prophets if we err by stressing the external dimension of success to the detriment of the internal spirit of charity and Godly motives. When the external dimension of the Church is emphasized to the exclusion of the internal spirit, the result can be doing the right deed for the wrong reason which is "the greatest treason," as T.S. Elliot reminds us in *Murder in the*

---

[69] Patrick Madrid, *Search and Rescue*, loc. 214.
[70] Patrick Madrid, *Search and Rescue*, loc. 214-455.

Cathedral through Thomas Becket's fourth tempter.[71] De Lubac described this temptation as "the most subversive temptation," for on the outside all seems to be well but is not since the "spiritual perfections" and good acts that are being done are for man's glory and not for God's.[72] In

---

[71] T.S. Eliot, *Murder in the Cathedral* (Orlando: Harcourt Brace & Company, 1963), 44. "The last temptation is the greatest treason. To do the right deed for the wrong reason."

[72] Henri de Lubac, *The Splendor of the Church*, trans. Michael Mason (San Francisco: Ignatius Press, 1999), Location 4075-4081 of 8029. "That is Mary; and so also is the Church our Mother-the perfect worshipper; there lies the focal point of the analogy between them, for there the same spirit is at work in both. But whereas this humble and lofty perfection shines dazzlingly in supreme purity in Mary, in ourselves (who are as yet barely touched by the Spirit) it scarcely struggles to the light at all. The Church-as-Mother is never at the end of her labor to deliver us to the life of the Spirit, and the greatest danger we are to the Church, the most subversive temptation, the one that is ever and insidiously reborn when all the rest are overcome, and even strengthened by those victories, is what Abbot Vonier called the temptation to 'worldliness of the mind... the practical relinquishing of other-worldliness, so that moral and even spiritual standards should be based, not on the glory of the Lord, but on what is the profit of man; an entirely anthropocentric outlook would be exactly what we mean by worldliness. Even if men were filled with every spiritual perfection, but if such perfections were not referred to God (suppose this hypothesis to be possible) it would be unredeemed worldliness. If this spiritual worldliness were to invade the Church and set to work to corrupt her by attacking her very principle, it would be something infinitely more disastrous than any worldliness of the purely moral

reference to these words of De Lubac, the future pope Francis, Cardinal Bergoglio, responded to the question, "what is the worst thing that can happen in the Church?" with, "It is what De Lubac calls 'spiritual worldliness'. It is the greatest danger for the Church, for us, who are in the Church. 'It is worse,' says De Lubac, 'more disastrous than the infamous leprosy that disfigured the dearly beloved Bride at the time of the libertine popes.' Spiritual worldliness is putting oneself at the center. It is what Jesus saw going on among the Pharisees: 'You glorify yourselves. Who give glory to yourselves, the ones to the others.'"[73]

Despite the spiritual dangers apologists face, primarily within themselves, nonetheless some are genuinely called by God to defend the faith which the term apologetics conveys. The English word apologetics comes from the Greek word *apologia* which signifies a type of speech which defends a position.[74] In affirming that some are called to be

---

order-even worse than the hideous leprosy that at certain moments in history inflects so cruel a disfigurement on the Bride; when religious seems to set up the scandalous 'in the sanctuary itself....'" Location 4075-4081 of 8029.

[73] Sefania Falasca, "What I would have said at the Consistory: An Interview with Cardinal Jorge Mario Bergoglio, Archbishop of Buenos Aires," *30Days*, Issue no. 11 (2007), 30giorni.it, http://www.30giorni.it/articoli_id_16457_l3.htm (accessed June 16, 2016).

[74] "Apology," Etymonline.com, http://etymonline.com/ index.php?allowed_in_frame=0&search=apology (accessed on July 23, 2016). "early 15c., 'defense, justification,' from Late Latin apologia, from Greek

defenders of the faith, to be apologists, Vatican Council II states:

> It is quite unbecoming for the Church's children idly to permit the message of salvation to be thwarted or impeded by the technical delays or expenses, however vast, which are encountered by the very nature of these media. Therefore, this sacred Synod advises them of the obligation they have to maintain and assist Catholic newspapers, periodicals and film projects, radio and television programs and stations, whose principal objective is to spread and defend the truth and foster Christian influence in human society. At the same time, the Synod earnestly invites those organizations and individuals who possess financial and technical ability to support these media freely and generously with their resources and their skills, inasmuch as they contribute to genuine culture and the apostolate.[75]

---

apologia 'a speech in defense,' from apologeisthai 'to speak in one's defense,' from apologos 'an account, story,' from apo- 'from, off' (see apo-) + logos "speech" (see lecture (n.)). The original English sense of "self-justification" yielded a meaning 'frank expression of regret for wrong done,' first recorded 1590s, but this was not the main sense until 18c. The old sense tends to emerge in Latin form apologia (first attested in English 1784), especially since J.H. Newman's 'Apologia pro Vita Sua' (1864)."

[75] Vatican Council II, "Decree on the Media of Social Communications *Inter Mirifica*" 1963, chap. 2, no. 17,

This affirmation of Vatican Council II is in continuity with tradition. St. Peter in his first letter clearly states, that we are "Always be ready to make your defense to anyone who demands from you an accounting for the hope that is in you; yet do it with gentleness and reverence." 1 Peter 3:15-16 NRSV) In fulfillment of our duty to make a defense of the faith, saints from the early Christian times to modern times have done so "in season and out of season" convincing, rebuking and exhorting while being "unfailing in patience and in teaching." (2 Timothy 4:2 RSV). The three principle means they have used to defend the faith as reasonable are Scripture, history and logic.[76] Notable saintly defenders of the faith include, St. Peter, St. Paul, St. Justin Martyr, St. Athanasius, St. Augustine, St. Bernard of Clairvaux, St. Aquinas, St. Bonaventure, St. Robert Bellarmine, to name just a few.

Quiz 2

1. Distinguish between rational arguments and non-rational arguments. Do so by providing three concrete examples.

The Vatican, http://www.vatican.va/archive/hist_councils/ii_vatican_council/documents/vat-ii_decree_19631204_inter-mirifica_en.html (accessed December 31, 2014).

[76] Patrick Madrid, *Answer Me This* (Patrick Madrid: www. PatrickMadrid.com, 2003).

2. Fill in the following chart. In addition, provide example in the second column titled "Expressions of the Mind's Acts".

Acts of the Mind	Expressions of the Mind's Acts
1.	1.
2.	2.
3.	3.

3. Diagram the five ways faith and reason can relate to one another while indicating which one is the Catholic position.

4. What is apologetics and why is it important? In answering do the following. Define the word apologetics by tracing it back to its Greek root. Refer to the three means of apologetics that are stated to in lecture one. Explain, with specific reference to at least one person and one era, how apologetics has been important in the history of the Church. Explain the role of apologetics according to Vatican II. Finally, describe temptations an apologist may face especially when the apologist is successful.

Additional Activities and Resources

1. Respond to the following. Do so according to the Socratic method of gathering, clarifying and challenging questions.

- Faith and reason are unrelated. It is possible, therefore, to have truths of faith that differ from truths of reason without contradiction.
- Faith can teach me everything that I can discover by reason.
- Only that which can be known by reason alone is legitimate to believe in by faith.
- The only way a person can be led into faith is with intellectual argumentation along with the gift of grace.
- Worldliness of the moral order is a much greater evil than spiritual worldliness. Don't be overly worried about doing good deeds for Godly reasons, just focus on doing good.

Readings

Chapters One and Two from Madrid, Patrick. *Search and Rescue*. Manchester: Sophia Institute Press, 2001.

Chapters One and Two from Kreeft, Peter, and Ronald K. Tacelli. *Handbook of Christian Apologetics: Hundreds of Answers to Crucial Questions*. Downers Grove, IL: InterVarsity Press, 1994.

II-II, Q. 1 from Aquinas, Thomas. *Summa Theologica*.

Fr. Peter Samuel Kucer, MSA

Chapter Three: God's Existence

Introduction

God's existence is the most fundamental reality that apologetics defends as eminently reasonable to believe. In this chapter, you will be introduced to a number of arguments from reason for the existence of God. We will begin with ways stemming from the physical world. This will be followed by ways stemming from the human person.

The *Catechism of the Catholic Church* refers not only to ways but also to "proofs for the existence of God," and it clarifies this terminology by adding that arguments for the existence of God are not to be understood "in the sense of proofs in the natural sciences, but rather in the sense of 'converging and convincing arguments', which allow us to attain certainty about the truth."[77]

---

[77] "Catechism of the Catholic Church, no. 31, Vatican.va,

Fr. Peter Samuel Kucer, MSA

Five Ways of Aquinas

In his *Summa Theologica,* Aquinas presents five convergent ways all of which indicate the high reasonableness of God' existence. Notice that these ways are like multiple roads that lead to and converge in one point, God's existence. When taken in isolation from one another, these indicators may seem weak but when seen together they provide ample evidence for God's existence. In his five ways, Aquinas argues for the existence of God from motion, from cause and effect, from possibility and necessity, from the gradation of being, and from design.

The phrase "nothing can give itself that which it does not have" can help to understand the first argument from motion. Nothing can go from being potentially in motion to being actually in motion unless it receives motion from another being. A marble in a state of rest can be put in motion but only if it receives motion from outside of itself, from something in the state of motion. The ultimate first mover did not receive motion from any other source since He is pure act. This is God.

The second way from cause and effect is similar to the first. The following analogy helps to understand this argument. Unless there is a librarian with books to lend no one can borrow a single book. The librarian and the books represent God who as existence, as the first cause itself, who

---

http://www.vatican.va/archive/ccc_css/archive/catechism/p1s1c1.htm (accessed July 26, 2016).

as pure act gives us existence and being by allowing us to borrow, or participate in His being, His existence. We only have existence. We only have being. God, in contrast, is being, is existence. As being itself God is equivalent to that He is, to His existence. In contrast, what we are, human beings, is not equivalent to that we are, for what we are can always potentially be more actualized, for example by actualizing our knowledge by reading books we borrow from a library. Finally, Aquinas points out, it is not possible for efficient causes to go on for infinity, for to do so would eliminate causes that mediate the effect of the first cause. As he explains, "[n]ow to take away the cause is to take away the effect."[78] In other words, explains Frank Sheed, it is not possible for there to be an infinite chain of receivers of existence since this implies there is no ultimate giver. If everything is only is a receiver, then how can anything be passed on since nothing has been given?[79]

The third way is from possibility and necessity. According to this argument since nothing comes from nothing, there must be an absolutely necessary being who did not receive his existence from anything else since He is existence. This being is God who brought into existence all subsequent beings. These subsequent beings are all contingent

---

[78] Thomas Aquinas, *Summa Theologica*, I, Q. 2, Art. 3, newadvent.org, http://www.newadvent.org/summa/1002.htm (accessed July 25, 2016).

[79] Frank Sheed, *Theology and Sanctity* (No location given: Catholic Way Publishing, 2014), loc. 494-519.

(from the Latin *contingere* meaning to touch) beings.

The fourth way is from the gradation of being. In nature we see that that which has the maximum degree of intensity is the cause of that which has less intensity. For example, the sun is the cause of the various degrees of heat we feel. There must, therefore, be a being in which all perfections exist to their highest degree. God is this being, who as pure act with no potentiality, contains all perfections.

The fifth way argues from intelligent design. The intelligent design in the universe points to an intelligent designer. It is less reasonable to claim that what we identify as a rational design, such as the periodic chart, is only due to chance. Furthermore, our concept of chance, Kreeft points out, is understood within the larger context of order. If I say, "That occurred by chance," I am doing so in order to indicate that it turned out in an unexpected manner, implying that there is an expected manner that it ought to have turned out. This reasoning applies to Darwin's theory of evolution since "the survival of the fittest presupposes the arrival of the fit."[80]

Below are the five ways as Aquinas presents them. Notice that all of these arguments proceed from the effects of God and not from the cause of the effects since the existence of God, asserts

---

[80] Peter J. Kreeft and Ronald K. Tacelli, *Handbook of Catholic Apologetics* (San Francisco: Ignatius Press, 2009), loc. 565.

Aquinas, "is not self-evident to us."[81]

~ Aquinas's Five Ways ~

I answer that, the existence of God can be proved in five ways.

The first and more manifest way is the argument from motion. It is certain, and evident to our senses, that in the world some things are in motion. Now whatever is in motion is put in motion by another, for nothing can be in motion except it is in potentiality to that towards which it is in motion; whereas a thing moves inasmuch as it is in act. For motion is nothing else than the reduction of something from potentiality to actuality. But nothing can be reduced from potentiality to actuality, except by something in a state of actuality. Thus that which is actually hot, as fire, makes wood, which is potentially hot, to be actually hot, and thereby moves and changes it. Now it is not possible that the same thing should be at once in actuality and potentiality in the same respect, but only in different respects. For what is actually hot cannot simultaneously be potentially hot; but it is simultaneously

---

[81] Thomas Aquinas, *Summa Theologica,* I, Q. 2, Art. 2, newadvent.org, http://www.newadvent.org/summa/1002.htm (accessed July 25, 2016).

potentially cold. It is therefore impossible that in the same respect and in the same way a thing should be both mover and moved, i.e. that it should move itself. Therefore, whatever is in motion must be put in motion by another. If that by which it is put in motion be itself put in motion, then this also must needs be put in motion by another, and that by another again. But this cannot go on to infinity, because then there would be no first mover, and, consequently, no other mover; seeing that subsequent movers move only inasmuch as they are put in motion by the first mover; as the staff moves only because it is put in motion by the hand. Therefore, it is necessary to arrive at a first mover, put in motion by no other; and this everyone understands to be God.

The second way is from the nature of the efficient cause. In the world of sense we find there is an order of efficient causes. There is no case known (neither is it, indeed, possible) in which a thing is found to be the efficient cause of itself; for so it would be prior to itself, which is impossible. Now in efficient causes it is not possible to go on to infinity, because in all efficient causes following in order, the first is the cause of the intermediate cause, and the intermediate is the cause of the ultimate cause, whether the intermediate cause be several, or only one. Now to take away the cause is to take away the effect. Therefore, if there be no first cause among efficient causes, there will be no ultimate, nor any intermediate cause. But if in efficient causes it is possible to go on to infinity, there will be no first efficient cause, neither will there be an ultimate effect, nor any intermediate efficient causes; all of which is plainly false. Therefore, it is necessary to admit a first efficient cause, to which everyone gives the name of God.

The third way is taken from possibility and necessity, and runs thus. We find in nature things that are possible to be and not to be, since they are found to be generated, and to corrupt, and consequently, they are possible to be and not to be. But it is impossible for these always to exist, for that which is possible not to be at some time is not. Therefore, if everything is possible not to be, then at one time there could have been nothing in existence. Now if this were true, even now there would be nothing in existence, because that which does not exist only begins to exist by something already existing. Therefore, if at one time nothing was in existence, it would have been impossible for anything to have begun to exist; and thus even now nothing would be in existence — which is absurd. Therefore, not all beings are merely possible, but there must exist something the existence of which is necessary. But every necessary thing either has its necessity caused by another, or not. Now it is impossible to go on to infinity in necessary things which have their necessity caused by another, as has been already proved in regard to efficient causes. Therefore, we cannot but postulate the existence of some being having of itself its own necessity, and not receiving it from another, but rather causing in others their necessity. This all men speak of as God.

The fourth way is taken from the gradation to be found in things. Among beings there are some more and some less good, true, noble and the like. But "more" and "less" are predicated of different things, according as they resemble in their different ways something which is the maximum, as a thing is said to be hotter according as it more nearly resembles that which is hottest; so that there is something which is truest, something best, something noblest and, consequently, something which is uttermost being; for those things that are greatest in truth are greatest in being, as it is written in Metaph. ii. Now the maximum in any genus is the cause of all in that genus; as fire, which is the maximum heat, is the cause of all hot things. Therefore, there must also be something which is to all beings the cause of their *being*, goodness, and every other perfection; and this we call God.

The fifth way is taken from the governance of the world. We see that things which lack intelligence, such as natural bodies, act for an end, and this is evident from their acting always, or nearly always, in the same way, so as to obtain the best result. Hence it is plain that not fortuitously, but designedly, do they achieve their end. Now whatever lacks intelligence cannot move towards an end, unless it be directed by some being endowed with knowledge and intelligence; as the arrow is shot to its mark by the archer. Therefore some intelligent being exists by whom all natural things are directed to their end; and this being we call God.[82]

Additional Ways from the Physical World

The five ways of Aquinas, and other similar ways, are described by the *Catechism of the Catholic Church* as "'ways' of approaching God from creation." Coming to the knowledge of God's existence by way of creation has, further explains the *Catechism*, "a twofold point of departure: the

---

[82] Thomas Aquinas, *Summa Theologica*, I, Q. 2, Art. 3, newadvent.org, http://www.newadvent.org/summa/1002.htm (accessed July 25, 2016).

physical world, and the human person."[83] Aquinas's five ways begin from the physical world. His ways may be supplemented by additional ways from the physical world and by ways from the human person. We will begin with the former.

Contingency, the Kalam argument, the World as an Interacting Whole

Some other ways from the physical world include the following: Contingency, the Kalam argument, the World as an Interacting Whole, and Miracles. As explained by Kreeft, the argument from contingency is as follows:

> 1. If something exists, there must exist what it takes for that thing to exist. 2. The universe – the collection of beings in space and time – exists. 3. Therefore, there must exist what it takes for the universe to exist. 4. What it takes for the universe to exist cannot exist within the universe or be bounded by space and time. 5. Therefore, what it takes for the universe to exist must transcend both space and time.[84]

---

[83] "Catechism of the Catholic Church, no. 31, Vatican.va, http://www.vatican.va/archive/ccc_css/archive/catechism/p1s1c1.htm (accessed July 26, 2016).

[84] Peter J. Kreeft and Ronald K. Tacelli, *Handbook of Catholic Apologetics* (San Francisco: Ignatius Press, 2009), loc. 620-625.

The Kalam argument is similar to the Contingency argument. This argument for God's existence originated from medieval Arabic scholasticism. A modern formulation of the Kalam argument by William L. Craig is as follows:

1. Everything that begins to exist has a cause of its existence.
2. The universe began to exist.
3. Therefore, the universe has a cause of its existence.[85]

Another similar argument is called by Kreeft as "The World as an Interacting Whole". According to this argument no part of the universe is self-sufficient but depends on others, on the whole for its existence. This means that since no part is self-sufficient, all the parts taken together as a whole cannot be self-sufficient since nothing can give that which it does not have. The existence of the entire universe, therefore, must come from outside itself and this ultimate cause we identify as God.[86]

Miracles

Finally, an argument that is not directly related

---

[85] William L. Craig, *The Kalam Cosmological Argument* (Eugene: Wipf and Stock Publishers, 1979), 63.
[86] Peter J. Kreeft and Ronald K. Tacelli, *Handbook of Catholic Apologetics* (San Francisco: Ignatius Press, 2009), Loc. 651-662.

to the just mentioned three directly interrelated arguments is from miracles. Since there is sufficient, credible data supporting the occurrence of miracles, it is reasonable to maintain that their occurrence is due to God. For example, the International Medical Committee at Lourdes, France, has documented sixty-nine credible, miraculous cures that are not capable of being explained by modern science. The rigorous stages that an unexpected cure goes through before being declared as miracle by this committee are as follows:

Stages of Recognition

- Beginning with spontaneous and voluntary declarations made to the Medical Bureau by people who claim that they have been cured thanks to the intercession of Our Lady of Lourdes, the specialists of the International Medical Committee (CMIL), during their meeting in Paris on 27 and 28 November last decided to put in place the following 3 stages for examining files.

    Stage 1: From the "Declared" Cure to the "Unexpected" Cure

    All possible information is gathered from the person who believes they have received the grace of a cure by the medical officer of the Medical Bureau who then proceeds with a primary evaluation:

- To build up a file on the illness with a report on the current state of health to judge the person's personality in order to rule out trickery, acting, illusion, a possible hysterical or delirious pathology.
- To judge if this cure is clearly beyond the normal medical provisions of the illness in question note the circumstances of the cure itself and to verify if it happened according to extraordinary, unforeseen, striking or remarkable conditions. Some of these declarations will be marked "no follow-up" or "pending" or registered as "unexpected cure" to be studied.
- The bishop of the diocese where the person claiming to be cured lives will be informed that this cure is the subject of an enquiry and a doctor nominated by him can also be informed.

Stage 2: from the "Unexpected" Cure to the "Confirmed" Cure.

- The files of the "unexpected cures" are studies to complete the authentication inquiry which consists of a comparative study of the medical documents before and after the cure. This is to ensure that there was an indisputable change from a precise medical diagnosis of a known illness to a situation of restored health. They will also look to see if this cure shows signs of being completely out of character with the development of this illness. The opinion of a large number of professional specialists will be sought by a member of the CMIL before the file is presented to a gathering of the CMIL. In the end, the CMIL will classify the cure as no follow-up or they will validate this cure which they feel has been "thoroughly discussed and confirmed"

Stage 3: Opinion for Recognizing an Unexpected Cure.

- This is the final stage where the CMIL will affirm the "exceptional character" of a cure according to present scientific knowledge. The file is then sent by the Bishop of

Tarbes and Lourdes to the bishop of the diocese where the person who was cured lives. The support of the Lambertini criteria will assure that the cure has been found complete and lasting, from a serious illness which is incurable or of an unfavorable prognosis and that it happened in a sudden way.[87]

Ways from the Human Person

Ways to the knowledge of God's existence from the human person include human intelligence, the human sense of morality and human desire. This section will conclude with the clever argument known as Pascal's Wager.

Human Intelligence and the True

With respect to human intelligence the following question has been raised. How is it possible for human beings to understand material processes that occur in the brain which do not understand themselves? How is it possible for human beings to perceive the material world in an intelligent manner when we are also material?

---

[87] "Recognition of a Miracle," en.lourdes-france.org, http://en.lourdes-france.org/deepen/cures-and-miracles/recognition-of-a-miracle (accessed July 26, 2016).

Since nothing can give that which it does not have, in order for us to transcend physical processes, it is reasonable to conclude that our intellects are in part immaterial. We are able to understand material processes that do not understand themselves because we are in part immaterial. If we rule out that chance is an unreasonable explanation of why there is an intelligible universe capable of being understood by intelligent minds, it is also reasonable to conclude that the intelligibility of the universe and our intellects are products of a creating intelligence we call God.[88]

With reference to "abstraction," Aquinas explains how the immaterial aspect of our minds understand the intelligibility of the universe. As explained by the Dominican H.D. Gardeil in his classic work on Thomistic metaphysics, there are various degrees of abstraction in which the intellect abstracts matter away.[89] One way to begin understanding what Gardeil means by abstraction is to etymologically define the term. Abstraction is made up of two Latin words, the prefix *ab*, which means away from, and the verb *trahere*. Literally, therefore, abstraction means drawing away from. What is being drawn away? That which is physical

---

[88] Peter J. Kreeft and Ronald K. Tacelli, *Handbook of Catholic Apologetics* (San Francisco: Ignatius Press, 2009), Loc. 702.

[89] H.D. Gardeil, *Introduction to the Philosophy of St. Thomas Aquinas: IV. Metaphysics*, trans. John A. Otto (St. Louis: B. Herder Book Co., 1967), 295.

is being progressively drawn away from that which is immaterial. When I abstract, my mind strips away physical matter from an object in order to reveal its immaterial and universal aspects.

In the first degree of abstraction (physical), I only strip away some physical aspects but not all. For example, if I am thinking about the universal concept of dog I have abstracted all characteristics that pertain only to Fido my pet dog, color of his hair and eyes, etc., while leaving those physical characteristics that pertain to all dogs: a dog is a mammal who eats meat, etc.

In the second degree of abstraction (mathematical), I might be looking at the nose of my dog Fido and think that it is round. With the mathematical concept of roundness, I have removed all physical attributes from my pet dog Fido while retaining only the concept of a circle that is applicable to all physical things, whether wood, cement or dust, which can be made into a circular object.

In the third degree of abstraction (metaphysical), I abstract away even mathematical concepts that are only understood in relationship to physical matter, but in a general way. For example, I may think to myself, Fido is a beautiful dog, who is good, honest and faithful. The terms good, honest and faithful can be understood to referring to realities that exist in some material reality but not all, or do not exist in matter at all since they exist in their highest form in God. This third and last degree of abstraction is called metaphysics, which in Greek means literally after the physical.

Even atheists must rely on our immaterial ability to abstract. If atheists want to argue with logic that God does not exist, then they need to do so by abstracting out immaterial logical laws from the material world. But by so doing, they are accepting in practice the existence of immateriality that implies an immaterial creator who is God. Similarly, if an atheistic mathematician acknowledges that the idea of a perfect equilateral triangle[90] exists in his mind, he is in practice accepting that his mind is in part immaterial since a purely material mind cannot contain an immaterial object. By so doing he is accepting the existence of immateriality that implies an immaterial creator who is God.

Sense of Morality and the Good

Many atheists appeal to a universal standard by which to judge our actions. This universal moral standard, however, cannot be found in the material world. Where, then, does our moral sense originate from? If it comes from the material world, then how can it obligate an individual in a universal manner since the material world by being physical is particular? After all, something greater, in this case morality, does not come from something less, the particularity of the physical world. It is reasonable to conclude, therefore, that the common sense of a

---

[90] The sides of an equilateral triangle are perfectly equivalent and each angle is exactly sixty degrees

universally obliging moral law comes from God who is outside of the physical world. [91]

Desire for the Infinite

St. Augustine wrote in his spiritual classic *Confessions*, "our hearts are restless till they find rest in You."[92] With this phrase, he expressed the common human experience of not being satisfied by any amount of what this world can offer us whether this consists of money, power, pleasure or honors. It seems that we are all born with a natural desire for an infinite reality that does not exist in this material, finite reality. Where does this desire come from, and since our experience is that our natural desires can be met by natural ends why can't this fundamental desire by satisfied by a natural end? A reasonable answer is that we are not simply physical but also spiritual and the desire to be satisfied in an infinite manner can only be satisfied by that which is infinite goodness who is God.

---

[91] Peter J. Kreeft and Ronald K. Tacelli, *Handbook of Catholic Apologetics* (San Francisco: Ignatius Press, 2009), Loc. 778-855.

[92] Augustine, "Confessions," Book I, Chapter 1, newadvent.org, http://www.newadvent.org/fathers/110101.htm (accessed July 27, 2016). The following source was cited. Translated by J.G. Pilkington. From Nicene and Post-Nicene Fathers, First Series, Vol. 1. Edited by Philip Schaff. (Buffalo, NY: Christian Literature Publishing Co., 1887.) Revised and edited for New Advent by Kevin Knight. http://www.newadvent.org/fathers/110101.htm

Pascal's Wager

According to what is known as Pascal's Wager, it is risky to be an atheist and live in accordance with an atheistic moral view which ultimately entails no universally binding moral law since this cannot be found in the particular, material world. This amoral position is risky to live by since what happens if the atheist is mistaken and after dying comes face to face with God whom he has repeatedly offended? For the sake of a brief moment of finite existence on earth, during which the atheist bet on God's not existing, the atheist is now at risk of suffering eternally in hell.

~ Blaise Pascal ~

> Who then will blame Christians for not being able to give a reason for their belief, since they profess a religion for which they cannot give a reason? They declare, in expounding it to the world, that it is a foolishness, *stultitiam*; and then you complain that they do not prove it! If they proved it, they would not keep their word; it is in lacking proofs that they are not lacking in sense. "Yes, but although this excuses those who offer it as such and takes away from them the blame of putting it forward without reason, it does not excuse those who receive it." Let us then examine this point, and say, "God is, or He is not." But to

which side shall we incline? Reason can decide nothing here. There is an infinite chaos which separated us. A game is being played at the extremity of this infinite distance where heads or tails will turn up. What will you wager? According to reason, you can do neither the one thing nor the other; according to reason, you can defend neither of the propositions.

Do not, then, reprove for error those who have made a choice; for you know nothing about it. "No, but I blame them for having made, not this choice, but a choice; for again both he who chooses heads and he who chooses tails are equally at fault, they are both in the wrong. The true course is not to wager at all."

Yes; but you must wager. It is not optional. You are embarked. Which will you choose then? Let us see. Since you must choose, let us see which interests you least. You have two things to lose, the true and the good; and two things to stake, your reason and your will, your knowledge and your happiness; and your nature has two things to shun, error and misery. Your reason is no more shocked in choosing one rather than the other, since you must of necessity choose. This is one point settled. But your happiness? Let us weigh the gain and the loss in wagering that God is. Let us estimate these two chances. If you gain, you gain all;

if you lose, you lose nothing.

Wager, then, without hesitation that He is. "That is very fine. Yes, I must wager; but I may perhaps wager too much." Let us see. Since there is an equal risk of gain and of loss, if you had only to gain two lives, instead of one, you might still wager. But if there were three lives to gain, you would have to play (since you are under the necessity of playing), and you would be imprudent, when you are forced to play, not to chance your life to gain three at a game where there is an equal risk of loss and gain. But there is an eternity of life and happiness.

And this being so, if there were an infinity of chances, of which one only would be for you, you would still be right in wagering one to win two, and you would act stupidly, being obliged to play, by refusing to stake one life against three at a game in which out of an infinity of chances there is one for you, if there were an infinity of an infinitely happy life to gain. But there is here an infinity of an infinitely happy life to gain, a chance of gain against a finite number of chances of loss, and what you stake is finite. It is all divided; where-ever the infinite is and there is not an infinity of chances of loss against that of gain, there is no time to hesitate, you must give all. And thus, when one is forced to play, he must renounce reason to preserve his life, rather than risk it for infinite gain, as likely to happen as the loss of nothingness.

...

According to the doctrine of chance, you ought to put yourself to the trouble of searching for the truth; for if you die without worshipping the True Cause, you are lost. "But," say you, "if He had wished me to worship Him, He would have left me signs of His will." He has done so; but you neglect them. Seek them, therefore; it is well worth it.[93]

Quiz 3

1. Explain the five ways of St. Thomas Aquinas for God's existence.

2. State and then explain another two ways for God's existence that Aquinas does not refer to with his five ways.

3. Argue why there cannot be an infinite number of events.

4. Argue why it is impossible for the universe to come into existence on its own.

---

[93] Blaise Pascal, "Pensees, Section III: Of the Necessity of the Wager," 233-236, ccel.org, http://www.ccel.org/ccel/pascal/pensees.iv.html (accessed July 27, 2016).

5. Explain why when atheists write books in which they argue that their materialistic world view is true they are contradicting a central presupposition of their world view. Also, explain why the materialistic world view of atheists is unreasonable. Include in your answer the following: material world, immaterial ideas, three degrees of abstraction, mathematics, and logic.

Additional Activities and Resources

1. Respond to the following. Do so according to the Socratic method of gathering, clarifying and challenging questions.

   - Cause and effect can be traced back to infinity.
   - Something can come from nothing since the universe began after the Big Bang.
   - Since there is chance in the world, such as evolution that operates by random mutation, the world is not intelligently designed.
   - Intelligence is only due to chemical processes in the brain.
   - Ultimately it doesn't make a difference if you believe in God or not, if you are moral or not. We're all going to die, so why just enjoy ourselves as much as possible while we still can?

Readings

Chapters Three from Kreeft, Peter, and Ronald K. Tacelli. *Handbook of Christian Apologetics: Hundreds of Answers to Crucial Questions.* Downers Grove, IL: InterVarsity Press, 1994.

I, Q. 2, Art. 3 from Aquinas, Thomas. *Summa Theologica.*

Chapter Four: Objections of Atheists

Introduction

Despite being confronted with the many converging ways that indicate God's existence, atheists still object to God's existence. In this chapter, we will discuss one of the most common objections of atheists to God's existence, the objection that since there is evil in the world God cannot exist. Then, we will discuss atheists' rejection of miracles. Finally, we will see why the claim of scripture that atheism is foolishness is reasonable.

Evil

When atheists appeal to evil in order to reject the existence of God, it can be argued that they are contradicting their materialism. According to materialism, only that which is physical exists. But what is physical is particular and not universal.

Furthermore, according to atheistic materialism, physical matter is in a constant state of change since it randomly evolves. This means that it is not possible to find universal laws, such as a universal, moral standard, in what is physical because something cannot give that which it does not have. Similarly, since an effect does not bring about something greater than its cause, a universal reality cannot be produced by a cause that is made up by randomly, evolving matter. This basic principle is important to keep in mind when someone claims that something is evil because in the process of doing so they are implicitly making a reference to what is good, to a standard of goodness, which is a universal reality. According to Catholicism, and other believers in God, the ultimate standard of goodness is the immaterial God.[94]

Atheistic non-God Standards of Goodness

Atheists claim that a non-God standard of goodness exists by which it is possible to determine what is evil from what is good without any reference to God. Patrick Madrid and Kenneth Hensley in *The Godless Delusion* identify a number of these atheistic standards. Standards atheists appeal to include reference to happiness, doing no harm, majority rule, experts, and reason.[95] Accord-

---

[94] Kenneth Hensley, *Answering Atheism* CD (Augustine Institute).
[95] Patrick Madrid, and Kenneth Hensley, *The Godless Delusion: A Catholic Challenge to Modern*

ing to the "happiness standard" the morality of action is determined by what will lead to the greatest happiness to the greatest number of people. According to this standard, anything may be done to the individual as long as the group increases in happiness. The following practical question, though, remains unresolved. Who determines what actions make the group the happiest? Even if individuals within species are naturally inclined both to compete and to mutually aid one another, as the evolutionary theorist Peter Kropotkin demonstrates, what is the rationale for labelling individualistic competition evil and cooperative, mutual aid good when both are equally the result, according to evolutionary theorists, of evolution?[96]

Atheism (Huntington: Our Sunday Visitor Publishing Division, 2010), 93-125.
[96] The Russian, evolutionary theorist Peter Kropotkin disagreed with Darwin's thesis that competition is at the basis for the survival of a species. In order to survive, animals do not primarily ruthlessly compete, argued Kropotkin, but instead naturally band together in order to defend and support each other. Since Kropotkin identified himself with anarchism he was opposed to the formation of a strong world political power. In defending his thesis that mutual aid and not competition is the most basic principle he argues:
> Don't compete!—competition is always injurious to the species, and you have plenty of resources to avoid it!" That is the tendency of nature, not always realized in full, but always present. That is the watchword which comes to us from the bush, the forest, the river, the ocean. "Therefore combine—practice mutual aid! That

is the surest means for giving to each and to all the greatest safety, the best guarantee of existence and progress, bodily, intellectual, and moral." That is what Nature teaches us; and that is what all those animals which have attained the highest position in their respective classes have done. That is also what man—the most primitive man—has been doing; and that is why man has reached the position upon which we stand now, as we shall see in the subsequent chapters devoted to mutual aid in human societies.

Peter Kropotkin, *Mutual Aid a Factor of Evolution*, Project Gutenberg, http://www.gutenberg.org/cache/epub/4341/pg4341.html (accessed September 28, 2014), ch. 2.

Also read in chapter 2.

The idea which permeates Darwin's work is certainly one of real competition going on within each animal group for food, safety, and possibility of leaving an offspring. He often speaks of regions being stocked with animal life to their full capacity, and from that overstocking he infers the necessity of competition. But when we look in his work for real proofs of that competition, we must confess that we do not find them sufficiently convincing. ...In such cases what is described as competition may be no competition at all. One species succumbs, not because it is exterminated or starved out by the other species, but because it does not well accommodate itself to new conditions, which the other does. ...Happily enough, competition is not the rule either in the animal world or in mankind. It is limited among animals to exceptional periods, and natural selection finds better fields for its activity. Better conditions are created by the elimination of competition by means of mutual aid and mutual Support. In the great struggle for life—for the greatest possible

Upon examination, another supposed atheistic standard by which to determine morality also fails at being reliable. This is the "do no harm standard." According to this ethical standard, one may do whatever they want as long as the actions chosen do not cause undue harm to others. Who determines, though, what constitutes excessive harm? Often

---

> fullness and intensity of life with the least waste of energy—natural selection continually seeks out the ways precisely for avoiding competition as much as possible. The ants combine in nests and nations; they pile up their stores, they rear their cattle—and thus avoid competition; and natural selection picks out of the ants' family the species which know best how to avoid competition, with its unavoidably deleterious consequences. Most of our birds slowly move southwards as the winter comes, or gather in numberless societies and undertake long journeys—and thus avoid competition. Many rodents fall asleep when the time comes that competition should set in; while other rodents store food for the winter, and gather in large villages for obtaining the necessary protection when at work. The reindeer, when the lichens are dry in the interior of the continent, migrate towards the sea. Buffaloes cross an immense continent in order to find plenty of food. And the beavers, when they grow numerous on a river, divide into two parties, and go, the old ones down the river, and the young ones up the river and avoid competition. And when animals can neither fall asleep, nor migrate, nor lay in stores, nor themselves grow their food like the ants, they do what the titmouse does, and what Wallace (Darwinism, ch. v) has so charmingly described: they resort to new kinds of food—and thus, again, avoid competition...

moral choices involve harming one person while benefitting another. For example, is it morally wrong for a physician to inform an intimate partner of a patient that the patient has AIDS? What if the patient has not given permission to the physician for this information to be revealed? If the physician honors his patient/physician confidentiality agreement he avoids harming his patient while harming, by omission, the patient's lover.[97]

Also, some actions may appear to cause no immediate harm to others but over time their harm becomes apparent. For example, sexual activity outside of marriage may result in a pregnancy that may be aborted, causing great harm to the unborn baby, to the mother and to others. If the baby is brought to term, often the baby will be brought up by a single mother and will experience the pain of not knowing a father. Even if conception does not occur by a non-marital sexual act, those involved in the act may experience pain in such an act not taking place in the protective, loving context of a marriage. Finally, this do no harm standard cannot be found in the natural world, of which atheists claim we are completely part. For example, due to territorial competition, male chimpanzees have been reported to kill male chimpanzees who are not part of their group while female chimpanzees have killed and even eaten the infant chimpanzees of

---

[97] Jonathan Baron, "Do no harm," in D. M. Messick & A. E. Tenbrunsel (Eds.), *Codes of Conduct: Behavioral Research into Business Ethics* (New York: Russell Sage Foundation, 1996), 197-213.

female competitors.[98]

One way to determine if an action is excessively harmful and immoral is by majority decision. What happens if the majority turns upon a minority, such as occurred during World War II ending in the murder of millions? Most people, including atheists, do not attempt to justify the Nazi concentration camps in which genocide occurred. In addition, since polls indicate that majority opinions change frequently, is majority rule a reliable enough standard to determine morality by? If so, then how often should polls be taken and on what issues? In addition, where in the natural world, in which animals struggle to survive by beating out competitors, is this moral principle evident?

In response to the above objections to majority rule that can quickly end up in mob rule an atheist may respond by claiming that highly trained experts in ethics are to determine what is moral from what is not. What is to prevent experts from devising moral laws that serve their own interests in order to experience the most amount of pleasure, and to acquire the greatest amount of power, along with the greatest amount of distinction? Why would they act otherwise, or at least have a tendency in this direction, once the power to establish moral laws are placed in their few hands?

---

[98] Charles Q. Choi, "Female Chimps Kill Infants," May 14, 2007, livescience.com, http://www.livescience.com/1518-female-chimps-kill-infants.html (accessed July 29, 2016).

A response by atheists may be to simply appeal to reason as the standard to determine what is moral from what is immoral. However, it matters not if an expert, if the majority, or a minority agrees with the standard established by reason since they all can act irrationally. Furthermore, how do we determine what is reasonable from what is not? What is the basis out of which universal truth claims can be determined according to reason if the human mind is simply made up by chemical reactions in the brain that are based upon randomly driven evolution? The only way for an atheist to be logically consistent with their materialism is to bring morality into conformity with the random, chemical reactions of the brain that reason, according to materialism, from which it is derived. By so doing, however, atheists lack a universal standard of goodness to appeal to when determining what is true from what is false and what is good from what is evil.

The "Unjust" Distribution of Evil

Kreeft points out that some atheists fine tune their argument by claiming that they do not reject the existence of God due to the presence of evil in the world but because evil is unfairly distributed and is present in an excessive amount. Like the previous objections, this objection is problematic since a standard is needed in order determine not only what is good from what is evil but also what constitutes an unjust distribution of evil from a just distribution of evil.[99]

Another more refined argument by atheists against God's existence was answered by Aquinas a few hundred years ago. In succinctly capturing this objection, Aquinas writes:

> It seems that God does not exist; because if one of two contraries be infinite, the other would be altogether destroyed. But the word 'God' means that He is infinite goodness. If, therefore, God existed, there would be no evil discoverable; but there is evil in the world. Therefore, God does not exist.[100]

For a chart representation of this objection see below. Do the two columns necessarily contradict one another?

1. God exists	1. Evil exists
2. God is completely good	
3. God is all powerful (omnipotence)	

In order to answer this objection, the terms goodness, evil and omnipotence need to be carefully defined. We will begin with the term

---

[99] Peter J. Kreeft and Ronald K. Tacelli, *Handbook of Catholic Apologetics* (San Francisco: Ignatius Press, 2009), 1405-1412.

[100] Thomas Aquinas, *Summa Theologica* I (Fathers of the English Dominican Province, 1920), art. 2, q. 3, obj. 1.

goodness. In reference to Aristotle, Aquinas defines the essence of goodness as that which "is in some way desirable. Hence the Philosopher says (Ethic. i): 'Goodness is what all desire.'"[101]

Evil is the "absence of the good, which is natural and due to a thing."[102] Since evil has no being and only exists as an absence in a being (convertible with good), God did not create it.[103]

The above two pithy phrases were interpreted as referring to moral evil. Physical evil needs to be distinguished from moral evil. Physical evil is something from which we suffer but for which we are not directly responsible. For example, my mother was not responsible for suffering from cancer.

Moral evil is something we are responsible for. St. Augustine defines moral evil as disordered love that we choose and which leads to disordered relationships. Aquinas further develops Augustine's thought by identifying truth as the object of the

---

[101] Thomas Aquinas, *Summa Theologica* I (Fathers of the English Dominican Province, 1920), I, q. 5, art. 1.

[102] Thomas Aquinas, *Summa Theologica* I (Fathers of the English Dominican Province, 1920), I, q. 49, art. 1.

[103] Peter J. Kreeft and Ronald K. Tacelli, *Handbook of Catholic Apologetics*, 140. Kreeft demonstrates that by defining evil as the absence of the good logically means that the corruption of the best things are the worst things (*Corruptio optimi pessima*). Another way of phrasing this, he further explains, is "Lilies that fester smell far worse than weeds." The reason for this is because, according to this definition of evil, the degree we can be evil, i.e. immoral, depends to what extent we are ontologically good.

intellect and good as the object of the intellectual appetite, the will.[104] In order for the will to be properly ordered, the goods it desires need to be ordered according to truth. When we commit a moral evil we choose a good in a manner disordered to the ultimate good who is God and ultimate truth who likewise is God. God permits us this freedom since he wants our love and in order for this to occur we need to be free. In his infinite wisdom as an all-powerful loving Father, God wants us in our fallen state to discover how to order goods according to truth.

That God is all powerful does not mean that he can contradict himself. He cannot cease to exist or choose to be imperfect since this is contrary to his nature of perfect existence. God cannot contradict himself since he is by nature consistent and true. Nothing, including God can be and not be in the same respect. To claim otherwise is to claim something that is without meaning.[105]

In his infinite power, God providentially allows evil and in so doing draws good out of it as Romans states, "We know that all things work together for good for those who love God, who are called according to his purpose." (Romans 8:28) This phrase indicates that evil is in a certain sense relative, that is depends on the perspective of who experiences or witnesses evil. Aquinas explains the

---

[104] Thomas Aquinas, *De Veritate*, q. 1, art. 9; *De potential Dei*, q. 3, art. 15.
[105] Peter J. Kreeft and Ronald K. Tacelli, *Handbook of Catholic Apologetics*, loc. 1631.

relative nature of physical and moral evil as follows. When an antelope meets a hungry tiger, it views the hungry tiger as an evil, but the tiger views the antelope as a good. The analogous relativity of moral evil is evident in the relationship of the tyrant to the martyr, for without the tyrant there are no martyrs.[106]

---

[106] Robert Barron, *The Mystery of God: Who God is and Why He Matters*, DVDs (Word on Fire, 2015). Thomas Aquinas, *Summa Theologica,* I, q. 22, art. 2, reply to Obj. 2, New Advent, http://www.newadvent.org/summa/1022.htm (accessed October 3, 2015). "It is otherwise with one who has care of a particular thing, and one whose providence is universal, because a particular provider excludes all defects from what is subject to his care as far as he can; whereas, one who provides universally allows some little defect to remain, lest the good of the whole should be hindered. Hence, corruption and defects in natural things are said to be contrary to some particular nature; yet they are in keeping with the plan of universal nature; inasmuch as the defect in one thing yields to the good of another, or even to the universal good: for the corruption of one is the generation of another, and through this it is that a species is kept in existence. Since God, then, provides universally for all being, it belongs to His providence to permit certain defects in particular effects, that the perfect good of the universe may not be hindered, for if all evil were prevented, much good would be absent from the universe. A lion would cease to live, if there were no slaying of animals; and there would be no patience of martyrs if there were no tyrannical persecution. Thus Augustine says (Enchiridion 2): "Almighty God would in no wise permit evil to exist in His works, unless He were so almighty and so good as to produce good even from evil." It would appear that it was on account of these two arguments to which we have just replied, that some were persuaded to consider corruptible things--e.g. casual and

Although the above way of carefully defining terms in order to respond intelligently to atheism is a good way to answer atheism, one of the best ways to respond to the problem of evil is by directing the objector's attention to an image of Christ on the cross. Here, in faith, we see God who became one of us, who suffered with us, as Bishop Barron so well explains.[107] The title Emmanuel (Greek form of the Hebrew word *Immanuel*) of Jesus that we often use during Christmas time means exactly that God is with us for the Hebrew word Immanuel is formed from "*im*" which means with "*manu*" meaning us and "*el*" meaning God.[108]

By being with us in our very hearts, which is the spiritual center of our being, Jesus is with us in the most intimate way possible. In order not to be disappointed by Jesus' presence within our hearts as our closest friend (John 15:15), it is necessary to know what He offers us. Jesus offers to be our redeemer who will transform our experience of reality that our Heavenly Father permits us to experience as the Father, respecting human freedom, allowed his son to suffer and then to be raised from the dead. Jesus' intimate friendship is not, therefore, as Fr. Rolheiser teaches, a rescuer who saves us from suffering and death but rather

---

evil things--as removed from the care of divine providence."

[107] Robert Barron, *The Mystery of God: Who God is and Why He Matters*, DVDs (Word on Fire, 2015).

[108] "Emmanuel," eymonline.com, http://www.etymonline.com/index.php?term=Emmanuel (accessed April 30, 2016).

one who redeems us, who gives us the way, as The Way, for our sufferings and even death are to be transformed by His life for He has truly suffered, died and risen from the dead.[109]

Atheistic World View

To understand why atheists are so insistent that their belief that God does not exist because there is evil in the world is a rational claim, we need to examine their world view. What is a world view? As defined by Benedict XVI, writing as a theologian, "a world-view is always a synthesis of knowledge and values, which together propose to us a total vision of the real, a vision whose evidence and power of persuasion rest upon the fusion of knowledge and value."[110] Knowledge in this context refers to verifiable conclusions drawn from experience. Values are subjective perceptions that determine for a person what is important from what is not important. One value judgment of atheistic materialism is that the spiritual is not important. This assertion, though, is not based on knowing whether the immaterial exists or not. It is impossible to disprove that an immaterial world

---

[109] Ron Rolheiser, "The Resurrection as Revealing God as Redeemer, not as Rescuer," March 24, 2013, ronrolheiser.com, http://ronrolheiser.com/the-resurrection-as-revealing-god-as-redeemer-not-as-rescuer/#.VySsN2PXvnh (accessed 04/30/ 2016).

[110] Joseph Ratzinger, *Daughter Zion: Meditations on the Church's Marian Belief* (San Francisco: Ignatius Press, 1983), 57.

exists. Simply because I deem something is unimportant does not mean it does not exist. As is commonly held, including by atheists, minds do not determine existence; minds are part of existence.

An atheist may object that since the idea of a perfect God is unimaginable to the finite human mind God cannot exist. How can a tiny, little human being imagine a being who is greater than the entire universe and sustains it in existence? A response to this, as Frank Sheed explains, is to distinguish what is inconceivable from what is unimaginable. What is inconceivable is not the same as what is unimaginable. For example, since our mind relies on the imagination, with visually-based ideas, it is unimaginable that the soul has no color, size, weight or shape. However, due to our ability to abstract from the physical world in order to understand it, we can conceive that the soul has no color, size, weight or shape. This means that the truth of the spiritual reality needs to be discerned by the intellect with its ability to abstract and not by the imagination alone.[111]

Unlike what is unimaginable, what is inconceivable, as defined by Sheed, is nothing and does not and cannot exist. For example, a four-sided triangle is inconceivable since it is nothing. For God to create a four-sided triangle, all He needs to do is do nothing since a four-sided triangle is self-contradictory and meaningless in a similar way that blah, blah, bo, be, goteror, te is a meaningless

---

[111] Frank Sheed, *Theology and Sanctity* (No location given: Catholic Way Publishing, 2014), 13-15.

phrase, signifying nothing.[112]

What prevents atheists from admitting that while God is not imaginable he is conceivable and that it is reasonable to believe in his existence due to many converging reasons? The answer once again lies in the atheistic world view which devalues spiritual realities to such an extent that atheists assume that they know the immaterial/the spiritual does not exist. When the atheistic world view is judged by the standard of actual lived experience its unreasonableness quickly becomes apparent. According to the atheistic materialism, ultimate meaning is fictional, universal moral truths do not exist, abstract knowledge does not exist, and love and a sense of beauty do not actually exist since these are only chemical brain reactions. However, in actual life experience, including of atheists, a universal moral code is accepted and lived by, ultimate meaning is sought after, and love and beauty are affirmed as more than just chemical reactions in the brain. Since the materialistic atheistic world view is not in accordance with the vast majority of how people actually live life, it is, therefore, highly unreasonable.[113]

When the atheistic materialism is reduced to its logical conclusion the result is quite interesting. This manner of argumentation is called *Reductio*

---

[112] Frank Sheed, *Theology and Sanctity*, 15.

[113] Patrick Madrid, and Kenneth Hensley, *The Godless Delusion: A Catholic Challenge to Modern Atheism* (Huntington: Our Sunday Visitor Publishing Division, 2010), 180-232.

Ad Absurdum. Reducing atheistic materialism to a logical absurd conclusion entails the following steps. According to materialistic atheism, the process of thinking is entirely made up by random chemical reactions in the brain. Logically, therefore, books written by atheists are only the result of random chemical reactions. This means, according to atheists, books written by atheists are irrational and meaningless. Why then write them? In addition, since atheists write books, and in the process of writing the books they implicitly ground their arguments in logical, universal laws they are assuming the existence of a spiritual, non-material reality while arguing for a matter-only universe absent of God. This is highly contradictory.[114]

Similarly, when atheists reject God by arguing that God cannot exist since evil exists, they are once again appealing to an immaterial, non-particular, universal reality (universal goodness), who ultimately is God since as truth and goodness itself, He is the standard of all truth and goodness. As pithily put forth by Madrid, "for the atheist wanting to raise the problem of evil: He has to sit on God's lap before he can slap God in the face."[115] Using another image, Madrid also points out the inner contradiction in atheistic reasoning by arguing that since atheists reason, debate, and write books against the existence of God due to the presence of

---

[114] Patrick Madrid, and Kenneth Hensley, *The Godless Delusion*, 141.
[115] Patrick Madrid, and Kenneth Hensley, *The Godless Delusion*, 92.

evil in the world, they are similar to people who claim that gravity does not exist while at the same time living as if it does and expecting others to live as if gravity exists.[116]

To phrase this in another way, according to atheistic materialism, human reason is merely determined by random, ever changing chemical reactions. This means that there is no standard by which to judge anything as more right/true or good/evil than something else. Therefore, when atheists write books in which they argue that their materialistic world view is true they are contradicting their presupposition that a standard of truth does not exist.[117] As pointed out by Hensley, in order for the inner tension in atheists to be resolved between what they profess (materialism) and how they live (morally according to a theistic world view) and argue (as if truth is capable of being known) they need either to accept God's existence or reject morality as universal and cease arguing that one position is more true than another.[118]

Miracles

Atheists reject the possibility of miracles for a

---

[116] Patrick Madrid, and Kenneth Hensley, *The Godless Delusion*, 51.
[117] Patrick Madrid, and Kenneth Hensley, *The Godless Delusion*, 134.
[118] Kenneth Hensley, *Answering Atheism* CD (Augustine Institute).

variety of reasons that all are based on atheistic materialism. Kreeft identifies a number of atheistic objections to miracles and their responses. These include the following.

A miracle, an atheist may claim, is impossible since it is a contradiction to an ordered universe. In order to respond to this objection, the term contradiction needs to be defined. Aristotle defines the law of non-contradiction as follows. "It is, that the same attribute cannot at the same time belong and not belong to the same subject and in the same respect."[119] For example, a person cannot walk on water and not walk on water in the same respect, in

---

[119] "It is, that the same attribute cannot at the same time belong and not belong to the same subject and in the same respect; we must presuppose, to guard against dialectical objections, any further qualifications which might be added. This, then, is the most certain of all principles, since it answers to the definition given above. For it is impossible for anyone to believe the same thing to be and not to be, as some think Heraclitus says. For what a man says, he does not necessarily believe; and if it is impossible that contrary attributes should belong at the same time to the same subject (the usual qualifications must be presupposed in this premise too), and if an opinion which contradicts another is contrary to it, obviously it is impossible for the same man at the same time to believe the same thing to be and not to be; for if a man were mistaken on this point he would have contrary opinions at the same time. It is for this reason that all who are carrying out a demonstration reduce it to this as an ultimate belief; for this is naturally the starting-point even for all the other axioms.'" Aristotle, *Metaphysics*, book IV, part 3, trans. W.D. Ross, Classics MIT, http://classics.mit.edu/Aristotle/metaphysics.mb.txt (accessed December 28, 2014).

other words at the same time with his one body. To claim this occurred is to claim nonsense, to claim something that signifies nothing. To claim that someone walked on water, although highly unlikely, is not a contradiction. Instead it is a logical possibility. Furthermore, miracles are not contrary to the observation that the universe is ordered. A miracle only makes sense when it is assumed that nature is orderly. The order of nature is the standard used to determine a miracle. With nature as a standard, a miracle is an exception to this standard. If nature was not ordered and predictable than a miracle would be meaningless since it would no longer be an exception to what is ordinary and predictable but would be how nature ordinarily occurs, chaotically and randomly. In such a universe, the exception is the norm and miracles can be expected to occur regularly.

An atheist may counter by objecting that since all that exists is matter and science has shown that the material world operates according to predictable laws then miracles are not possible since they break these laws. In response, one may point out that once the intelligent order of the universe is credited to an intelligent designer, who is God, then God as the designer of the universe can suspend creation's laws since he is their author. To this an atheist may object by claiming that such a belief in divine intervention entails the rejection of the scientific method and hence is irrational. Kreeft wisely points out that this claim is not reasonable since belief in miracles only requires recognizing the limits of the scientific method.[120]

In a final attempt to reject miracles, an atheist may even appeal to God's existence by arguing that presuming that a perfect God exists a miracle would mean that God created an imperfect creation indicating that He is not perfect. One may respond by explaining that God is not restricted from creating a universe in which he cannot intervene. He may choose to create a universe that gradually, in time reveals His infinite wisdom, goodness, and truth.[121]

Atheism and Foolishness

As has been explained, atheism is rooted in materialism which claims all that exists is physical matter. If, however, physical matter is all that exists, then it is not possible that universal concepts of truth and goodness exist since matter is only particular and individualized and never universal. This also means that if a standard that determines the degree to which something is false and lacking in goodness does not exist, then falsehood and evil likewise do not exist since there is nothing to determine what is false from what is true and what is evil from what is good. Atheistic arguments that reject God because evil exists do not, consequently, make sense. Within such an argument both a

---

[120] Peter J. Kreeft and Ronald K. Tacelli, *Handbook of Catholic Apologetics*, loc. 1284.
[121] Peter J. Kreeft and Ronald K. Tacelli, *Handbook of Catholic Apologetics*, 1261-1293.

universal standard of goodness is appealed to which determines what is evil and the existence of a universal standard of goodness is rejected. As the phrase goes, you can't have your cake and eat it, too. Something cannot be and not be in the same respect. For this reason, and others, atheism is foolishness.

Scripture's association of atheism with foolishness is, consequently, reasonable. In describing the foolishness of atheists Psalm fourteen writes, "Fools say in their hearts, 'There is no God.'" (Psalm 14:1 NRSV) In explaining why atheists are fools, St. Paul asserts in his letter to the Romans that those who deny God are foolish even though they claim to be wise since "what can be known about God is plain to them." The context of this quote is as follows:

> For the wrath of God is revealed from heaven against all ungodliness and wickedness of those who by their wickedness suppress the truth. For what can be known about God is plain to them, because God has shown it to them. Ever since the creation of the world his eternal power and divine nature, invisible though they are, have been understood and seen through the things he has made. So they are without excuse; for though they knew God, they did not honor him as God or give thanks to him, but they became futile in their thinking, and their senseless minds

were darkened. Claiming to be wise, they became fools; and they exchanged the glory of the immortal God for images resembling a mortal human being or birds or four-footed animals or reptiles. (Roman 1:18-23 NRSV)

With reference to the above scriptural passage, Hensley argues that atheists are fools because they suppress the abundant evidence of God's existence they daily encounter in how they reason (by abstracting universal, immaterial ideas from the physical world) and in their acceptance of objective moral laws. Despite the foolishness of their position, atheists continue to spend time arguing their position is better than another position. Why do they exert this effort if reason is only many biochemical reactions in the brain? How, according to their basic materialistic premise, is it possible to know something is more true than something else? In order for this to occur, I need the capacity to transcend that which is material in order to judge it. This, though, is precisely what atheists deny and yet they keep on thinking, reasoning and arguing.[122]

Compassion for Atheists

In demonstrating that belief in God is highly reasonable, we need to be cautious not to present belief in God as equivalent to knowledge we obtain

---

[122] Kenneth Hensley, *Answering Atheism* CD (Augustine Institute).

through observation and study of the physical world. As St. Paul writes in his letter to the Corinthians, while in this life "we see in a mirror, dimly." Only after we die will we "see face to face." (1 Corinthians 13:12 NRSV) Due to not seeing God as we are promised to in the beatific vision, it is very likely we experience difficulty in believing. Even with his great faith and towering intellect, Blessed John Henry Newman experienced difficulty in believing. However, he made a clear distinction between these difficulties and doubt, in its fullest sense. "Ten thousand difficulties," he wrote, "do not make one doubt..."[123]

The great saint and doctor of the Church Thérèse of Lisieux even experienced the "worst temptations of atheism." In summarizing her struggles, Benedict XVI, writing as a theologian, states:

---

[123] John Henry Newman, "Apologia Pro Vita Sua (1865)," Chapter 5. Position of my Mind since 1845, newmanreader.org, http://www.newmanreader.org/works/apologia65/chapter5.html (accessed August 3, 2016). "Ten thousand difficulties do not make one doubt, as I understand the subject; difficulty and doubt are incommensurate. There of course may be difficulties in the evidence; but I am speaking of difficulties intrinsic to the doctrines themselves, or to their relations with each other. A man may be annoyed that he cannot work out a mathematical problem, of which the answer is or is not given to him, without doubting that it admits of an answer, or that a certain particular answer is the true one. Of all points of faith, the being of a God is, to my own apprehension, encompassed with most difficulty, and yet borne in upon our minds with most power."

Yet this very saint, a person apparently cocooned in complete security, left behind her, from the last weeks of her passion, shattering admissions that her horrified sisters toned down in her literary remains and that have only now come to light in the new verbatim editions. She says, for example, "I am assailed by the worst temptations of atheism". Her mind is beset by every possible argument against the faith; the sense of believing seems to have vanished; she feels that she is now "in sinners' shoes." In other words, in what is apparently a flawlessly interlocking world someone here suddenly catches a glimpse of the abyss lurking—even for her—under the firm structure of the supporting conventions. In a situation like this, what is in question is not the sort of thing that one perhaps quarrels about otherwise—the dogma of the Assumption, the proper use of confession—all this becomes absolutely secondary. What is at stake is the whole structure; it is a question of all or nothing. That is the only remaining alternative; nowhere does there seem anything to cling to in this sudden fall. Wherever one looks, only the bottomless abyss of nothingness can be seen.[124]

---

[124] Joseph Ratzinger, *Introduction to Christianity*, Revised Edition (San Francisco: Ignatius Press, 2004),

At the time she experienced these temptations, St. Thérèse of Lisieux also paradoxically continued to believe with a faith that was far greater than believers who do not experience temptations like hers. Despite these struggles, her faith was certain for as the *Catechism of the Catholic Church* states: "Faith is certain. It is more certain than all human knowledge because it is founded on the very word of God who cannot lie. To be sure, revealed truths can seem obscure to human reason and experience, but the certainty that the divine light gives is greater than that which the light of natural reason gives.'"[125]

Even if our temptations against faith are but a faint resemblance of St. Thérèse of Lisieux's heroic struggles, these trials can help us to have compassion for atheists. In other words, we can suffer with atheists, which the Greek basis of word compassion literally means. This compassion for atheists is a way to challenge atheists to rethink what they think is certain. In re-examining their conviction that God does not exist, they may encounter what Benedict XVI, writing as a theologian, describes as "the eerie feeling induced

---

42-43.

[125] *Catechism of the Catholic Church*, no. 157, ccc.usccb.org, http://www.usccb.org/beliefs-and-teachings/what-we-believe/catechism/catechism-of-the-catholic-church/epub/index.cfm (accessed August 4, 2016).

by the words 'Yet perhaps it is true.'"[126]

In trying to persuade atheists to open themselves to the gift of faith, to belief in God, our humbly admitting, at least to ourselves, our own difficulties with the faith may help bring about conversions. This humility is key, for as Pope Francis said:

> If a person says that he met God with total certainty and is not touched by a margin of uncertainty, then this is not good. For me, this is an important key. If one has the answers to all the questions—that is the proof that God is not with him. It means that he is a false prophet using religion for himself. The great leaders of the people of God, like Moses, have always left room for doubt. You must leave room for the Lord, not for our certainties; we must be humble. Uncertainty is in every true discernment that is open to finding confirmation in spiritual consolation.[127]

---

[126] Joseph Ratzinger, Introduction to Christianity, Revised Edition (San Francisco: Ignatius Press, 2004), 46.

[127] Pope Francis, "Interview with Pope Francis by Fr Antonio Spadaro," August 19, 2013, The Vatican, http://w2.vatican.va/content/francesco/en/speeches/2013/september/documents/papa-francesco_20130921_intervista-spadaro.html (accessed August 7, 2015).

Quiz 4

1. Argue in at least two ways that Scripture's assertion that atheists are fools is reasonable.

2. Explain why in order for atheists to be logically consistent with their materialistic world view they cannot argue that atheism is more reasonable than theism. Include in your answer the following: the human mind, transcendence, abstraction, truth, goodness and judgment.

3. Argue against the following:

   - Objection 1: Miracles contradict nature.
   - Objection 2: Miracles can't happen since nature follows predictable, scientifically shown patterns.
   - Objection 3: In order to believe in miracles, it is necessary to reject the scientific method.
   - Objection 4: Those who believe in miracles are foolish since they are believing in a contradiction. The contradiction is that a perfect God created an imperfect creation. An imperfect creation that needs to be perfection, however, indicates that its maker is imperfect.

Additional Activities and Resources

Respond to the following. Do so according to the Socratic method of gathering, clarifying and challenging questions.

- Since evil exists God cannot possibly exist.
- Since there is so much evil and evil happens to good people, God does not exist.
- St. Thérèse of Lisieux was atheistic.
- I saw an innocent young boy being murdered before my eyes. Where was your God then?
- You don't need God in order to have a universal standard for truth and goodness.
- Miracles contradict nature.
- Knowledge alone can prove God does not exist.
- I can't image God exists therefore He does not.
- I am so convinced that God does not exist I am going to write a book proving conclusively that this is true.
- Miracles can't happen since nature follows predictable, scientifically shown patterns.
- In order to believe in miracles, it is necessary to reject the scientific method.
- Those who believe in miracles are foolish since they are believing in a contradiction. The contradiction is that a perfect God

created an imperfect creation. An imperfect creation that needs to be perfection, however, indicates that its maker is imperfect.

Readings

Chapters Five and Six from Kreeft, Peter, and Ronald K. Tacelli. *Handbook of Christian Apologetics: Hundreds of Answers to Crucial Questions*. Downers Grove, IL: InterVarsity Press, 1994. Loc. 1261-1293.

Chapters Three, Four, Five, and Six from Madrid, Patrick, and Kenneth Hensley. *The Godless Delusion: A Catholic Challenge to Modern Atheism*. Huntington: Our Sunday Visitor Publishing Division, 2010.

Chapters Two, and Ten through Fourteen from Sheed, Frank. *Theology and Sanctity*. Catholic Way Publishing, 2014.

Audio

Hensley, Kenneth, *Answering Atheism CD*. Augustinian Institute.

Chapter Five: Faith and Science

Introduction

Many atheists and agnostics claim that science provides abundant reasons not to believe in a God. We will examine a number of the most frequently referred to supposedly scientifically-based arguments that attempt to portray faith in God as at best not needed and at worst irrational. The following will be discussed: the Galileo Affair, the Scientific Method, evolution, modern physics, chance, and human intelligence in relationship to animal intelligence and computer intelligence.

The Galileo Affair

Knowing the historical context will help to properly interpret why the Church placed Galileo Galilei under house arrest. Galileo's heliocentric model was based on an earlier heliocentric model proposed by Nicholas Copernicus (1473-1543). This

Polish mathematician and astronomer developed a heliocentric (sun-centered) theory in his book *On the Revolutions of the Celestial Spheres*.[128] His theory was not a brand-new theory, for it had been proposed even before the birth of Christ by the Greek Mathematician and astronomer Aristarchus (c. 310-230 BC).[129]

In contrast to how the Church responded to Galileo, the Church treated Copernicus's

---

[128] Nicholas Copernicus, *On the Revolutions of the Heavenly Spheres*, trans. Charles Glenn Wallis (Amherst: Prometheus Books, 1995).

[129] Archimedes (c. 287-212 BC), a Greek mathematician and physicist, describes refers to Aristarchus and his heliocentric theory:

> You are aware ['you' being King Gelon] that 'universe' is the name given by most astronomers to the sphere, the center of which is the center of the earth, while its radius is equal to the straight line between the center of the sun and the center of the earth. This is the common account ... as you have heard from the astronomers. But Aristarchus brought out a book consisting of a certain hypothesis, wherein it appears, as a consequence of the assumptions made, that the universe is many times greater than the 'universe' just mentioned. His hypotheses are that the fixed stars and the sun remain unmoved, that the earth revolves about the sun in the circumference of a circle, the sun lying in the middle of the orbit...

Thomas Heath, *Aristarchus of Samos: The Ancient Copernicus* (Oxford: Clarendon Press, 1913), 301-302. See the following source: archive.org, https://archive.org/stream/aristarchusofsamooheatuoft#page/n5/mode/2up.

heliocentric theory with great respect as is evident in the foreword to Copernicus's 1542 edition of *On the Revolutions of the Celestial Spheres*. In the foreword is a letter by Cardinal Schönberg, written in 1536. It reads:

~ Cardinal Schönberg 1536 letter to Copernicus ~

Some years ago word reached me concerning your proficiency, of which everybody constantly spoke. At that time, I began to have a very high regard for you, and also to congratulate our contemporaries among whom you enjoyed such great prestige. For I had learned that you had not merely mastered the discoveries of the ancient astronomers uncommonly well but had also formulated a new cosmology. In it you maintain that the earth moves; that the sun occupies the lowest, and thus the central, place in the universe; that the eighth heaven remain perpetually motionless and fixed; and that, together with the elements included in its sphere, the moon, situated between the heavens of Mars and Venus, revolves around the sun in the period of a year. I have also learned that you have written an exposition of this whole system of astronomy, and have computed the planetary motions and set them down in tables, to the greatest admiration of all. Therefore, with the utmost earnestness I entreat you, most learned sir, unless I inconvenience you, to communicate this discovery of yours to scholars, and at the earliest possible moment to send me your writings on the sphere of the universe together with the tables and whatever else you have that is relevant to this subject. Moreover, I have instructed Theodoric of Reden to have everything copied in your quarters at my expense and dispatched to me. If you gratify my desire in this matter, you will see that you are dealing with a man who is zealous for your reputation and eager to do justice to so fine a talent. Farewell.[130]

Why did the Church praise Copernicus and punish Galileo? The answer is that unlike Galileo, Copernicus did not insist on presenting the heliocentric theory as proven but instead cautiously presented this theory as only a possible explanation that needed further verification. Currently, we have abundant evidence that verifies the heliocentric

---

[130] Nicholas Copernicus, *On the Revolutions*, trans. Edward Rosen (Baltimore: John Hopkins University Press, 2008), WebExhibits, http://www.webexhibits.org/calendars/year-text-Copernicus.html (accessed November 11, 2014); In 1616, after Copernicus had died, the Catholic Church decided for prudential reasons to place Copernicus's book, *On the Revolutions of the Celestial Spheres*, on the Index. In 1835 this book was finally removed from the Index. Jack Repcheck, *Copernicus' Secret: How the Scientific Revolution Began* (New York: Simon & Schuster, 2007), 194.

Catholic Apologetics

theory, but such evidence was lacking both at the time of Copernicus and at the time of Galileo. Another explanation is due to the differing styles of Copernicus and Galileo. Copernicus was respectful to Church authority while Galileo mocked Church authority. In his book *Dialogue Concerning the Two Chief World Systems*, Galileo even poked fun at Pope Urban VIII by having the character *Simplicio* (simpleton) speak words that the Pope once spoke.[131] Finally, due to the Protestant Reformers' tendency to literally interpret Scriptural passages that phenomenologically describe the sun rotating around the earth, the Church did not want to lend support to the heliocentric theory until there was greater verification for the theory. For these and other reasons, the Church brought Galileo to trial, accused him of heresy, required him to recant and then placed him under house arrest.[132]

In criticizing the Church's actions towards Galileo, many forget that the historical context at the time of Galileo differed significantly from ours.[133] In pointing this out, Cardinal Ratzinger in a

---

[131] Galileo Galilei, *Dialogue Concerning the Two Chief World Systems*, trans. Stillman Drake (New York: The Modern Library, 2001), xvi.

[132] Galileo Galilei, *Dialogue Concerning the Two Chief World Systems*, xiii-xxiii.

[133] Cardinal Bellarmine, head of the Holy Office of the Roman Inquisition at the time of Galileo, even indicated his openness to the heliocentric theory but wanted more verification. He said:

Feb. 15, 1990, speech at Sapienza University of Rome stated:

> The Church at the time of Galileo kept much more closely to reason than did Galileo himself, and she took into consideration the ethical and social consequences of Galileo's teaching too. Her verdict against Galileo was rational and just and the revision of this verdict can be justified only on the grounds of what is politically opportune.[134]

With hindsight gained from history, many in the Church, including those in the highest office, wish that the Church was less harsh in punishing Galileo. Taking our current historical perspective into account, on October 31, 1992, Pope John Paul II expressed remorse for the Church's punishment

---

If there were a real proof that the Sun is in the center of the universe...and that the Sun does not go around the Earth but the Earth round the Sun, then we should have to proceed with great circumspection in explaining passages in Scripture which appear to teach the contrary, and admit that we did not understand them...But as for myself, I shall not believe that there are such proofs until they are shown to me.

Christopher Baglow, *Faith, Science & Reason, Theology on the Cutting Edge* (Woodridge: Midwest Theological Forum, 2009), 81. Baglow refers to the following source: Robert Bellarmine, *Letter to Foscarini*, as quoted in Barr, *Modern Physics*, 8.

[134] Ratzinger, *Turning Point for Europe* (Ignatius Press, 2010), 104.

of Galileo.[135]

The Scientific Method

The English philosopher and scientist Francis Bacon (1561-1626) greatly contributed to what is now called the scientific method. His method promoted the careful analysis of sensory data obtained by experimentation in order "establish degrees of certainty."[136] A simplified description of how scientists currently obtain various degrees of certainty is as follows:

1. Find a natural phenomenon to be accounted for.
2. Frame a hypothesis that if true would account for the phenomenon in question.

---

[135] Discorso Di Giovanni Paolo Ii Ai Partecipanti Alla Sessione PlenariaDella Pontificia Accademia Delle Scienze Sabato, 31 ottobre 1992 http://www.vatican.va/holy_father/john_paul_ii/speeches/1992/october/documents/hf_jp-ii_spe_19921031_accademia-scienze_it.html accessed 01/10/ 2014.

[136] Francis Bacon, *The New Organon*, eds. Lisa Jardine, and Michael Silverthorne (Cambridge: Cambridge University Press, 2000), 28. "Our method, though difficulty to practice, is easy to formulate. It is to establish degrees of certainty, to preserve sensation by putting a kind of restraint on it. But to reject in general the work of the mind that follows sensation; and rather to open and construct a new and certain road for the mind from the actual perceptions of the senses."

3. Derive a directly observable result from the hypothesis, given a set of initial conditions.
4. Set up an experiment that brings about those initial conditions and check to see if the observable result occurs.
5. If the observable result does not occur, reject the hypothesis deductively ...; go back to step 2 and frame a new hypothesis.
6. If the observable result does occur, the hypothesis receives inductive support; go back to step 3 and test again.[137]

Madrid observes that nowhere in the scientific method is a particular philosophy adopted. Just as a recipe book can be followed with equal results by a materialist and by a Platonist so can the scientific method be followed by people of diverse philosophical assumptions. A recipe and a method is not a the same as a philosophy. Unfortunately, when it comes to the scientific method some people erroneously assume that the scientific method is necessarily supportive of philosophical materialism. This is not the case since as a method it neither affirms or denies a particular philosophical approach.[138]

In addition, the scientific method can only be

---

[137] Steven Gimbel, *Exploring the Scientific Method: Cases and Questions* (Chicago: University of Chicago Press, 2011), 93.

[138] Patrick Madrid, *The Godless Delusion*, 28-29.

applied to the material, observable world. It cannot be applied to God and other immaterial realities since modern science is limited to studying physical matter. The scientific method's attempt to falsify its starting hypothesis also means that it only deals with varying degrees of probability and not with certainties. The method always remains open to exceptions being discovered and if discovered to return to the hypothesis in order either to modify or reject it. The inherent skepticism within this method means that according to this method of acquiring knowledge simply because something has not been discovered does not mean it does not exist.[139]

As pithily explained by Father Robert Spitzer, a scientist cannot know what he doesn't know until he knows it.[140] Once he knows something he did not previously know, the scientific method can be used

---

[139] Patrick Madrid, *The Godless Delusion*, 216-217.

[140] Patrick Madrid, *The Godless Delusion*, 29, 216-217. Similarly, Madrid argues the absence of conclusive evidence of God's existence does not means there is definitive evidence that God does not exist. For example, after I search my room for ants I cannot reasonably conclude that since I did not find a single ant in my room that there are no ants in my room. They may be hiding beneath the floor boards. Also, an atheistic professor may reason that since no student in his class has heard, smelled, seen, touched, or tasted God that means that God exists. A reply could be that since no student in the class has heard, smelled, touched or tasted the professor's brain that means that the professor has no brain. Likewise, would a car mechanic be considered sane if he claimed that since he has only worked with cars he is convinced that only cars exist?

once again to discover more knowledge that was previously not known. Logically, therefore, the scientific method can neither disprove or prove with certainty that God exists since, as evident in the above steps, scientific findings are always subject to being modified and re-examined. This is because science is based on degrees of probability not on certainty, for it is primarily an inductive science, based on probabilities and on particular observations, and not a deductive science, based on certain conclusions that follow certain premises. Furthermore, adds Spitzer, a scientist cannot use evidence within the universe to disprove existence of something outside the universe.[141]

Evolution

As cautiously presented by the Catholic International Theological Commission in *Communion and Stewardship: Human Persons Created in the Image of God*, around 15 billion years ago the universe exploded into existence. Gradually, the exploding particles coalesced into galaxies and stars. Then around 10 billion years ago, the first planets were formed. Planet earth and its solar system was formed about 4.5 billion years

---

[141] Robert Spitzer, "Teaching Science and Faith – Conflict or Confluence? For High School Science and Religion Teachers," Institute for Theological Encounter with Science and Technology and the Magis Center, http://mp125118.cdn.mediaplatform.com/125118/wc/mp/4000/5592/5599/40716/Lobby/default.htm (accessed February 28, 2015).

ago. Around 3.5-4 billion years ago the first living organism evolved on planet earth. According to the consensus of biologists, all living organisms on earth are descendants of this first living organism. About 150,000 years ago the *homo sapiens*, the first man and woman, evolved out of hominids.[142]

---

[142] "International Theological Commission Communion and Stewardship: Human Persons Created in the Image of God," vatican.va, http://www.vatican.va/roman_curia/congregations/cfaith/cti_documents/rc_con_cfaith_doc_20040723_communion-stewardship_en.html (accessed August 6, 2016).

"63. According to the widely accepted scientific account, the universe erupted 15 billion years ago in an explosion called the "Big Bang" and has been expanding and cooling ever since. Later there gradually emerged the conditions necessary for the formation of atoms, still later the condensation of galaxies and stars, and about 10 billion years later the formation of planets. In our own solar system and on earth (formed about 4.5 billion years ago), the conditions have been favorable to the emergence of life. While there is little consensus among scientists about how the origin of this first microscopic life is to be explained, there is general agreement among them that the first organism dwelt on this planet about 3.5-4 billion years ago. Since it has been demonstrated that all living organisms on earth are genetically related, it is virtually certain that all living organisms have descended from this first organism. Converging evidence from many studies in the physical and biological sciences furnishes mounting support for some theory of evolution to account for the development and diversification of life on earth, while controversy continues over the pace and mechanisms of evolution. While the story of human origins is complex and subject to revision, physical anthropology and molecular biology combine to make a convincing case for the origin of the human species in Africa about 150,000 years ago in a humanoid

Fr. Peter Samuel Kucer, MSA

This Catholic International Theological Commission explanation of man's origin is based on evolutionary theory.[143] According to this theory, as outlined above around 150,000 years ago a hominid called the *Homo sapiens* emerged out of ape like creatures called hominids. In Latin *Homo sapiens* means wise man. They received this name because of their high degree of intelligence in comparison with other hominids.

As explained by Baglow, the symbolic artifacts of the *Homo sapiens* from around 45,000 to 77,000 years ago demonstrate that because of their intelligence that they differed in kind and not simply in degree from their ancestors. Some of the artifacts the *Homo sapiens* left behind indicate they

---

population of common genetic lineage. However it is to be explained, the decisive factor in human origins was a continually increasing brain size, culminating in that of homo sapiens. With the development of the human brain, the nature and rate of evolution were permanently altered: with the introduction of the uniquely human factors of consciousness, intentionality, freedom and creativity, biological evolution was recast as social and cultural evolution."

[143] Also see the following documents written by modern popes which affirm the evolutionary theory. Pope Pius XII 1950 encyclical *Humani Generis*, especially number 36-37; Pope St. John Paul II's General Audience of April 16, 1986 titled "Humans are Spiritual and Corporeal Beings"; Pope St. John Paul II October 22, 1996 address to the Pontifical Academy of Sciences titled, "Evolution and the Church's Magisterium," and Benedict XVI's July 27, 2007 question-and-answer session.

were developing language which in turn indicates that they had the capacity to form universal concepts. The ability to form universal concepts requires the capacity to spiritually transcend the material world including the particular matter of the brain in order to judge it.

This unique capacity of the first man and first woman to transcend the material world cannot come from the material world since the material world is individualized and not universal. Nothing can give that which it does not have. Since the capacity to reason did not come from themselves, or from biological evolution, it is reasonable to conclude that it came as a gift from outside the physical world, from God. This is what the Catholic Church teaches. According to the Catholic Church, the human, immaterial soul with its capacity to transcend the material world is not a product of biological evolution but rather is given to man by God in a special act of creation. In this special creation, called ensoulment, God intervened in history by creating and infusing two spiritual souls into the first man and first woman. Findings in modern genetics have even roughly identified the first man and first woman by tracing every human being's genetic material to but only one male and one female. As He did with Adam and Eve, at the conception of every human being God continues his special intervention by creating an immaterial soul and infusing this soul into the human life that is developing within the womb of the mother.[144]

Modern Physics: Gravity and a Multi-Universe

The noted physicist Stephen Hawking has famously claimed that the universe could have originated from nothing. He wrote, "Because there is a law like gravity, the universe can and will create itself from nothing …. Spontaneous creation is the reason there is something rather than nothing, why the universe exists, why we exist. It is not necessary to invoke God to light the blue touch paper and set the universe going."[145]

The Jesuit Robert Spitzer counters Hawking's assertion by pointing out that this claim "betrays Hawking's fundamental assumption about the universe, namely that it came from nothing."[146] Hawking, explains Spitzer, can only hold this assumption if "he believes that there are reasons for

---

[144] Christopher Baglow, *Faith, Science & Reason, Theology on the Cutting Edge* (Woodridge: Midwest Theological Forum, 2009), 251-258; Tia Ghose, "Genetic 'Adam' and 'Eve' Uncovered," livescience.com, http://www.livescience.com/ 38613-genetic-adam-and-eve-uncovered.html (accessed August 7, 2016).

[145] Stephen Hawking, and Leonard Mlodinow, *The Grand Design* (New York: Bantam 2010), 180.

[146] Robert Spitzer, "The Curious Metaphysics of Dr. Stephen Hawking," catholiceducation.org, http://www.catholiceducation.org/en/science/faith-and-science/the-curious-metaphysics-of-dr-stephen-hawking.html (accessed August 7, 2016).

thinking that the universe had a beginning."[147] In deducing this Spitzer states, "If Dr. Hawking does not believe that there is any reason to think that the universe had a beginning (from physics or philosophy), then why does he even bother to speculate about how the universe could spontaneously create itself from nothing?"[148]

Now, once it is accepted that the universe had a beginning, then who or what was responsible for the beginning of the universe? This question can only be answered by appealing to a non-material reality that is not the subject matter of physics. Physics cannot study nothing since nothing has no physical properties. Metaphysics, which is beyond or after physics, can reflect on the possibility of nothingness and in so doing conclude there must have been some necessary intelligent being that created the universe out of nothing since nothing comes from nothing.

Hawking, however, confuses nothing with something physical by identifying it with the law of gravity. Is gravity nothing? Of course not, Spitzer argues, for:

> It has a specific constant associated with it and specific characteristics, and it has specific effects on mass-energy and even on space-time itself. This is a very curious

---

[147] Robert Spitzer, "The Curious Metaphysics of Dr. Stephen Hawking."

[148] Robert Spitzer, "The Curious Metaphysics of Dr. Stephen Hawking."

definition of 'nothing.' Therefore, Dr. Hawking's phrase should be restated to say something like, 'Because there is a law such as gravity, the Universe has unfolded and developed.' But what must be avoided are the rest of the statements – 'can and will create itself from nothing' and 'Spontaneous creation is the reason there is something rather than nothing,' etc. Now, if we rephrase Dr. Hawking's statement in the above fashion, then he has clearly not explained why there is something rather than nothing. He has only explained that something comes from something (i.e. the universe from physical laws such as the law of gravity).[149]

Hawking does not only appeal to the laws of gravity in order to dismiss the need of a creating God but also appeals to the multi-universe theory. In an article first published in the *Washington Times*, Bruce L. Gordon, associate professor of science and mathematics at the King's College, argues against Hawking's belief in the multi-universe theory. Hawking relies on this theory in order to explain the astonishing fine-tuning of the universe. From a Catholic perspective, relying on reason, the fine-tuning of the universe indicates the need of an intelligent mind who established precisely the right conditions for life, especially

---

[149] Robert Spitzer, "The Curious Metaphysics of Dr. Stephen Hawking."

human life, to be possible.[150] In countering Hawking's argument, Gordon writes:

> [I]n the machinations of multiverse cosmology to "explain" cosmological fine-tuning, [c]osmic inflation is invoked to "explain" why our universe is so flat and its background radiation so uniform. All possible solutions of string theory are invoked to "explain" the incredible fine-tuning of the cosmological constant. But the evidence for cosmic inflation is both thin and equivocal; the evidence for string theory and its extension, M-theory, is nonexistent; and the idea that conjoining them demonstrates that we live in a multiverse of bubble universes with different laws and constants is a mathematical fantasy. What is worse, multiplying without limit the opportunities for any event to happen in the context of a multiverse - where it is alleged that anything can spontaneously jump into existence without cause - produces a situation in which no absurdity is beyond the pale.
>
> For instance, we find multiverse cosmologists debating the "Boltzmann Brain" problem: In the most "reasonable" models for a multiverse, it is immeasurably more

---

[150] Christopher Baglow, *Faith, Science & Reason, Theology on the Cutting Edge* (Woodridge: Midwest Theological Forum, 2009), 151-152.

likely that our consciousness is associated with a brain that has spontaneously fluctuated into existence in the quantum vacuum than it is that we have parents and exist in an orderly universe with a 13.7 billion-year history. This is absurd. The multiverse hypothesis is therefore falsified because it renders false what we know to be true about ourselves. Clearly, embracing the multiverse idea entails a nihilistic irrationality that destroys the very possibility of science.

Universes do not "spontaneously create" on the basis of abstract mathematical descripttions, nor does the fantasy of a limitless multiverse trump the explanatory power of transcendent intelligent design. What Mr. Hawking's contrary assertions show is that mathematical savants can sometimes be metaphysical simpletons.[151]

The Bolzmann brain that Gordon refers to is a hypothetical self-conscious being which supposedly arose out of an original chaos of random fluctuations. This concept was named after the

---

[151] Bruce L. Gordon, "Hawking's Irrational Arguments: Theoretical Physicist Takes Leave of his Senses" The Washington Times October 5, 2010 http://www.washingtontimes.com/news/2010/oct/1/hawking-irrational-arguments/ accessed 01/25/2014. Also see http://www.discovery.org/a/15481 accessed 01/25/2014.

physicist Ludwig Boltzmann (1844-1906) who argued that the universe originated from random fluctuations.[152]

Chance

Due to the advent of quantum physics, randomness or chance is frequently appealed to in arguments that reject God. Acknowledging, however, the existence of chance and randomness is not contrary to at the same time believing in an intelligent creator.[153] At first, this may seem to be

---

[152] Dennis Overbye, "Big Brain Theory: Have Cosmologist Lost Theirs?" January 15th, 2008, nytimes.com, http://www.nytimes.com/2008/01/15/science/15brain.html?_r=0 (accessed August 7, 2016).

[153] For two Biblical references to chance see Ecclesiastes 9:11, and Proverbs 16:33. Also, see Thomas Aquinas, *Summa Contra Gentiles*, Book 3, Chapters 73 and 74, dhspriory.org, http://dhspriory.org/thomas/ContraGentiles3a.htm#73 (accessed August 7, 2016). "Chapter 73 THAT DIVINE PROVIDENCE DOES NOT EXCLUDE FREEDOM OF CHOICE

[1] From this it is also evident that **providence is not incompatible with freedom of will.**

[2] Indeed, the **governance of every provident ruler is ordered either to the attainment, or the increase, or the preservation of the perfection of the things governed.** Therefore, **whatever pertains to perfection is to be preserved by providence rather than what pertains to imperfection and deficiency**. Now, among inanimate things the contingency of causes is due to imperfection and deficiency, for by their nature they are determined to one result which they always achieve, unless there be some impediment arising either from a weakness of their

power, or on the part of an external agent, or because of the unsuitability of the matter. And for this reason, natural agent causes are not capable of varied results; rather, in most cases, they produce their effect in the same way, failing to do so but rarely. Now, the fact that the will is a contingent cause arises from its perfection, for it does not have power limited to one outcome but rather has the ability to produce this effect or that; for which reason it is contingent in regard to either one or the other. **Therefore, it is more pertinent to divine providence to preserve liberty of will than contingency in natural causes.**

[3] **Moreover, it is proper to divine Providence to use things according to their own mode.** Now, the mode of acting peculiar to each thing results from its form, which is the source of action. Now, the form whereby an agent acts voluntarily is not determined, for the will acts through a form apprehended by the intellect, since the apprehended good moves the will as its object. Now, the intellect does not have one form determined to an effect; rather, it is characteristic of it to comprehend a multitude of forms. And because of this the will can produce effects according to many forms. Therefore, it does not pertain to the character of providence to exclude liberty of will.

[4] Besides, by the governance of every provident agent the things governed are led to a suitable end; hence, Gregory of Nyssa says of divine providence that it is the "will of God through which all things that exist receive a suitable end." But the ultimate end of every creature is to attain the divine likeness, as we showed above. **Therefore, it would be incompatible with providence for that whereby a thing attains the divine likeness to be taken away from it.** Now, the voluntary agent attains the divine likeness because it acts freely, for we showed in Book One [88] that there is free choice in God. Therefore, freedom of will is not taken away by divine providence.

[5] **Again, providence tends to multiply goods among the things that are governed. So, that whereby many goods are removed from things does not pertain to providence. But, if freedom of will were taken away, many goods would be removed. Taken away, indeed, would be the praise of human virtue which is nothing, if man does not act freely.** Taken away, also, would be justice which rewards and punishes, if man could not freely do good or evil. Even the careful consideration of circumstances in processes of deliberation would cease, for it is useless to dwell upon things that are done of necessity. Therefore, it would be against the very character of providence if liberty of will were removed.

[6] Hence it is said: "God made man from the beginning and left him in the hand of his own counsel"; and again: "Before man is life and death, good and evil, that which he shall choose shall be given him" (Sirach 15:14, 18).

[7] Now, by these considerations the opinion of the Stoics is set aside, for they said that all things come about by necessity, according to an irrevocable order of causes, which the Greeks called ειμαρμενη.

Chapter 74
THAT DIVINE PROVIDENCE DOES NOT EXCLUDE FORTUNE AND CHANCE

[1] It is also apparent from the foregoing that **divine providence does not take away fortune and chance from things.**

[2] For it is in the case of things that happen rarely that fortune and chance are said to be present. **Now, if some things did not occur in rare instances, all things would happen by necessity**. Indeed, things that are contingent in most cases differ from necessary things only in this: they can fail to happen, in a few cases. **But it would be contrary to the essential character of divine providence if all things occurred by necessity, as we showed. Therefore,**

it would also be **contrary to the character of divine providence if nothing were to be fortuitous and a matter of chance in things.**

[3] **Again, it would be contrary to the very meaning of providence if things subject to providence did not act for an end**, since it is the function of providence to order all things to their end. Moreover, it would be against the perfection of the universe if no corruptible thing existed, and no power could fail, as is evident from what was said above. Now, due to the fact that an agent fails in regard to an end that is intended, it follows that **some things occur by chance**. So, it would be contrary to the meaning of providence, and to the perfection of things, if there were no chance events.

[4] Besides, the large number and variety of causes stem from the order of divine providence and control. But, granted this variety of causes, one of them must at times run into another cause and be impeded, or assisted, by it in the production of its effect. **Now, from the concurrence of two or more causes it is possible for some chance event to occur, and thus an unintended end comes about due to this causal concurrence.** For example, the discovery of a debtor, by a man who has gone to market to sell something, happens because the debtor also went to market. Therefore, it is **not contrary to divine providence that there are some fortuitous and chance events among things**.

[5] Moreover, what does not exist cannot be the cause of anything. Hence, each thing must stand in the same relation to the fact that it is a cause, as it does to the fact that it is a being. So, depending on the diversity of order in beings, there must also be a **diversity of order among causes**. Now, it is necessary for the perfection of things that there be among things not only substantial beings but also accidental beings. Indeed, **things that do not possess ultimate perfection in their substance must obtain such perfection**

contradictory. Is not randomness contrary to an intelligent design? How can chance be reflective of God's reason reflected in what he has created?

Baglow answers these questions in three ways. First, he demonstrates that in some ways chance is

---

through accidents, and the more of these there are, the farther are they from the simplicity of God. From the fact, then, that a certain subject has many accidents it follows that it is a being accidentally, because a subject and an accident, and even two accidents of one substance, are a unit and a being accidentally; as in the example of a white man, and of a musical, white being. **So, it is necessary to the perfection of things that there should also be some accidental causes. Now, things which result accidentally from any causes are said to happen by chance or fortune.** Therefore, it is not contrary to the rational character of providence, which preserves the perfection of things, for certain things to come about as a result of chance or fortune.

[6] Furthermore, **that there be order and a gradation of causes is important to the order of divine providence.** But the higher a cause is, the greater is its power; and so, its causality applies to a greater number of things. Now, the natural intention of a cause cannot extend beyond its power, for that would be useless. So, the particular intention of a cause cannot extend to all things that can happen. **Now, it is due to the fact that some things happen apart from the intention of their agents that there is a possibility of chance or fortuitous occurrence.** Therefore, the order of divine providence requires that there be chance and fortune in reality.

[7] Hence it is said: "I saw that the race is not to the swift ... but time and chance in all" (Sirach 9:11), that is, among things here below. "

in the eye of the beholder.[154] For example, if I know the exact order of every card in a deck prior to dealing it, then from my perspective handing out the cards is not chance but from the perspective of those receiving the cards it is. Now, this way of understanding how chance fits into God's providential designs is not sufficient. It makes chance appear completely fictional. Chance does actually exist and, along with man's free will, co-exists with God's omniscience. Ultimately, how chance, freedom, providence and God's ability to know everything in advance relate to one another is a mystery. Since it is mysterious, a variety of explanations, offering different perspectives, will help our finite minds to gain insight into this paradox.

Baglow, consequently, presents two other explanations. First, he shows how the presence of randomness does not necessarily reflect a lack of intelligent order but may actually be intelligently willed in order to serve a greater order.[155] For example, even though the random way of distributing fish food by throwing it in a tank does not mean that my choice to throw the fish food in the tank was random.

Second, if there were no randomness/chance, then the world would only have a single pattern and direction similar to auto-programming a destina-

---

[154] Christopher Baglow, *Faith, Science & Reason, Theology on the Cutting Edge* (Woodridge: Midwest Theological Forum, 2009), 175.

[155] Christopher Baglow, *Faith, Science & Reason, Theology on the Cutting Edge*, 177.

tion on a missile.[156] Unless the missile is shot down or there is a program failure, it will reach its destination. This is because the missile is not free, unlike humans, and is analogous (that is similar and with a difference) to random aspects of creation. Human, animals and even creation itself are all free in various degrees and kinds precisely because God allows an element of randomness and chance to co-exist with his intelligent, providential plans reflected in nature. These aspects reflect the unconditional freedom of their creator.

By directing our attention to the macro level of physics, Baglow complements his emphasis on chance at the micro level. Mathematicians and physicists, including the English mathematical physicist Roger Penrose, have demonstrated that the universe is so delicately fine-tuned to support the existence of life that it is more reasonable to conclude that it was a product of intelligent design than a result of mere chance. This is because the odds that the universe would have occurred in a manner that supports life, above all human life, are overwhelming against this fine tuning occurring by chance. Atheists counter this argument by asserting that there may exist an infinite number of undetectable universes caused by chance of which ours is one of the few or only one that has life. This argument is very weak since there is no evidence that these universes exist, and even if they do exist it still does not answer the question of what or who

---

[156] Christopher Baglow, *Faith, Science & Reason, Theology on the Cutting Edge*, 178.

caused them to exist.[157]

With respect to the multi-universes theory, Fr. Spitzer adds the following. Although the principle that the simpler, more elegant, and non-redundant explanations are to be preferred is not scientifically provable and only serves as a guide to scientist it, nonetheless is repeatedly observed in nature.[158] Nature has a pronounced tendency to be simple, and not bloated, or contradictory. The multi-universe theory, though, is a complex, and convoluted explanation. In addition, the multi-universe theory does not provide an answer to what caused the fine tuning of the multi-universe. For a multi-universe to exist there has to be an initial condition that was highly fine-tuned for it to form. In addition, for a multi-universe to continue existing there needs to be constant ongoing fine tuning in order to prevent multi-universes from clashing into and destroying one another. Since nothing comes from nothing, there must be, even with a multi-universe, something or someone who as uncaused cause brought forth the effect of creation.[159]

---

[157] Christopher Baglow, *Faith, Science & Reason, Theology on the Cutting Edge*, 151-152.

[158] This principle is called Occam's razor after the English Franciscan William of Ockham (c. 1287-1347).

[159] Robert Spitzer, "Teaching Science and Faith – Conflict or Confluence? For High School Science and Religion Teachers," Institute for Theological Encounter with Science and Technology and the Magis Center, http://mp125118.cdn.mediaplatform.com/125118/wc/mp/4000/5592/5599/40716/Lobby/default.htm (accessed February 28, 2015).

In arguing for the necessity of an uncaused, completely self-sufficient first cause of the universe Bishop Barron explains that matter only exists in forms that are filled with potentiality to be formed in other ways. This reality of matter as necessarily in a form leads to the question why is matter in this form and not in another? For example, why is a podium in this form and not in another form? It is in this particular form because all sorts of causes came together in order for this configuration of matter to occur. Since matter necessarily depends on causes in order to exist it leads to another question of who caused matter. Matter could not have caused itself since it is by nature dependent on causes for it to be in forms. Therefore, some reality that is not contingent on anything else must exist that is the cause. In other words, this non-contingent being is being itself *ipsum esse*, God who created out of nothing.[160]

Human Intelligence, Animal Intelligence and Computer Intelligence

It has just been explained how a version of evolutionary theory can be fully consistent with the Catholic faith. Sometimes, though, people approach evolutionary theory and religious faith in a creating God from an either-or stance. According to this understanding, if evolutionary theory is correct then God does not exist. Those who see

---

[160] Robert Barron, *The Mystery of God: Who God is and Why He Matters*, DVDs (Word on Fire, 2015).

evolutionary theory as a replacement explanation for the origin of the universe, view human beings as merely highly evolved animals whose intelligence only differs in degree and not in kind from animal intelligence.

In his book *Faith, Science & Reason, Theology on the Cutting Edge*, Baglow demonstrates how unreasonable this atheistic assumption is. Baglow argues that what appears to be rationality in animals is only the result of their highly tuned sense perception. For example, tests done on the German horse dubbed Clever Hans demonstrated that the horse's apparent ability to solve math problems was not because the horse was solving math problems but rather was due to the horse responding to its keeper's reaction of relaxing when the horse had tapped out the right number of times. The horse was not able to solve a single math problem when the possibility of the keeper unintentionally cueing the horse was eliminated by either blindfolding the horse or by selecting a person who did not know the answer to ask the horse a math question. Baglow also points out that the supposed high degree of animal intelligence observed in lab settings, at the coaxing of trainers, has never spontaneously occurred in the wild.

How does our intelligence differ in kind from animal intelligence? Baglow answers this by going through five human qualities that distinguish human intelligence from animal intelligence. These five qualities are "self-consciousness, awareness of time, appreciation of the beautiful, a sense of morality and responsibility, and the development of culture."[161]

The first quality, self-consciousness, is our ability to be self-aware. As a self-aware being, I can transcend myself by viewing myself as a subject. This ability is due to the human ability of abstracttion: physical, mathematical and metaphysical.[162]

The second quality, our awareness of time, is unique since no evidence has been found that indicates that animals have created a way of measuring time, such as using a calendar. Our awareness of time is due to our ability to abstract mathematically. As explained previously, mathematical abstraction refers to our ability to understand universal concepts (circles, squares, triangles) that are applicable to all physical things and not just to a certain kind of thing (such as certain types of trees or dogs).[163]

The third quality, our appreciation of beauty, is evident even in Stone Age tools. These ancient tools were not made only for functional reasons but also were made in an aesthetically pleasing manner. Due to our human ability to abstract metaphysically, we can appreciate beauty that is reflective of all physical things and also transcends the created world, for it points us to the source of all beauty,

---

[161] Christopher Baglow, *Faith, Science & Reason, Theology on the Cutting Edge*, 225.

[162] Christopher Baglow, *Faith, Science & Reason, Theology on the Cutting Edge*, 225.

[163] Christopher Baglow, *Faith, Science & Reason, Theology on the Cutting Edge*, 226.

God.[164]

The fourth quality, our sense of morality and responsibility, is also due to our ability to abstract in a metaphysical manner, but in this case with respect to goodness and not to beauty.[165] This goodness is not, borrowing from Dietrich von Hildebrand, simply subjectively satisfying but also objectively fulfilling. Animals pursue the good in so far as it is subjectively satisfying. Humans, though, can pursue the good in a moral sense in so far as it is objectively fulfilling. An example of something merely subjectively satisfying is eating a hamburger. An example of something objectively fulfilling is an encounter of Christ through prayerful meditation on Christ crucified on the cross. When meditating on the love of Christ, we can experience our disordered love being re-arranged and re-ordered in accordance with the love of Christ.

The fifth quality, development of culture, is evident in the thousands of human cultures that, although experiencing change and development, also are passed on as a unifying principle from one generation to the next. In contrast, animals only learn from their own species or from other species

---

[164] Christopher Baglow, *Faith, Science & Reason, Theology on the Cutting Edge*, 226-227. The universal transcendent characteristics of beauty, as explained by Baglow, are integrity, harmony, consonance and splendor.

[165] Christopher Baglow, *Faith, Science & Reason, Theology on the Cutting Edge*, 227.

by mirroring the behavior of what they see.[166]

In arguing how computer intelligence also differs in kind and not simply in degree from human intelligence, Baglow again relies on the three degrees of abstraction. The mathematician Kurt Gödel has convincingly demonstrated a computer can only solve problems by following a set of rules created by a programmer. Since computers are restricted by these rules, they cannot act beyond or think about these rules. For example, when programmed to do so, a computer can rapidly add up millions of numbers in short time. However, it cannot think about the meaning of 0 and 1 in an objective manner since it cannot abstract mathematically. Due to our ability to abstract physically, mathematically and metaphysically we are not trapped by rules that others create. Instead we can think about the rules themselves, and, if we chose to do so, modify them, change them, and discover new rules.[167]

Finally, following the basic Thomistic principle that grace builds on nature, Baglow argues that the existence of human freedom is supported by the modern quantum theory. According to quantum theory, the universe on the subatomic level is not deterministic but probabilistic. If everything, even down to the minutest subatomic particle of electrons, protons, neutrons and quarks, inflexibly

---

[166] Christopher Baglow, *Faith, Science & Reason, Theology on the Cutting Edge*, 227-228.
[167] Christopher Baglow, *Faith, Science & Reason, Theology on the Cutting Edge*, 228-232.

followed pre-determined laws, then how could the human soul, representing freedom, interact with the human mind, which in this case would be completely determined down to the sub-atomic level? The probabilistic and non-deterministic aspect of matter is highly fitting for non-deterministic human freedom to be rooted in and build upon.[168]

Quiz 5

1. Compare and contrast how the Church reacted to Copernicus with how it later reacted to Galileo. Include the following in your response: geocentric theory, heliocentric theory, Cardinal Schönberg, Dialogue Concerning the Two Chief World Systems, Protestants.

2. How does the scientific method differ from a philosophy, and why is this difference important with respect to religious belief? Include the following in your response: method, philosophy, materialism, the essential steps of the scientific method, God and immaterial realities.

3. Defend the position that human beings differ in kind and not simply in degree from

---

[168] Christopher Baglow, *Faith, Science & Reason, Theology on the Cutting Edge*, 233.

highly evolved apes and computers. Include the following in your answer: evolution, ensoulment, abstraction, transcendence, programming and rules.

4. Counter Stephen Hawking's claim that the universe could have originated from nothing. Include the following in your answer: gravity, multi-universe theory, and fine tuning.

5. Why is presence of chance not contrary to an intelligent design by an intelligent creator? Include the following in your response: eye of the beholder (explain this), end, and freedom.

6. Why is the multi-universe a highly unlikely explanation of reality? Include the following in your answer: Occam's razor (see footnote), fine tuning, origin.

Additional Activities and Resources

Respond to the following. Do so according to the Socratic method of gathering, clarifying and challenging questions.

- The Church has a long tradition of repressing scientific reasoning. Just look at what happened to Galileo.

- "Because there is a law like gravity, the universe can and will create itself from nothing …. Spontaneous creation is the reason there is something rather than nothing, why the universe exists, why we exist. It is not necessary to invoke God to light the blue touch paper and set the universe going."
- Randomness within the universe is contrary to an intelligent design.
- How can chance be reflective of God's reason reflected in what he has created?
- Who created the designer?
- Why are there shooting stars, and other random events if there is an intelligent designer?
- Why are we headed to nothing?
- What is the meaning behind the sun that will explode, the Andromeda Galaxy that will collide with our Galaxy, and the fact that our universe is ever expanding?[169]

---

[169] "Debate – William Lane Craig vs Christopher Hitchens – Does God Exist?," Craig vs. Hitchens Debate at Biola University, April 4, 2009, youtube.com, https://youtu.be/4KBx4vvlbZ8 (accessed August 8, 2016). The last four objections were raised by Hitchens. Craig argued that the idea God does not exist since we are headed towards nothingness is not a necessary conclusion. Temporal duration is irrelevant to the possibility that what currently exists was created. Finally, the question why would God create something that will go extinct is answered by theism. God did not create something that will cease to exist since there is life

Readings

Chapters Five, Seven, Eight, Ten, Eleven from Baglow, Christopher T. *Faith, Science, and Reason: Theology on the Cutting Edge*. Woodridge, IL: Midwest Theological Forum, 2009.

Chapters Five from Kreeft, Peter, and Ronald K. Tacelli. *Handbook of Christian Apologetics: Hundreds of Answers to Crucial Questions*. Downers Grove, IL: InterVarsity Press, 1994.

Websites

Robert Spitzer, "The Curious Metaphysics of Dr. Stephen Hawking," catholiceducation.org, http://www.catholiceducation.org/en/science/faith-and-science/the-curious-metaphysics-of-dr-stephen-hawking.html

Robert Spitzer, "Teaching Science and Faith –

---

beyond death and we are promised a new heavens and a new earth.

In addition, as eloquently phrased by Frank Sheed, "the universe is not crashing towards a chaos, for it would not have been consonant with God's all-wisdom and all-knowledge to bring something into existence which would escape His control and by its own aimlessness mock Him rather than mirror Him. The universe is not crashing towards a chaos but growing towards a harmony. All that anything is, all that anything does, has its part in the harmony." Frank Sheed, *Theology and Sanctity* (No location given: Catholic Way Publishing, 2014), loc. 2204.

Conflict or Confluence? For High School Science and Religion Teachers," Institute for Theological Encounter with Science and Technology and the Magis Center, http://mp125118.cdn.mediaplatform.com/125118/wc/mp/4000/5592/5599/40716/Lobby/default.htm

Video

"Debate – William Lane Craig vs Christopher Hitchens – Does God Exist?," Craig vs. Hitchens Debate at Biola University, April 4, 2009, youtube.com, https://youtu.be/4KBx4vvlbZ8

Chapter Six: Divinity and Resurrection of Christ

Introduction

Many who believe in God's existence do not believe in the divinity of Christ nor in His resurrection from the dead. Some even claim that it is against reason to believe Christ is divine and that He rose from the dead. In this chapter, we will examine from the standpoint of reason to what extent this claim is warranted. We will begin with Christ's divinity.

Who Christ Identified Himself As

Christ indicated himself that He is the Son of God, that He is equal to the Father, and as equal to the Father is God. He indicated He is the Son of God in a variety of ways. With the Apostle Peter, Jesus elicits His identify from Peter and then confirms Peter's answer. "He [Jesus] said to them,

'But who do you say that I am?' Simon Peter answered, 'You are the Messiah, the Son of the living God.' And Jesus answered him, 'Blessed are you, Simon son of Jonah! For flesh and blood has not revealed this to you, but my Father in heaven.'" (Matthew 16: 15-17 NRSV) Jesus also identifies himself as the Son of God by referring to himself as the fulfillment of the Son of Man of whom the prophet Daniel had a vision. "But Jesus was silent. Then the high priest said to him, 'I put you under oath before the living God, tell us if you are the Messiah, the Son of God.' Jesus said to him, 'You have said so. But I tell you, from now on you will see the Son of Man seated at the right hand of Power and coming on the clouds of heaven.' (Matthew 26:63-64 NRSV)

In order to interpret this passage properly the terminology Son of Man needs to be carefully defined. At times, the term Son of Man, in Hebrew *ben adam*, is used in the bible to contrast a human being with God, for example in Psalm Eight (Psalm 8: 4-5). At other times it is used to signify the divine and not the human, for example, the Old Testament's description of the prophet Daniel's vision uses the term Son of Man [in Aramaic *kebar enosh*] to signify a divine being. "I saw in the night visions, and behold, with the clouds of heaven there came one like a son of man, and he came to the Ancient of Days and was presented before him. And to him was given dominion and glory and kingdom, that all peoples, nations, and languages should serve him; his dominion is an everlasting dominion, which shall not pass away, and his kingdom one that shall not be destroyed." (Daniel 7:13-14 RSV) The latter meaning is the one Jesus is clearly referring to with his reference to the Son of Man "coming on the clouds of heaven." Also see Matthew 24:30-31, 37-39; and Luke 17:22-30. In these passages the terminology Son of Man is once again referring to Daniel chapter seven and the judgment associated with the Son of Man's coming.[170]

Jesus indicated he is equal to the Father and is divine in many ways. In the Gospel of John Jesus clearly states, "The Father and I are one." (John 10:30 NRSV) In this same Gospel Jesus tells Philip, "Jesus said to him, 'Have I been with you all this time, Philip, and you still do not know me? Whoever has seen me has seen the Father. How can you say, 'Show us the Father'? Do you not believe that I am in the Father and the Father is in me? The words that I say to you I do not speak on my own; but the Father who dwells in me does his works. Believe me that I am in the Father and the Father is in me; but if you do not, then believe me because of

---

[170] Jodi Magness, *Jesus and His Jewish Influences*, Course Transcript (Chantilly: The Great Courses, 2015), 176-178. "That is why the Lord proclaims himself the Son of Man, the one who renews in himself that first man from whom the race born of woman was formed; as by a man's defeat our race fell into the bondage of death, so by a man's victory we were to rise again to life." St. Irenaeus, "From a Treatise Against Heresies, book 5, 19," *Liturgy of the Hours*, Volume 1 (New York: Catholic Book Publishing Company, 1975), 244.

the works themselves.'" (John 14:9-11 NRSV) Another way Jesus indicated his equality with God the Father, and hence His divinity, was by forgiving sins. After witnessing Jesus forgive sins they said, "Who can forgive sins but God alone?" (Luke 5:21 NRSV)

Bishop Barron points out subtle ways by which Jesus reveals He is equal to the Father. Jesus by saying, "You've heard it said, but I say to you..." is asserting that the Torah, received by Moses, is not the final appeal. Instead, Jesus is the final appeal since Jesus as God is the author and giver of Torah. Another example is when Jesus says, "Heaven and Earth will pass away but my words will not pass away." (Matthew 24:35 NRSV) Only the words of God will not pass away. Human beings' words will pass away since they like the earth are created realities. Another example is when Jesus says, in reference to Himself, "I tell you, something greater than the temple is here." (Matthew 12:6 NRSV) The Jewish people at the time of Jesus believed the Jerusalem Temple was the place where God lived. This means that if Jesus is greater than where God lives, then Jesus is God. Still another example is when Jesus says, "Whoever loves father or mother more than me is not worthy of me." (Matthew 10:37) In a culture that greatly valued parents, this claim made no sense unless Jesus was identifying Himself with a good greater than that affirmed in the Fourth Commandment by identifying himself as the highest good, God, to whom Commandments

One through Three refer.[171]

Jesus also indicated his divinity by performing miracles, by forgiving sins, by changing names (an action only God may do according to the Jewish mind of the time) and by rising from the dead.[172] We will now carefully examine the reasonableness of Christ's claim that He is God.

Reasonableness of Christ's Claim to Divinity

Kreeft counters four arguments against Christ's claim that He is divine.[173] In a nutshell they are that Jesus was a liar; Jesus was crazy, Jesus was a guru, and Jesus is a myth. According to the first argument, Jesus claimed he was divine but knew he was not and hence lied. In contrast, the second argument maintains that Jesus did not lie that He is divine since he was a lunatic who was convinced He was divine when he actually was not. Similarly, the third argument states that Jesus did not lie when he indicated he is divine since he only meant his assertion to be interpreted mystically in the sense that we all are divine since we all are God. The fourth argument also does not accuse Jesus of being a liar because, this argument claims, he never existed and the myth of Jesus does not present him

---

[171] Robert Barron, *The Mystery of God: Who God is and Why He Matters*, DVDs (Word on Fire, 2015).

[172] Peter J. Kreeft and Ronald K. Tacelli, *Handbook of Catholic Apologetics*, loc. 1756.

[173] Peter J. Kreeft and Ronald K. Tacelli, *Handbook of Catholic Apologetics*, loc. 1745-2103.

as a liar. Kreeft counters these arguments in the following ways.

First, Jesus was known for being a good person. As a good person He lacked the psychological profile of a liar. Habitual liars have a great tendency to be selfish. Jesus, though, was loving, and so unselfish that He was willing to die for others and die for what He affirmed as true. After Pentecost, Jesus' disciples demonstrated similar loving, unselfish traits even to the point of death.

Second, Jesus lacked the psychological profile of an insane person. Crazy people are known for being highly impractical and untrustworthy. Jesus, though, was eminently practical. His practical nature was repeatedly demonstrated by His attentiveness to other's concrete needs. People also readily trusted in Jesus. Finally, Jewish people have consistently defended the transcendence of God against the pagan polytheistic teaching of extreme divine immanence. Examples, of pagan, extreme divine immanence teaching include emperor and pharaoh worship and the belief that there are many gods who at times come down on earth and act as badly as humans do, by fornication, murder, etc. Since Jesus was born of a Jewish woman, He knew that it was crazy for a Jewish person to claim that He was divine since this claim, if believed by the person, is totally at odds with Jewish belief. Since, despite this knowledge He claimed that He is divine, and He did not exhibit traits of liars, it is reasonable to conclude that Jesus claimed He is divine as a sane, and truthful person.[174]

Third, Jesus' Jewish upbringing indicates that His claim to be divine was not similar to a guru who claims to be divine. Gurus, who often are followers of religions from India, claim that not only are they divine but all people are divine since ultimately God is everything that exists. It was, and to the most part still is, contrary to Jewish thought for a Jew to claim to be enlightened in such way. This is because the belief that all are divine and will experience being brought into harmony with the universe once they realize their divinity is directly contrary to the Jewish belief in God's transcendence. Furthermore, gurus typically do not believe in eternal punishment. Rather, they teach that we are given multiple possibilities to be reborn until we finally are enlightened that there is no distinction between God and the world. Once this occurs we, according to the teaching, will vanish into the reality of God and all our suffering and false sense of identity and difference will vanish like a mirage. Jesus, though, referred to judgment and eternal damnation and never once taught reincarnation.

Fourth, if Jesus was a myth, asks Kreeft, then who was the author of the myth and what was author's motive? Since up until the 313 A.D. Edict of Milan, Christians were routinely martyred, what could motivate someone to invent such a myth?

---

[174] Kreeft adds that those who wrote the New Testament were not lunatics since the writings of the New Testament does not resemble the writings of crazy people.

What did the author have to gain from creating this supposed myth? Kreeft also points out that according to scientific standards applied to other ancient texts, the New Testament texts are the most reliable of ancient texts. In contrast, there exists only one known ancient copy of Tacitus' *Annals*, written during the first century A.D. The *Annals* provides historians significant understanding of first century history of the Roman Empire, and no reputable historian has ever called this historical document of early Roman times into question.[175]

Continuing this line of reasoning, Kreeft points out that all reputable scholars, Christian and non-Christian, agree that almost all of the New Testament, in particular the letters of Paul, was written during the first century AD. For a myth to be invented and believed by a group of followers, it would have to be created after all the first followers had died; otherwise, it would be easily refuted. The writings on the divinity of Christ, however, date before the first followers had died. This indicates that it is very reasonable to hold that the early Christians believed in Christ's divinity and that Jesus actually claimed He is divine. His claim to be God explains why the Jews insisted that He be put to death.

Another reason, argues Kreeft, against a mythic layer being added to the New Testament text is that the New Testament was not written according to the style of ancient myths but rather according to

---

[175] Peter J. Kreeft and Ronald K. Tacelli, *Handbook of Catholic Apologetics*, loc. 1929.

accounts of eyewitnesses. Also, the genre of realistic fantasy was invented in modern times and did not exist at the time of Jesus.

In conclusion, the above argumentation demonstrates from reason that the truthfulness of Christ's claim to be God is not only possible but is highly probable. Kreeft also refers his readers to the practice of Christian life in order to further demonstrate the reasonableness of Christ's claim. Belief in Christ's divinity has consistently transformed people's lives for the better, according to common understanding of what is good behavior from what is not.[176]

In addition, those who refuse to believe in Christ's divinity often do so for non-rational reasons. Like Gandhi, some refuse to believe in Christianity because of the unfortunate immorality of many Christians. Second, some fear the moral demands of Christ's teachings. Others fear the uncontrollable nature of the supernatural. Still others are afraid of what others will think if they believe, and yet still others choose not to believe because of their high regard for democracy and equality.

Kreeft points out that all of these reasons are

---

[176] With reference to Aquinas, Kreeft states, "if the incarnation did not really happen, then an even more unbelievable miracle happened: the conversion of the world by the biggest lie in history and the moral transformation of lives into unselfishness, detachment from world pleasures and radically new heights in holiness all by a mere myth." Peter J. Kreeft and Ronald K. Tacelli, *Handbook of Catholic Apologetics*, loc. 166.

based more on emotional responses rather than on reason.[177]

Christ's Resurrection

Catholics believe that Christ rose in his body from the dead by His power as God. His resurrection differs significantly from Mary's assumption. In Mary's assumption, Mary was taken up into heaven not by her power but by the power of God. Kreeft identifies three common objections to this belief in Christ's resurrection. They are as follows: Jesus swooned on the cross, the disciples lied about the resurrection and created a resurrection myth and the disciples had a hallucination that Jesus rose from the dead.[178]

First, since Romans took very careful measures to make sure that those they crucified died it was highly improbable for anyone to have survived a Roman crucifixion. The care is evident in the Roman legal practice of punishing a soldier with death if he was responsible for allowing a person sentenced to crucifixion to escape or if a soldier failed to ensure after crucifixion the crucified died. That the Roman soldiers did not break Jesus' legs indicates they were certain that He had died. Legs were broken in order to hasten the death of the crucified who were still breathing. Once the legs

---

[177] Peter J. Kreeft and Ronald K. Tacelli, *Handbook of Catholic Apologetics*, loc. 1745-2103.

[178] Peter J. Kreeft and Ronald K. Tacelli, *Handbook of Catholic Apologetics*, loc. 2115-2434.

were broken, it was much more difficult to raise the chest in order to take a breath of air. It also is recorded in the Gospels (John 19:34) that blood and water came out from Jesus heart after it was pierced by a soldier's lance, and that Jesus' body was completely wrapped by sheets, including his mouth and nose (John 19:38-42). The flowing of blood and water, argues Kreeft, demonstrates that the lungs of Jesus had collapsed. Even if they had not and He was still breathing, which was highly unlikely, the sheets that were tightly wrapped around his entire body would have prevented Him from breathing. Even if Jesus still was able to breathe underneath the sheets, which is even more unlikely, how could He have in such a weakened state shoved aside a heavy boulder from the entrance of His tomb and then overpowered the Roman guards who were guarding the tomb?[179]

Second, even after being tortured, no follower of Jesus ever said or wrote that the resurrection was a deliberate lie. Also, what motive did Jesus' followers have for lying that their master had risen from the dead? They knew that exalting Jesus in this manner greatly increased the likelihood they would be martyred. Even radical Muslim Jihadists are motivated to die because they believe Islam is true. It is highly unreasonable to maintain that radical Muslim Jihadists are willing to die for something they know is a lie. Also, if Jesus' followers did lie, then why didn't Jewish people

---

[179] Peter J. Kreeft and Ronald K. Tacelli, *Handbook of Catholic Apologetics*, loc. 2211-2227.

who were opposed to Christianity produce Jesus' body? Finally, points out Kreeft, history repeatedly teaches us that given time lies are eventually uncovered, and yet an early Christian lie in the resurrection of Jesus has never been uncovered.[180]

With respect to the claim that early Christians created a myth that Jesus rose from the dead, it is important to note that the Gospels were written according to an eye witness account and not in the style of a myth. That the gospels were actually written by eyewitness is made evident by the following. The gospels contain a detailed description of Jerusalem prior to its destruction by the Romans in 70 A.D. The gospels describe Jesus' human, non-sinful weakness and describe His disciples' sins and imperfections. A later forger would have likely harmonized the gospels and removed descriptions about Jesus' and his disciples' weaknesses. A forger also very likely would have included anachronistic elements that would have latter been uncovered. No anachronism has been convincingly discovered in the gospel accounts.

Furthermore, as pointed out earlier, the New Testament is the most reliable ancient text we have. Not only that but the New Testament quotations of the early Church Fathers, in close succession to one another, essentially match. It would have been nearly impossible for someone to alter all the New Testament texts, and if there was an attempt,

---

[180] Peter J. Kreeft and Ronald K. Tacelli, *Handbook of Catholic Apologetics*, loc. 2227-2259.

Christians would have noticeably protested. There is no historical evidence of such a protest.

In continuity with the gospel accounts, St. Peter in a letter explicitly denies that the resurrection is a myth. "For we did not follow cleverly devised myths when we made known to you the power and coming of our Lord Jesus Christ, but we had been eyewitnesses of his majesty." (2 Peter 1:16 NRSV) As pointed out earlier, in order for such a myth not to have been dismissed by early Christians, at least a generation would have had to have passed by. However, much of the New Testament, in particular Paul's letters, were written during the first century. With reference to Julius Muller's study, Kreeft points out that there is not a single example in history of a myth arising about a historical person thirty years after they died.[181] The dating of Paul's earliest letter, First Thessalonians, is established at around 51 A.D., well within the range of thirty years after the death of Christ.[182] In the first letter to the Thessalonians we read, "For the people of those regions report about us what kind of welcome we had among you, and how you turned to God from idols, to serve a living and true God, and to wait for his Son from heaven, whom he raised from the

---

[181] Peter J. Kreeft and Ronald K. Tacelli, *Handbook of Catholic Apologetics*, loc. 2328-2336. Kreeft cites Julius Muller, *Theory of Myths in its Application to the Gospel History Examined and Confuted* (London: John Chapman, 1844), 26.

[182] Ron Witherup, St. Paul: His Life, Faith and Legacy, A Now You Know Media Written Guide (http://www. nowyouknowmedia.com, 2010), 23.

dead—Jesus, who rescues us from the wrath that is coming." (1 Thessalonians 1:9-10 NRSV)

If we look outside of the bible, we will not find any documentary evidence that a mythological layer was added to the New Testament writings. On the contrary, Christ's resurrection was consistently taught in non-biblical writings including in the letters of Ignatius of Antioch (c. 35– c. 98), in *The Epistle of Barnabas* (written 70-131), in the *Letter to a Church at Corinth* by Pope Clement (r. 92-99), and in writings of Justin Martyr (100-165). Finally, adds Kreeft, if a resurrection myth was invented, due to their historical conditioning the inventors would have very likely described men and not women as testifying to the resurrection. This is because at the time of Jesus the witness of a woman was seen as almost worthless.[183]

Third, with respect to the claim that the disciples had a hallucination that Jesus rose from the dead, Kreeft counters that contrary to the private nature of hallucinations, Scripture records Christ appearing publicly to people and once to 500 people at the same time. (1 Cor. 15:3-8) In addition, hallucinations are for a short duration, but Jesus stayed around for 40 days. (Acts 1:3) Also, unless a person is insane, an individual will seldom experience them, but Jesus repeatedly appeared to simply, ordinary, people who, it is reasonable to conclude, were sane. Typical characteristics of hallucinations are their resemblance of past

---

[183] Peter J. Kreeft and Ronald K. Tacelli, *Handbook of Catholic Apologetics*, loc. 2294-2382.

memories and their unrealistic dreamlike quality. Jesus, though, is described in Scripture as appearing in a non-dreamlike state as someone who engages in thoughtful, long conversations and even eats.[184]

Quiz 6

1. Demonstrate why four of the five following options are unreasonable and then argue why it is reasonable to believe in Christ's resurrection while emphasizing the need for grace. The options are: Jesus was a liar, or crazy, or a guru, or a myth, or is the Son of God.

2. Distinguish between resuscitation, assumption and resurrection.

3. Counter the following assertions in at least two different ways for each one:

   - Jesus swooned on the cross.
   - The disciples hallucinated that Jesus rose from the dead.
   - Early Christians invented a resurrection myth.
   - The disciples lied that Jesus rose from the dead.

---

[184] Peter J. Kreeft and Ronald K. Tacelli, *Handbook of Catholic Apologetics*, loc. 2258-2289.

Additional Activities and Resources

Respond to the following. Do so according to the Socratic method of gathering, clarifying and challenging questions.

- The New Testament does not teach that Jesus is God. This was a later teaching invented by the early Church and promoted by the emperor Constantine.
- Jesus said he was only a son of a man. He never claimed to be the Son of God.
- Jesus swooned on the cross.
- Jesus lied that He is divine.
- Jesus was insane.
- Jesus taught everyone is God. That's why he said he is God.
- Jesus never existed.
- The disciples hallucinated that Jesus rose from the dead.
- So what if early Christians were willing to die for their faith, so do some Muslims.
- Early Christians invented a resurrection myth.
- The disciples lied that Jesus rose from the dead.

Readings

Chapters Seven and Eight from Kreeft, Peter, and Ronald K. Tacelli. *Handbook of Christian*

Apologetics: Hundreds of Answers to Crucial Questions. Downers Grove, IL: InterVarsity Press, 1994.

Fr. Peter Samuel Kucer, MSA

Chapter Seven: *Sola Scriptura*, *Traditio*, Magisterium

Introduction

The previous chapters approached apologetics from the standpoint of atheistic objections to belief in God. Starting with this chapter, we will focus our attention on debates among those who believe in God. We will begin with Protestant objections to the Catholic faith. The topic this chapter will address is the reasonableness of the Protestant *Sola Scriptura* teaching.

Definition of *Sola Scriptura*

According to the *Sola Scriptura* teaching, the bible is the sole, infallible rule of faith for Christians. This means that since the bible alone is sufficient to teach Christians the essential salvific truths of faith, an unwritten apostolic tradition that helps to interpret the Bible is not needed. All that is needed is a believer and his bible. Most Protestants will acknowledge that the community of believers, commonly called a Church, has a legitimate role but it is always subordinate to Scripture. As a community of believers, Christians are to individually and collectively obey written Scripture that is sufficient by itself since it is, Protestants claim, self-interpreting.[185]

That Scripture is sufficient by itself, according to *Sola Scriptura*, does not mean that Protestants think that every verse of scripture is clear to everyone. Instead, Sola Scriptura teaches that only what is necessary for salvation is clear to all who read scripture. Protestants also maintain that the Church does have an interpretive role to Scripture but never in a way that is above Scripture. Protestants deny, therefore, that any person, any group, or succession of people has an authoritative role above Scripture. St. Paul, according to a common Protestant claim, explicitly teaches *Sola Scriptura* with, "All scripture is inspired by God and is useful for teaching, for reproof, for correction, and for training in righteousness, so that everyone who belongs to God may be proficient, equipped for every good work." (2 Timothy 3:16-17 NRSV) Since similar New Testament passages use a different Greek word than ἄρτιος for "equipped," also translated as

---

[185] "Does the Bible Teach Sola Scriptura? James White vs Patrick Madrid," Published Sept. 7, 2014, youtube.com, https://youtu.be/2IJYWqFjKb0 (accessed August 18, 2016).

complete, this passage, argues Protestants, applies to Scripture in a unique manner.[186]

Catholic Response to *Sola Scriptura*

Patrick Madrid in a debate with James White responded to the *Sola Scriptura* doctrine by arguing the following. There is abundant evidence that no early Church Father ever taught *Sola Scriptura*. If a passage from a Church Father seems to teach Sola Scriptura, this is never the case once the context of the passage is taken into account. For example, St. Cyril of Jerusalem is sometimes quoted by Protestants as supposedly supportive of Sola Scriptura, but a careful reading of St. Cyril of Jerusalem's writings reveals that he actually affirmed the mutually subordinate role of the Church and Scripture. By the Holy Spirit, the Church exercises her authoritative role by recognizing what words and books are inspired Scripture and what words and books are not. By the Holy Spirit, the Catholic Church identifies, protects and defends the message behind the inspired written words of Scripture.[187] This message of

---

[186] "What Still Divides Us: Patrick Madrid & Team vs. Michael Horton & Team," CD 1, store.patrickmadrid.com, https://store.patrickmadrid.com/what-still-divides-us-a-catholicprotestant-debate/ (accessed August 20, 2016).

[187] In debating with White on the need for Church authority, Madrid distinguishes between three meanings of the scriptural term "word": the eternal Word of the Father spoken in the love of the Holy Spirit, the Word

Scripture, the form of Scripture, is what the Church is always subordinate to.

St. Cyril of Jerusalem on the Apostolic Tradition of the Canon of Scripture

> 33. Now these the divinely-inspired Scriptures of both the Old and the New Testament teach us. For the God of the two Testaments is One, Who in the Old Testament foretold the Christ Who appeared in the New; Who by the Law and the Prophets led us to Christ's school. For before faith came, we were kept in ward under the law, and, the law has been our tutor to bring us

---

made flesh, and the written Word of Scripture. A fourth meaning, referred to above, is the Church as the mystical body of Christ who is the Word of the father. The Church is able to recognize which meaning is being referred to when the term word is used. The authority that grants the Church an ability to recognize correct scriptural interpretations does not mean that the Church as an ultimate authority, by being the mystical body of Christ, is in tension with the ultimate authority of Sacred Scripture. The presence of more than one ultimate authority is not necessarily contradictory provided that the authorities are mutually subordinate to one another and mutually shed light upon one another as the two prophets, both contemporaries of one another, Jeremiah and Isaiah were in harmony with one another, and as is Scripture, Tradition and the Magisterium, and as were the four evangelists. "Does the Bible Teach Sola Scriptura? James White vs Patrick Madrid," Published Sept. 7, 2014, youtube.com, https://youtu.be/2IJYWqFjKb0 (accessed August 18, 2016).

unto Christ. And if ever thou hear any of the heretics speaking evil of the Law or the Prophets, answer in the sound of the Savior's voice, saying, Jesus came not to destroy the Law, but to fulfil it. Matthew 5:17 Learn also diligently, and from the Church, what are the books of the Old Testament, and what those of the New. And, pray, read none of the apocryphal writings: for why do you, who know not those which are acknowledged among all, trouble yourself in vain about those which are disputed? Read the Divine Scriptures, the twenty-two books of the Old Testament, these that have been translated by the Seventy-two Interpreters.[188]

23. It is called Catholic then because it extends over all the world, from one end of the earth to the other; and because it teaches universally and completely one and all the doctrines which ought to come to men's knowledge, concerning things both

---

[188] Cyril of Jerusalem, *Catechetical Lecture 4*, no. 33 New Advent, http://www.newadvent.org/fathers/310104.htm (accessed January 4, 2015). New Advent gives the following source information. Translated by Edwin Hamilton Gifford. From Nicene and Post-Nicene Fathers, Second Series, Vol. 7. Edited by Philip Schaff and Henry Wace. (Buffalo, NY: Christian Literature Publishing Co., 1894.) Revised and edited for New Advent by Kevin Knight. <http://www.newadvent.org/fathers/310104.htm>.

visible and invisible, heavenly and earthly ; and because it brings into subjection to godliness the whole race of mankind, governors and governed, learned and unlearned; and because it universally treats and heals the whole class of sins, which are committed by soul or body, and possesses in itself every form of virtue which is named, both in deeds and words, and in every kind of spiritual gifts.[189]

In more scholastic language, the above quotations teach that the Church is formally sufficient and Scripture is materially sufficient. Both the Church and Scripture, therefore, are complementary authorities. The material sufficiency of Scripture means that all doctrines of the Catholic Church necessary for salvation are either explicitly or implicitly contained in written Scripture. In affirming the material sufficiency of Scripture Pope Pius XII taught, "It is also true that theologians must always return to the sources of divine revelation: for it belongs to them to point out how the doctrine of the living Teaching Authority is to be found either explicitly or implicitly in the Scriptures and in Tradition."[190]

---

[189] Cyril of Jerusalem, *Catechetical Lecture 18,* no. 23 New Advent, http://www.newadvent.org/fathers/310118.htm (accessed January 4, 2015).

[190] Pius XII, *Humani Generis*, 1950, no. 21, The Vatican, http://w2.vatican.va/content/pius-xii/en/encyclicals/documents/hf_p-

Formal sufficiency of the Catholic Church is the Church's inspired ability to recognize what books are part of the bible that teach "universally and completely one and all the doctrines" pertaining to salvation, and what is the message, the form, that God intends the Christian to hear through the material words of Scripture.

Since it is not clear what Scripture teaches regarding some doctrines necessary for salvation, the magisterium of the Church, relying on living Tradition, is necessary. Examples of doctrines that are unclearly referred to in Scripture include scriptural references to infant baptism, to baptismal regeneration and to the Eucharist. The interpretation of these Scriptural references not only distinguish Catholics from Protestants but also Protestants from one another. If Scripture is not clear on these doctrines, then Scripture is clearly not formally sufficient. The belief that Scripture is formally sufficient (*sola scriptura*) has led to the many divisions within Protestantism since, as Madrid points out, "*Sola Scriptura* is a blue print for anarchy."

When interpreting difficult passages as a Catholic, I am not to rely only on myself or a biblical scholar, both of whom are fallible men, but on the Church, on Christ's mystical body, which is animated by the Holy Spirit, who gives unique guidance to the successors of the Apostles, the bishops. In accordance with this approach, St. Peter

---

xii_enc_12081950_humani-generis.html (accessed January 6, 2014).

teaches that reading the bible without reference to Church authority can lead one astray especially when reading the letters of St. Paul. He states, "So also our beloved brother Paul wrote to you according to the wisdom given him, speaking of this as he does in all his letters. There are some things in them hard to understand, which the ignorant and unstable twist to their own destruction, as they do the other scriptures. You therefore, beloved, since you are forewarned, beware that you are not carried away with the error of the lawless and lose your own stability." (2 Peter 3:15-17 NRSV)

Sola Scriptura is Unhistorical

Madrid further counters the Protestant belief in *Sola Scriptura* by systematically arguing that it is unhistorical, unbiblical, unworkable and is not followed in practice by Protestants. We will begin with his argument that this Protestant teaching is unhistorical.

As mentioned previously, the Church Fathers and the early Church Councils never taught *Sola Scriptura*. Sacred Scripture was understood by them to be materially sufficient but not formally sufficient. The form (interpretation) requires an external body, in other words the living tradition of the Church and her magisterial office.

Benedict XVI, writing as a theologian, explains

that the "external form"[191] of the living tradition of the Church are the bishops as a result of Apostolic Succession. The teaching authority of the bishops in union with the papacy is the means by which the "content"[192] of the living tradition is defined and the key that unlocks the meaning intended by God that stands behind the literal words of Scripture. These keys have historically taken place in the form of creeds, liturgical formulas, etc. In referring to this role of the bishops, St. Basil the Great (330-379) states:

> Of the beliefs and practices whether generally accepted or publicly enjoined which are preserved in the Church some we possess derived from written teaching others we have received delivered to us "in a mystery" by the tradition of the apostles; and both of these in relation to true religion have the same force.[193]

Other Church Fathers repeatedly refer to teachings Protestants claim are non-scriptural including: purgatory, the Mass as sacrifice, Real Eucharistic Presence, Sacramental Theology, Intercession of the Saints and Holy Orders.

---

[191] Joseph Ratzinger, *The Episcopate and the Primacy*, trans. Kenneth Barker (New York: Herder and Herder, 1962), 51.

[192] Joseph Ratzinger, *The Episcopate and the Primacy*, trans. Kenneth Barker, 51.

[193] St. Basil the Great, *The Book of Saint Basil on the Spirit*, Chapter XXVII.

Moving to the Medieval age to the great scholastic theologian, St. Thomas Aquinas, echoing the Church Fathers, understood Scripture and Tradition in a participative manner that is only rightly experienced in the context of the Catholic community. For Aquinas, Scripture and Tradition both participate in the one Divine Truth. Aquinas, therefore, never divided Scripture from Tradition. Understood in this way Tradition, as represented by many Protestants, is not understood as an external reality that imposes propositions to believers.

Vatican Council II in *Dei Verbum* officially taught the participative nature of Scripture, Tradition and the Magisterium by writing, in reference to the Magisterium, "This teaching office is not above the word of God, but serves it, teaching only what has been handed on, listening to it devoutly, guarding it scrupulously and explaining it faithfully in accord with a divine commission and with the help of the Holy Spirit, it draws from this one deposit of faith everything which it presents for belief as divinely revealed."[194] That all three participate in the one divine truth and are mutually subordinate to one another is made even clearer by the following passage of *Dei Verbum*, "It is clear, therefore, that sacred tradition, Sacred Scripture and the teaching authority of the Church, in accord with God's most wise design, are so linked and

---

[194] Vatican II, *Dei Verbum*, 1965, chap. 2, no. 10, The Vatican, http://www.vatican.va/archive/hist_councils/ii_vatican_council/documents/vat-ii_const_19651118_dei-verbum_en.html (accessed January 6, 2015).

joined together that one cannot stand without the others, and that all together and each in its own way under the action of the one Holy Spirit contribute effectively to the salvation of souls."[195]

In highlighting the role of the Magisterium and Tradition in interpreting the words of Scripture the council explains:

> Sacred Scripture is the word of God inasmuch as it is consigned to writing under the inspiration of the divine Spirit, while sacred tradition takes the word of God entrusted by Christ the Lord and the Holy Spirit to the Apostles, and hands it on to their successors in its full purity, so that led by the light of the Spirit of truth, they may in proclaiming it preserve this word of God faithfully, explain it, and make it more widely known. Consequently, it is not from Sacred Scripture alone that the Church draws her certainty about everything which has been revealed. Therefore both sacred tradition and Sacred Scripture are to be accepted and venerated with the same sense of loyalty and reverence.[196]

---

[195] Vatican II, *Dei Verbum*, 1965, chap. 2, no. 10, The Vatican, http://www.vatican.va/archive/hist_councils/ii_vatican_council/documents/vat-ii_const_19651118_dei-verbum_en.html (accessed January 6, 2015).

[196] Vatican II, *Dei Verbum*, 1965, chap. 2, no. 9, The Vatican, http://www.vatican.va/archive/hist_councils/ii_vatican_council/documents/vat-ii_const_19651118_dei-verbum_en.html (accessed December 10, 2015).

As stated above, the Church teaches that Scripture does not function alone as a sole authority but together with tradition and the Magisterium. With respect to the message of Scripture, the Magisterium and Tradition play a subordinate and servant role to scripture. However, with respect to the text that conveys the message, the Magisterium and Tradition do have an interpretative, authoritative role. By the Holy Spirit, the Magisterium and Tradition are able to recognize which words and books constitute Scripture, and what is the correct message that God intends to convey through the words of Scripture.[197]

That the text of Scripture is obscure at times and in great need of authority is testified by Peter, as previously shown. (2 Peter 3:15-17 NRSV) Catholics, in accordance with Peter, do not believe that all of God's teachings are clear. Catholics do not believe that theology has completely mastered understanding God's teachings. The Catholic use of the term *homooúsios* is an example of this cautious approach to theology. The non-biblical, Greek term

---

[197] An example of role of guarding Scripture that the Catholic Church has in order to ensure proper understanding of Scripture is evident in how Jehovah Witnesses interpret John 1:1. According to their New World Translation this verse reads, "In the beginning was the Word, and the word was with God, and the Word was **a** god." This false interpretation/ translation of the text conveys the Jehovah Witness's modern Arian belief that although Jesus is divine he is not equal and one with the Father since Jesus was created by the Father. Patrick Madrid, *Answer Me This*, loc. 619.

homooúsios was used in the early Church in order to clarify difficult to understand passages of scripture that Arians were erroneously interpreting.[198]

Sola Scriptura is Unbiblical

In contradiction to the *Sola Scriptura* teaching, the New Testament cites oral traditions that are not written in the Old Testament. For example, 2 Tim. 3:8 refers to Jannes and Jambres who opposed Moses and Aaron. The names of these men do not appear in the Old Testament. Their names do, though, appear in a non-biblical Jewish Targum (Jonathan Exodus 7:11-8:19).[199]

The New Testament writers also believed in and developed extra-biblical doctrines of Pharisaical Judaism such as: resurrection, the soul, the afterlife, eternal reward or damnation, angelology, and demonology. These same doctrines were all rejected by the Sadducees as testified by the ancient Jewish historian Josephus.[200]

In addition, the New Testament often cites

---

[198] "What Still Divides Us: Patrick Madrid & Team vs. Michael Horton & Team," CD 2-3, store.patrickmadrid.com, https://store.patrickmadrid.com/what-still-divides-us-a-catholicprotestant-debate/ (accessed August 20, 2016).

[199] Dave Armstrong, *100 Bible Arguments against Sola Scriptura* (San Diego: Catholic Answers Press, 2012), loc. 535.

[200] Dave Armstrong, *100 Bible Arguments against Sola Scriptura*, loc. 870.

deuterocanonical books (Tobit, Judith, Wisdom, Ecclesiastes, Baruch, 1 and 2 Maccabees, some parts of Daniel and some parts of Esther) which Protestants categorize as non-inspired and not part of the Bible. The following are two examples: Matthew 4:4 cites Wisdom 16:26, and Matthew 4:15 cites 1 Mac. 5:15.[201]

Finally, being faithful to tradition is explicitly taught in St. Paul's Second Letter to the Thessalonians. He writes, "So then, brothers and sisters, stand firm and hold fast to the traditions that you were taught by us, either by word of mouth or by our letter." (2 Thessalonians 2:15 NRSV) Since *Sola Scriptura* is explicitly unbiblical it is not a tradition reflective of Scriptural truths but rather a tradition of men which contradicts the word of God and therefore ought to be rejected.[202] (See Mark 7:8; 1 Cor. 11:2; 2 Thes. 2:15)[203]

---

[201] Dave Armstrong, *100 Bible Arguments against Sola Scriptura*, loc. 588.

[202] "What Still Divides Us: Patrick Madrid & Team vs. Michael Horton & Team," CD 2-3.

[203] "You abandon the commandment of God and hold to human tradition." (Mark 7:8 NRSV) "I commend you because you remember me in everything and maintain the traditions just as I handed them on to you." (1 Corinthians 11:2 NRSV); "So then, brothers and sisters, stand firm and hold fast to the traditions that you were taught by us, either by word of mouth or by our letter." (2 Thessalonians 2:15 NRSV). Jesus also teaches the importance of encountering His Divine truth not only in Scripture but also in the context of the living communal nature of the Church which provide the context for traditions to be passed down. "For where two

The argument that St. Paul in another letter (2 Timothy 3:16-17) explicitly teaches *Sola Scriptura* is readily seen to be unreasonable once the Scripture passage is looked at carefully. The Scripture passage in question is provided below with its original Greek wording:

> All scripture is inspired by God and is useful for teaching, for reproof, for correction, and for training in righteousness, so that everyone who belongs to God may be **proficient** [sufficient], **equipped for every good work**. (2 Timothy 3:16-17 NRSV)

> 16 πᾶσα γραφὴ θεόπνευστος καὶ ὠφέλιμος πρὸς διδασκαλίαν, πρὸς [f]ἐλεγμόν, πρὸς ἐπανόρθωσιν, πρὸς παιδείαν τὴν ἐν δικαιοσύνῃ, 17 ἵνα **ἄρτιος** ᾖ ὁ τοῦ θεοῦ ἄνθρωπος, πρὸς πᾶν ἔργον ἀγαθὸν **ἐξηρτισμένος**. (2 Timothy 3:16-17)

As pointed out in a debate between Catholics and Protestants on this very passage, even from a Protestant standpoint it is ambiguous whether this passage teaches *Sola Scriptura* or not. According to lexicons, the two words in bold have multiple meanings and yet Greek does have words that clearly indicate something is sufficient or not.

---

or three are gathered in my name, I am there among them." (Matthew 18:20 NRSV)

Would not Paul have chosen a word that more clearly means sufficient and would he not have explicitly made it clear that he was referring to Scripture? It is also difficult to determine the meaning of these two words in their scriptural context since this is the only time ἄρτιος, proficient, is used in the bible, and the word ἐξηρτισμένος, equipped for every good work, is only used once more in the Septuagint. In addition, the Scripture that Paul is referring to is the Old Testament and not the New Testament since it had not been yet written.

The context of the passage indicates the emphasis is not on whether Scripture is sufficient but on what will equip Timothy to be equipped. An earlier passage by Paul to Timothy indicates that other sources are necessary for Timothy to be equipped. The Bible does not, therefore, teach a quantitative sufficiency of Scripture.[204] In both 2 Timothy 1:13-14 and in 2 Timothy 2:2, Paul tells Timothy to keep what he has heard, and has been passed down to him and not only to heed what he has read. The oral tradition is another source with which Timothy is to equip himself. Through oral tradition, the Word of God is entrusted to reliable men, in particular bishops, who pass the message down to future generations.[205] To drive the point

---

[204] "What Still Divides Us: Patrick Madrid & Team vs. Michael Horton & Team," CD 2-3.

[205] "Hold to the standard of sound teaching that you have heard from me, in the faith and love that are in Christ Jesus. Guard the good treasure entrusted to you,

even further, if Protestants use the same logic they used for 2 Timothy 3:16-17 for James 1:4, then does this mean that only perseverance in good works and nothing else is all that is required to be saved? The point here is not that James 1:4 serves as an adequate parallel text since its context is significantly different but that the logic that Protestants apply to 2 Timothy 3:16-17 is faulty. Also, the Greek used in James 1:4 more clearly indicates than 2 Timothy 3:16-17 that an activity, in this case perseverance, is sufficient.[206]

Sola Scriptura is Unworkable

The many divisions within Protestantism is proof that *Sola Scriptura* does not work. Madrid counters the argument that most Protestants only accept *Sola Scriptura,* but the Anabaptist *solo scriptura* is not a convincing distinction because unless the Protestants can locate where the authority of the Church resides how can scripture

---

with the help of the Holy Spirit living in us." (2 Timothy 1:13-14 NRSV) "You then, my child, be strong in the grace that is in Christ Jesus; and what you have heard from me through many witnesses entrust to faithful people who will be able to teach others as well." (2 Timothy 2:1-2 NRSV)

[206] "My brothers and sisters, whenever you face trials of any kind, consider it nothing but joy, because you know that the testing of your faith produces endurance; and let endurance have its full effect, so that you may be mature and complete, lacking in nothing." (James 1:2-4 NRSV)

be adequately interpreted?[207] According to *solo scriptura,* the only location where truth resides is in Sacred Scripture. According to *Sola Scriptura,* truth is acknowledged as existing in places other than Sacred Scripture, but Scripture differs from these other locations in that it is "the only infallible and supreme criterion of truth."[208] These two definitions do not, though, specifically explain where non-biblical authority resides. If this is not clearly stated, then there is a risk for competing authorities to develop, leading to chaos and schisms.

Madrid also points out that the related Protestant teaching of the perspicuity of Scripture (the meaning of Scripture is clear to the ordinary reader) has never historically worked. For example, Protestants are divided on how to interpret passages on baptism (whether to baptize infants or not), on the Eucharist (some type of presence of Christ or only symbolic), on justification, baptismal regeneration, salvation, divorce, remarriage, etc.[209] If Scripture is clear to the reader on essential

---

[207] Madrid, *Envoy for Christ: 25 Years as a Catholic Apologist* (Cincinnati: Servant Books, 2012), 47.

[208] Madrid, *Envoy for Christ: 25 Years as a Catholic Apologist,* 44. This is a quote from the Protestant Douglas Jones.

[209] For example, Lutherans believe that by baptism of water the baptized not only dies to sin but also is regenerated. Some Evangelicals, though, disagree on this fundamental issue concerning scriptural teaching on baptism. They believe that one needs to be baptized not only in water, where a Christian dies to sin, but also in the spirit, where a Christian is regenerated.

matters concerning faith, then why is there so much division among Protestants on an official level? By following the teaching of *Sola Scriptura*, Protestants have divided over significant matters and continue to do so. History demonstrates that living in accordance with *Sola Scriptura* results in fragmentation.[210]

Catholics also are divided but not in their official Catholic teaching. There is not one example of the Catholic Church ever officially dissenting from her doctrine. It is true that in a non-official manner many Catholics do not agree with other Catholics on theological doctrine. However, this reality is in accordance with the parable of Christ regarding the weeds and wheat growing in the field. The Catholic field resembles the Kingdom of God in its present earthly condition. Christ does not want Church officials to completely separate the wheat from the chaff since this role will be done by Christ at the end of time.[211]

Protestants do not in Practice or Follow *Sola Scriptura*

As emphasized by Madrid, for an authority to be formally sufficient it needs to have the ability to settle disputes. Catholics hold that the Magisterium has the authority to settle disputes on various interpretations of Scripture because it is a formally sufficient authority. Sacred Scripture alone does

---

[210] Patrick Madrid, *Answer Me This*, loc. 452.
[211] Patrick Madrid, *Answer Me This*, loc. 452.

not have the authority to settle disputes. If it did, then why do Protestants argue over passages of Scripture that directly pertain to essential aspects of salvation such as baptism? Logically, this means that in practice Protestants do not recognize Scripture as formally sufficient.

Other practices of Protestants that contradict their Sola Scriptura belief include their acceptance of the canon of Scripture that was determined by the early Christian Church. Scripture, after all, does not list an "inspired table of contents."[212] By accepting a particular book as inspired in the bible, one also implicitly is recognizing the authority that chose and considered this book as inspired. The authority that did this was the Church, specifically bishops who met together in councils. Catholics believe that the reason that the bishops were able to determine which books are inspired from books that are not is due to the special presence of the Holy Spirit at work in the Magisterium. Protestants also demonstrate in practice their faith in the Magisterium by their belief in the Trinity and by believing that Christ has two natures. Both of these doctrines were formulated by the Magisterium and are not explicitly stated in Scripture.[213]

---

[212] Madrid, *Envoy for Christ: 25 Years as a Catholic Apologist*, 47.

[213] "What Still Divides Us: Patrick Madrid & Team vs. Michael Horton & Team," CD 2-3.

The Catholic Church's Historical Relationship to Scripture

In defending their Sola Scriptura teaching, Protestants often depict the Catholic Church as preventing people from having access to the Scripture. What other reason, it is asked, did the Catholic Church have for chaining Scripture down and even burning bibles? A Catholic response to this question is that since monasteries and churches of medieval times saw the bible as precious, and since before the making of the Gutenberg Printing Press in 1440 there were very few books, relatively speaking, a common way to ensure bibles were not stolen was to chain them down. The bible, therefore, was not chained in order to prevent people from having access to it, but rather in order to ensure they would have access to it.[214]

With respect to bible burning, is true that the Catholic Church burned bibles but ones that were not authorized and which most likely contained errors in the text. In accordance with this logic, the Council of Trent (1545-1563) was not opposed to Scripture being in the vernacular but rather was opposed to unauthorized versions of Scripture. The Church has consistently encouraged the reading of Scripture, but of authorized versions whose translations are accurate and which contain all the inspired books. Similar to the Catholic Church,

---

[214] Patrick Madrid, *Answer Me This*, loc. 599.

Protestants also burned bibles they deemed unauthorized and possibly containing, consequently, errors. Calvin burned a bible of a fellow Protestant, Michael Servetus, and then burned Servetus as well. After declaring himself head of the Church of England, Henry VIII ordered Catholic bibles and Catholic religious texts to be burned. His daughter Elizabeth I did the same, with particular attention to the then recently released Catholic Rheims English translation of the New Testament.[215]

---

[215] Patrick Madrid, *Answer Me This*, loc. 659. Madrid also points out that before the Protestant Reformation, the Catholic Church commissioned and authorized vernacular translations of the bible including the following: Venerable Bede (672-735) translated the Bible into Saxon, which along with the Romance language of France, the English language is in part based upon; In the 1200s' the Spanish King Alfonso the Wise commissioned the bible to be translated into Spanish; The Italian, Catholic Archbishop Giacomo of Genoa translated the Bible into Italian in the 1200s; There were English translations of the bible prior to Wycliffe's translation. Wycliffe's translations were condemned because his translations were illicit not because the bible had been translated into English. The concern of those who condemned Wycliffe's translation was for quality and accuracy; In the 1400s the Polish Catholic Queen Hedwig commissioned a Polish Catholic translation of the bible; France had at minimum sixteen translations of the bible prior to 1547; Before Martin Luther's 1530 German translation, there were already at minimum 33 Catholic German translations of the bible in print. Madrid, *Envoy for Christ: 25 Years as a Catholic Apologist* (Cincinnati: Servant Books, 2012), 27, 28, 29, 31.

Quiz 7

1. With respect to Sacred Scripture and the Magisterium distinguish between formal sufficiency and material sufficiency.

2. Argue in four ways why the Catholic position of the mutual subordination of Scripture, Tradition, and Magisterium is more reasonable than the Protestant position of Sola Scriptura.

Additional Activities and Resources

Respond to the following. Do so according to the Socratic method of gathering, clarifying and challenging questions.

- St. Paul explicitly teaches Sola Scriptura. "All scripture is inspired by God and is useful for teaching, for reproof, for correction, and for training in righteousness, so that everyone who belongs to God may be proficient [sufficient], equipped for every good work." (2 Timothy 3:16-17 NRSV)
- If the Pope really has authority that Catholics claim he does than why can't he settle the very visible dissent among Catholics on important matters of the faith?

- Catholics hold that "We ought to believe because Rome says so." This is illogical, circular thinking.
- The Catholic Church locked up and burned bibles because it does not want people to read the bible.
- The ordinary person can simply read Scripture and find out by himself what sin is, who Christ is, what the cross means, and what it means to believe in Christ.

Readings

Armstrong, Dave. *100 Bible Arguments against Sola Scriptura*. San Diego: Catholic Answers Press, 2012.

"Scripture Alone? – *Questions 7-13*" from Madrid, Patrick. *Answer Me This*. Huntington: Our Sunday Visitor Publishing Division, 2003. Loc. 452

Section One Sola Scriptura from Madrid, Patrick. *Envoy for Christ: 25 Years as a Catholic Apologist*. Cincinnati: Servant Books, 2012 – 47 44

Vatican II, *Dei Verbum*, 1965, chap. 2, no. 10, The Vatican, http://www.vatican.va/archive/hist_councils/ii_vatican_council/documents/vat-ii_const_19651118_dei-verbum_en.html

Audio

"What Still Divides Us: Patrick Madrid & Team vs. Michael Horton & Team," store.patrickmadrid.com, https://store.patrickmadrid.com/what-still-divides-us-a-catholicprotestant-debate/

Video

"Does the Bible Teach Sola Scriptura? James White vs Patrick Madrid," Published Sept. 7, 2014, youtube.com, https://youtu.be/2IJYWqFjKb0

Fr. Peter Samuel Kucer, MSA

Chapter Eight: The Eucharist

Introduction

Protestants vary vastly in their understanding of the Eucharist. These differences were present right from the very beginning of Protestantism. For example, Martin Luther (1483-1546), who it is popularly held sparked the Protestant Reformation, believed that there is a real presence of Christ in the Eucharist.[216] In contrast, Luther's contemporary fellow Protestant Huldrych Zwingli (1484-1531)

---

[216] The following comes from the 1530 Augsburg Confession, that summarizes Lutheran beliefs. "The substance of the Eucharistic bread and wine is not changed, in the sense of transubstantiation, into the body and blood of Christ but rather both the reality of Christ and the reality of the bread are fully present. According to Lutheran theology what occurs is a consubstantiation by which Christ adheres in, with and under the bread and wine." "The Augsburg Confession", Christian Classics Ethereal Library, http://www.ccel.org/ccel/schaff/creeds3.iii.ii.html (accessed October 25, 2014), article 10.

taught that the Eucharist only symbolizes the presence of Christ.[217] While acknowledging the many different Protestant theologies concerning this sacrament, this chapter will provide Catholic responses to some of the most common Protestant objections to the Catholic understanding of the Eucharist. When reading this chapter, it is important, therefore, to bear in mind that these objections do not represent all the objections of Protestants to the Catholic Eucharistic belief. Some Protestants may agree with all the objections. Others may agree with only a few or have differing variations of the objections. We will begin by first presenting the Catholic Eucharistic belief before answering common Protestant objections to this belief.

Catholic Eucharistic Belief

Quoting the Council of Trent, which took place in the midst of the Protestant Reformation, the *Catechism of the Catholic Church* defines a key Catholic belief concerning the Eucharist as follows:

> The Council of Trent summarizes the Catholic faith by declaring: "Because Christ our Redeemer said that it was truly his body

---

[217] Johann Hottinger, *The Life and Times of Ulric Zwingli*, trans. Thomas Porter (Harrisburg: Theo. F. Scheffer, 1856), chapter 3, Project Gutenberg, http://www.gutenberg.org/files/31225/31225-h/31225-h.htm#div1_chap3 (accessed October 25, 2014).

that he was offering under the species of bread, it has always been the conviction of the Church of God, and this holy Council now declares again, that by the consecration of the bread and wine there takes place a change of the whole substance of the bread into the substance of the body of Christ our Lord and of the whole substance of the wine into the substance of his blood. This change the holy Catholic Church has fittingly and properly called transubstantiation."[218]

Shortly before the closure of Vatican Council II (December 8, 1965), Paul VI reaffirmed this teaching from the Council of Trent by teaching:

10. For We can see that some of those who are dealing with this Most Holy Mystery in speech and writing are disseminating opinions on Masses celebrated in private or on the dogma of transubstantiation that are disturbing the minds of the faithful and causing them no small measure of confusion about matters of faith, just as if it were all right for someone to take doctrine that has already been defined by the Church and consign it to oblivion or else interpret it in such a way as to weaken the genuine

---

[218] "Catechism of the Catholic Church," no. 1376, Vatican.va, http://www.vatican.va/archive/ccc_css/archive/catechism/p2s2c1a3.htm (accessed August 22, 2016).

meaning of the words or the recognized force of the concepts involved.

11. To give an example of what We are talking about, it is not permissible to extol the so-called "community" Mass in such a way as to detract from Masses that are celebrated privately; or to concentrate on the notion of sacramental sign as if the symbolism—which no one will deny is certainly present in the Most Blessed Eucharist—fully expressed and exhausted the manner of Christ's presence in this Sacrament; or to discuss the mystery of transubstantiation without mentioning what the Council of Trent had to say about the marvelous conversion of the whole substance of the bread into the Body and the whole substance of the wine into the Blood of Christ, as if they involve nothing more than "transignification," or "transfinalization" as they call it; or, finally, to propose and act upon the opinion that Christ Our Lord is no longer present in the consecrated Hosts that remain after the celebration of the sacrifice of the Mass has been completed.[219]

---

[219] Paul VI, "Mysterium Fidei, Encyclical of Pope Paul VI on the Holy Eucharist," no. 10-11, September 3, 1965, w2.vatican.va, http://w2.vatican.va/content/paul-vi/en/encyclicals/documents/hf_p-vi_enc_03091965_mysterium.html (accessed August 22, 2016).

In order to understand why Blessed Paul VI firmly held to the traditional terminology of transubstantiation, it is necessary to define what substance means in relationship to the related term accident. A simple definition of substance is what something truly is and not simply what it appears to be. A simple definition of accident is what something appears to be but is not. A standard, more complex scholastic definition of accident is "An attribute belonging to some nature but not constituting its essence or a part of its essence."[220] A standard scholastic definition of substance is, "A being that has existence in itself and by virtue of itself as an ultimate distinct subject of being."[221] A simple definition of transubstantiation that is based on the distinction of these substance and accident is that while the Eucharist appears to be bread and wine it actually is the body, blood, soul and divinity of the risen Jesus Christ. The official definition from the Council of Trent of transubstantiation is:

> [B]y the consecration of the bread and wine there takes place a change of the whole substance of the bread into the substance of the body of Christ our Lord and of the whole substance of the wine into the substance of his blood. This change the holy Catholic

---

[220] Bernard Wuellner, *Dictionary of Scholastic Philosophy* (Milwaukee: The Bruce Publishing Company, 1956), 2.
[221] Bernard Wuellner, *Dictionary of Scholastic Philosophy*, 119.

Church has fittingly and properly called transubstantiation.[222]

The following illustration from Bishop Barron helps to distinguish these two ways of perceiving reality. To a child looking through the back window of a car late at night, it might appear that the moon is chasing the car but it is not since this is only what appears to be happening and is not what is actually occurring.[223] Similarly, although the Eucharist appears to be ordinary bread and wine it actually is the body, blood, soul and divinity of the risen Christ.

Knowing the history of the term transubstantiation also helps to reveal why it is crucial term in understanding the mystery of the Eucharist properly. The term transubstantiation was used for the first time by the Church in an official ecclesial document in 1208 by Innocent III.[224] A few years later the Council of Lateran IV also used this term by stating, "There is one Universal Church of the faithful, outside of which there is absolutely no salvation. In which there is the same priest and sacrifice, Jesus Christ, whose body and blood are truly contained in the

---

[222] "Catechism of the Catholic Church," no. 1376, Vatican.va, http://www.vatican.va/archive/ccc_css/archive/catechism/p2s2c1a3.htm (accessed August 22, 2016).

[223] Robert Barron, *Eucharist: Catholic Spirituality for Adults* (New York: Orbis Books, 2008), loc. 1135.

[224] Robert Barron, *Eucharist: Catholic Spirituality for Adults*, loc. 1054.

sacrament of the altar under the forms of bread and wine; the bread being changed (*transsubstantiatio*) by divine power into the body, and the wine into the blood, so that to realize the mystery of unity we may receive of Him what He has received of us. And this sacrament no one can effect except the priest who has been duly ordained in accordance with the keys of the Church, which Jesus Christ Himself gave to the Apostles and their successors."[225]

One of the reasons for the use of this Greek term was due to errors concerning the Eucharist that some theologians had fallen into. On one end of a spectrum of errors, the French theologian Berengar of Tours (c. 999-1088) taught that the historical body of Jesus is essentially different from His Eucharistic body to such an extent that His Eucharistic presence is only symbolic of His historical body. Opponents to Berengar's Eucharistic theology reacted excessively in the opposite direction by teaching that Christ's Eucharistic body is his pre-resurrection body without any difference.[226]

The *Catechism of the Catholic Church* teaches that while the body, blood, soul and divinity "of the whole Christ is truly, really and substantially contained," Christ is present in his risen body and

---

[225] "Medieval Sourcebook: Twelfth Ecumenical Council Lateran IV 1215," sourcebooks.fordham.edu, http://sourcebooks.fordham.edu/halsall/basis/lateran4.asp (accessee August 25, 2016).

[226] Robert Barron, *Eucharist: Catholic Spirituality for Adults*, loc. 1054.

not in His pre-resurrection body that died on the cross:

> What material food produces in our bodily life, Holy Communion wonderfully achieves in our spiritual life. Communion with the flesh of the risen Christ, a flesh 'given life and giving life through the Holy Spirit,' preserves, increases, and renews the life of grace received at Baptism. This growth in Christian life needs the nourishment of Eucharistic Communion, the bread for our pilgrimage until the moment of death, when it will be given to us as viaticum.[227]

In stating the Church's Eucharistic doctrine, the *Catechism of the Catholic Church* refers to St. Thomas Aquinas's teaching. In his *Summa Theologica*, Aquinas makes a distinction between Christ's bodily presence according to His "proper species"[228] and His bodily presence "in a special

---

[227] "Catechism of the Catholic Church," 1371, 1392, vatican.va, http://www.vatican.va/archive/ccc_css/archive/catechism/p2s2c1a3.htm (accessed August 25, 2016).

[228] Thomas Aquinas, *Summa Theologica*, III, q. 75, art. 6, newadvent.org, http://www.newadvent.org/summa/4075.htm#article4 (accessed August 25, 2016). "Thirdly, it would be unbefitting this sacrament: because the accidents of the bread remain in this sacrament, in order that the body of Christ may be seen under them, and not under its proper species, as stated above (Article 5)."

manner which is proper to this sacrament."[229]

In reference to these passages of Aquinas, Bishop Barron explains that Christ's sacramental presence is substantial since He is present, body, blood, soul and divinity. This differs from a body being only physically present in body and blood and differs from mere spiritual presence of soul and divinity. He writes:

> Aquinas clarifies that the body of Christ is not in the sacrament of the Eucharist the way a body is ordinarily in a place, measured by its own dimensions and circumscribed by the contours of the space that it occupies. And thus, though we can say that Christ's body is on various altars at the same time, we shouldn't say that he is in various places at the same time, for this would be to confuse proper and sacramental modes of appearance. In a similar vein, Aquinas specifies that we shouldn't speak of

---

[229] Thomas Aquinas, *Summa Theologica*, III, q. 75, art. 1, ad. 3, newadvent.org, http://www.newadvent.org/summa/4075.htm#article4 (accessed August 25, 2016). "Christ's body is not in this sacrament in the same way as a body is in a place, which by its dimensions is commensurate with the place; but in a special manner which is proper to this sacrament. Hence we say that Christ's body is upon many altars, not as in different places, but 'sacramentally': and thereby we do not understand that Christ is there only as in a sign, although a sacrament is a kind of sign; but that Christ's body is here after a fashion proper to this sacrament, as stated above."

carrying around the body of Christ when we process with the Eucharist or of imprisoning Jesus when we put the sacramental elements in the tabernacle. To do so would be to conflate these two basic modes of presence. And this is why Thomas Aquinas and the mainstream of the Catholic tradition remain uneasy with that section of the anti-Berengarian oath that speaks of crunching Christ's body with one's teeth. In Aquinas's more precise language, when one consumes the Eucharist, one crunches the accidents of the bread with the teeth, not the body of Christ, since Christ is being received substantially but according to his sacramental species, not his proper species."[230]

Protestant Objections to Catholic Eucharistic Theology

A common Protestant objection to Catholic Eucharistic theology resembles Berengar's understanding. According to these Protestants, Christ intended that the Eucharist be understood only symbolically representing His presence and the early Church viewed the Eucharist in this symbolic manner.

One way Madrid responds to this objection is in reference to Scripture. In his *First Letter to the*

---

[230] Robert Barron, *Eucharist: Catholic Spirituality for Adults* (New York: Orbis Books, 2008), loc. 1109-1116.

Corinthians, St. Paul asserts that if someone takes the body and blood of Christ unworthily then they will be "answerable for the body and blood of the Lord."[231] In other words, they will be held guilty for sinning against the body and blood of the Lord. If I throw darts at a picture of someone, asks Madrid, am I guilty of physically harming them or for harming them in a symbolic manner?[232] The question is, of course, rhetorical. Throwing darts at a picture of someone does not harm the person who is depicted because the picture is not the actual person. Similarly, St. Paul is saying that when we take the Eucharist in an unworthy manner we are "answerable for the body and blood of the Lord" since the Eucharist is the body and blood of the Lord. Similarly, in the previous chapter, St. Paul refers to the Eucharist as the body and blood of Christ. He states:

> Therefore, my dear friends, flee from the worship of idols. I speak as to sensible people; judge for yourselves what I say. The

---

[231] "For I received from the Lord what I also handed on to you, that the Lord Jesus on the night when he was betrayed took a loaf of bread, and when he had given thanks, he broke it and said, "This is my body that is for you. Do this in remembrance of me." In the same way he took the cup also, after supper, saying, "This cup is the new covenant in my blood. Do this, as often as you drink it, in remembrance of me." For as often as you eat this bread and drink the cup, you proclaim the Lord's death until he comes." 1 Corinthians 11:23-26 NRSV.

[232] This image comes from Patrick Madrid. The source is unknown.

cup of blessing that we bless, is it not a sharing in the blood of Christ? The bread that we break, is it not a sharing in the body of Christ? Because there is one bread, we who are many are one body, for we all partake of the one bread. (1 Corinthians 10:14-17 NRSV)

The gospel of John chapter six describes Jesus as referring to the eating and drinking of His body and blood in a sense that exceeds mere symbolism. This reality was fulfilled when Jesus established the Eucharist.

The Jews then disputed among themselves, saying, "How can this man give us his flesh to eat?" So Jesus said to them, "Very truly, I tell you, unless you eat the flesh of the Son of Man and drink his blood, you have no life in you. Those who eat my flesh and drink my blood have eternal life, and I will raise them up on the last day; for my flesh is true food and my blood is true drink. Those who eat my flesh and drink my blood abide in me, and I in them. Just as the living Father sent me, and I live because of the Father, so whoever eats me will live because of me. This is the bread that came down from heaven, not like that which your ancestors ate, and they died. But the one who eats this bread will live forever." (John 6:52-58 NRSV)

Although these Scripture passages seem to indicate that the Eucharist is the body, blood, soul and divinity of the risen Christ they do not by themselves reveal to the individual reader with sufficient clarity the message, God's truth, that stands behind the words. For sufficient clarity on what is essential to our faith we, Catholicism maintains, need to read these Scriptural texts in light of Tradition and the Magisterium. In union with those God has ordained to be bishops we are, reminds St. Paul, to "stand firm and hold fast to the traditions that you were taught by us [the bishops], either by word of mouth or by our letter." (2 Thessalonians 2:15 NRSV)

Repeatedly in the sacred Tradition handed down in history by the bishops Christ's true, sacramental presence is taught. Below are but two early examples:

Bishop Ignatius of Antioch's Letter to the *Letter to the Smyrnaeans* c. 110 AD

Take note of those who hold heterodox opinions on the grace of Jesus Christ which has come to us, and see how contrary their opinions are to the mind of God ... They abstain from the Eucharist and from prayer because they do not confess that the Eucharist is the flesh of our Savior Jesus Christ, flesh which suffered for our sins and which that Father, in his goodness, raised up again. They who deny the gift of God are perishing in their disputes.[233]

St. Ignatius of Antioch's letter to the Romans AD 110

Chapter 7. Reason of desiring to die

The prince of this world would fain carry me away, and corrupt my disposition towards God. Let none of you, therefore, who are [in Rome] help him; rather be on my side, that is, on the side of God. Do not speak of Jesus Christ, and yet set your desires on the world. Let not envy find a dwelling-place among you; nor even should I, when present with you, exhort you to it, be persuaded to listen to me, but rather give credit to those things which I now write to you. For though I am alive while I write to you, yet I am eager to die. My love has been crucified, and there is no fire in me desiring to be fed; but there is within me a water that lives and speaks, saying to me inwardly, Come to the Father. I have no delight in corruptible food, nor in the pleasures of this life. I desire the bread of God, the heavenly bread, the bread of life,

---

[233] Alexander Roberts, James Donaldson, and A. Cleveland Coxe, *Ante-Nicene Fathers*, vol. 1, ed. Alexander Roberts, James Donaldson, and A. Cleveland Coxe (Buffalo, NY: Christian Literature Publishing Co., 1885) Revised and edited for New Advent by Kevin Knight. http://www.newadvent.org/fathers/0109.htm.

which is the flesh of Jesus Christ, the Son of God, who became afterwards of the seed of David and Abraham; and I desire the drink of God, namely His blood, which is incorruptible love and eternal life.[234]

The sacred, living Tradition concerning the Eucharist, which is testified to by the successors of the Apostles, builds upon and fulfills the traditions of the Jewish people that Jesus was born into. At the time of Jesus, celebrating the Passover was understood not simply as a sacrificial meal in which the Jewish people remember the Exodus, but also was understood as re-living the Exodus by making present the liberation that their ancestors had experienced after they were freed from Egyptian captivity. According to the Mishnah:[235]

> In each generation a man is obligated to regard himself as if he came forth out of Egypt, as it is written 'And you shall tell your son on that day, saying, 'It is because of that which the Lord did for me when I came forth out of Egypt' (Exodus 13:8). Therefore,

---

[234] Alexander Roberts, James Donaldson, and A. Cleveland Coxe, *Ante-Nicene Fathers*, vol. 1, ed. Alexander Roberts, James Donaldson, and A. Cleveland Coxe (Buffalo, NY: Christian Literature Publishing Co., 1885) Revised and edited for New Advent by Kevin Knight. http://www.newadvent.org/ fathers/0107.htm.

[235] The Mishnah is a collection of Jewish oral traditions put together by Rabbi Yehuda HaNasi around 217 AD.

we are obligated to thank, to praise, to laud, to glorify, to exalt, to adorn, to bless, to elevate, and to honor Him. Who did all these miracles for our fathers and for us; He brought us forth from slavery to freedom, from grief to joy, from mourning to Festival, from darkness to a great light, and from servitude to redemption.[236]

A modern day Hagadah, the liturgy for the Passover meal also known as the Seder, similarly states:

In every generation, each person should feel as though she or he were redeemed from Egypt, as it is said: "You shall tell your children on that day saying, 'It is because of what the Lord did for me when I went free out of Egypt.' For the Holy One redeemed not only our ancestors; He redeemed us with them."[237]

In fulfillment of the Jewish belief that the Passover meal transcends time, Catholics not only believe that the risen Christ is present in the Eucharist, but also maintain that during each mass

---

[236] Mishnah, Pesahim 10:5 http://www.emishnah.com/PDFs/Pesahim%2010.pdf; cf Brant Pitre, *Jesus and the Jewish Roots of the Eucharist* (New York: Doubleday, 2011), 64-65.

[237] Michael Strassfeld, *Jewish Holidays* (Harper Collins Publishers), loc. 154.

the sacrifice of Christ on the cross is mysteriously re-presented in the mass. In explaining this paradoxical mystery, Second Vatican Council states, "He did this in order to perpetuate the sacrifice of the Cross throughout the centuries until He should come again, and so to entrust to His beloved spouse, the Church, a memorial of His death and resurrection: a sacrament of love, a sign of unity, a bond of charity, a paschal banquet in which Christ is eaten, the mind is filled with grace, and a pledge of future glory is given to us."[238]

"Since Christ is risen how can he suffer again?" Protestants may object. Archbishop Sheen answers this objection by explaining that it is true that Christ has risen from the dead, yet his Mystical Body, the Church, continues Christ's presence, specifically by extending His sacrifice completed on Calvary throughout history.[239] Sheen explains, "Words are so fixed in their meaning that when we hear 'crucified,' our minds go back to a hill outside Jerusalem, which like the Battle of Waterloo, is gone forever."[240] This, understanding though is

---

[238] Vatican Council II, *Sacrosantum Concilium*, December 4, 1963, art. 47, The Vatican, http://www.vatican.va/archive/hist_councils/ii_vatican _council/documents/vat-ii_const_19631204_ sacrosanctum-concilium_en.html (accessed January 2, 2015).

[239] Charles P. Connor, *The Spiritual Legacy of Archbishop Fulton J. Sheen* (New York: Society of St. Paul, 2010), 119-120.

[240] Charles P. Connor, *The Spiritual Legacy of Archbishop Fulton J. Sheen*, 127. Connor cites the following: *Those Mysterious Priests* (Garden City, NY:

inaccurate, even from the Jewish standpoint that Catholicism fulfills. The Passion is not simply contained and located in a specific time and place but in addition has universally touched all of time, through Christ's mystical body.[241] The Mystical Body, anticipated by Israel, completes the sufferings of Christ the head of the Mystical Body.[242] According to Sheen, this is what St. Paul meant in Colossians when he wrote that "I am now rejoicing in my sufferings for your sake, and in my flesh I am completing what is lacking in Christ's afflictions for the sake of his body, that is, the church" (Colossians 1:24 NRSV):

> I fill up, I finish, I complete in my own body the sufferings that are wanting to the passion of Christ. Is there anything wanting in Christ's passion? Did he not redeem us completely? Did this not completely satisfy divine justice? How then could St. Paul say I am filling up a quota, a quota that has to be added to the suffering of Christ? Because our Blessed Lord in the Old Testament is sometimes presented as an individual and sometimes as Israel, the Church. He is

---

Doubleday & Company Inc., 1974; New York: St. Pauls/Alba House, 205), 101.

[241] Charles P. Connor, *The Spiritual Legacy of Archbishop Fulton J. Sheen*, 127. Connor cites the following: *Those Mysterious Priests*, 101.

[242] Charles P. Connor, *The Spiritual Legacy of Archbishop Fulton J. Sheen*, 128. Connor cites the following: *Those Mysterious Priests*, 107.

personal; he is the corporation of the people of God. In the New Testament he is our head, the Head of the Church He is the head of the corporation which is the Church. As he the head suffered for the Church and brought it into being, so we who are members of the Church, which is a continuation of His life, have to help redeem the Church. This is very much like creation. God created the world. He put the world into our hands. We have to complete it with our technology, with our arts, and with our sciences. So our Blessed Lord redeems us. We have to begin applying that redemption. He has given us the Word. We have to apply the acts. So the Church needs salvation. The Church needs redemption, and that is what St. Paul meant by saying that he finishes, he completes the work of redemption. Now this is something we never think about. It is one of the reasons why we have dropped reparation in the Church. We have reparation in the human body.[243]

Another passage from St. Paul to which Sheen refers when explaining that the sacrifice of Calvary is continued in the Mystical Body through time like rings of a tree that go all the way up and down a tree, is Christ's words to Paul, as Saul, prior to his

---

[243] Fulton J. Sheen, *A Voice from Calvary Audio Recording*.

conversion.[244] We read in Acts that as Saul was traveling to Damascus, a bright heavenly light flashed about him. Upon falling to the ground he heard the voice of Jesus say, "Saul, Saul, why do you persecute me?" (Acts 9:4 NRSV) In interpreting this passage, Sheen states, "How could Paul be persecuting Christ, now? Because the Church is Christ's body. That is why. If someone steps on your foot your head complains. Saul was touching part of the Church and the head complained."[245]

Quiz 8

1. Why in *Mysterium Fidei* did Paul VI affirm the term transubstantiation over transfinalization and transignification. Include the following in your answer: substance, accident, Berengar of Tours, the Council of Trent.

2. Explain Aquinas' distinction between Christ's bodily presence according to His "proper species"[246] and His bodily presence

---

[244] Fulton Sheen, *Vintage Sheen 16 Meditations*, CD 6 of a 13 Disc Set (Ramsey, N.J.:Keep the Faith-Latin Mass Magazine).CD 6.

[245] Fulton J. Sheen, *A Voice from Calvary Audio Recording*.

[246] Thomas Aquinas, *Summa Theologica*, III, q. 75, art. 6, newadvent.org, http://www.newadvent.org/summa/4075.htm#article4 (accessed August 25, 2016). "Thirdly, it would be unbefitting this sacrament: because the accidents of the bread remain in this sacrament, in

"in a special manner which is proper to this sacrament."[247] Include in your answer reference to Berengar of Tours and opponents of Berengar who reacted excessively in the opposite direction.

3. Respond to the Protestant objection that Christ and the early Church only understood the Eucharist symbolically. Do so in a biblical way with specific reference to Scripture, in reference to the early Church Fathers, and in reference to Judaism, specifically the Passover.

4. Respond to the following objection, "Since Christ is risen how can he suffer again?" Include in your answer the following: Archbishop Sheen, Mystical Body, Colossians 1:24 and Acts 9:4.

---

order that the body of Christ may be seen under them, and not under its proper species, as stated above (Article 5)."

[247] Thomas Aquinas, *Summa Theologica*, III, q. 75, art. 1, ad. 3, newadvent.org, http://www.newadvent.org/summa/4075.htm#article4 (accessed August 25, 2016). "Christ's body is not in this sacrament in the same way as a body is in a place, which by its dimensions is commensurate with the place; but in a special manner which is proper to this sacrament. Hence we say that Christ's body is upon many altars, not as in different places, but 'sacramentally': and thereby we do not understand that Christ is there only as in a sign, although a sacrament is a kind of sign; but that Christ's body is here after a fashion proper to this sacrament, as stated above."

Additional Activities and Resources

Respond to the following. Do so according to the Socratic method of gathering, clarifying and challenging questions.

- The Eucharist is only a symbol of Christ's presence.
- Nowhere in Scripture is it taught that the Eucharist is Christ's body and blood.
- How can Christ die again?
- Christ died once and for all. Therefore, it is impossible for Calvary to be reenacted during a Catholic mass.
- Christ has risen. He cannot suffer again in the mass.
- The terms transfinalization and transignification more accurately explain the Eucharistic mystery than transubstantiation.

Readings

Aquinas, Thomas. *Summa Theologica*, III, q. 75. newadvent.org, http://www.newadvent.org/summa/4075.htm#article4

Barron, Robert. *Eucharist: Catholic Spirituality for Adults*. New York: Orbis Books, 2008.

Catechism of the Catholic Church paragraphs 1322-1419

Paul VI, "Mysterium Fidei, Encyclical of Pope Paul VI on the Holy Eucharist," no. 10-11, September 3, 1965, w2.vatican.va, http://w2.vatican.va/content/paul-vi/en/encyclicals/documents/hf_p-vi_enc_03091965_mysterium.html

Audio

Hold Fast to the Traditions You Were Taught: Patrick Madrid vs. Rev. Frank Needham A Catholic/Protestant Debate on the Holy Eucharist and Sola Scriptura. MP3. store.patrickmadrid.com.

Winning Souls Not Just Arguments: Patrick Madrid & Curtis Martin. MP3. storepatrickmadrid.com

Fr. Peter Samuel Kucer, MSA

Chapter Nine: The Papacy

Introduction

In his book *Pope Fiction*, Patrick Madrid systematically answers thirty objections to the papacy. This chapter will present a concise version of these thirty objections.

Objections to the Papacy

Objection 1: Peter Was Never A Pope

Peter is referred to in the New Testament 195 times, more than any other Apostle. The second most named Apostle is John, 29 times. In addition, when the apostles are named, Peter is always named first, indicating his primacy. (Mat. 10:2-5; Mark 3:16-19; Luke 6:14-17; Acts 1:13) That Peter is the only Apostle whose name is changed by Christ also indicates his unique role among the Apostles, in a similar way that Abraham's and Jacob's names were changed to signify their leadership role. (Mat. 16:18)

The Apostle John acknowledged Peter as leader by his actions including waiting before the empty tomb in order to let Peter go before him. (John 20:6) In affirmation of Peter's leadership role, the risen Jesus appeared to Peter before the other Apostles. (Luke 24:34) Jesus also indicated Peter's leadership by preaching out of Peter's fishing boat. (Luke 5:3) Jesus singles out Peter by assuring that He will protect Peter's faith from the devil. (Luke 22:31-32) A Catholic explanation for this is that Jesus protects Peter's faith in order to preserve truth in at least one Apostle. Catholics additionally believe that all subsequent official Papal teachings on faith and morals are protected by Christ from error for this same reason.

Other scriptural passages that support the Catholic belief in Peter's primacy include Jesus' giving Peter the role of "feeding my sheep" (John 21:15-17), Peter's leading the other Apostles in choosing Matthias (Acts 1:13-26) and Peter's leading the Apostles by preaching on Pentecost. (Acts 2:14) Afterwards, Peter performs the first Pentecost miracle. (Acts 3:6) Still later, Paul acknowledges Peter's leadership by meeting with Peter, who then confirms Paul's faith. (Gal. 1:18) Paul's reference to Peter as a fellow presbyter in 1 Peter 5:1 does not mean that Paul was rejecting Peter's authority over the Twelve, which he had previously acknowledged. Rather, Paul was simply referring to Peter as a spiritual brother.[248]

Objection 2: The Original Greek New Testament Language Indicates that Jesus Did Not Build His Church on Peter as a Rock

According to this objection, since *petra* in Greek means large rock and *petros* means small rock, when Jesus said he would build his Church on a large rock (*petra*) and then refers to Peter as a little rock (*petros*) he was implying that Peter is not the large rock upon which the Church will be built. This large rock is Christ, as indicated by St. Paul (1 Corinthians 10:4).

In Matthew chapter sixteen, Peter's primacy over the Apostles is demonstrated in three ways. First, unlike the others he correctly identifies Christ as the Son of God. Second, Jesus explains that Peter's correct answer comes from God the Father, who chose to reveal to Peter Jesus' identity. Third, the truth about Christ's identity was revealed through Peter and did not come directly from the Father or directly from Christ.

With respect to the distinction between *petros* and *petra* as big rock and little rock, this distinction did not exist at the time of Christ.[249] The word that

---

[248] Patrick Madrid, *Pope Fiction* (Dallas: Basilica Press, 1999), 21-36.

[249] Madrid cites the Protestant scripture scholars, D.A. Carson and Oscar Cullmann who both acknowledge the absence at the time of Christ between the Greek nouns *petros* and *petra*. This distinction was not used in

was used in ordinary Greek at the time for small rock is *lithos*, but it was not used. Furthermore, Jesus did not speak to the Apostles in Greek but in Aramaic. Chapter sixteen of Matthew, therefore, contains a Greek version of a conversation that originally took place in Aramaic where Peter was called *Kephas*, which in Aramaic means rock. (cf. John 1:41-42) The Aramaic language does not distinguish between a masculine and feminine form for the noun rock. The reason why the masculine form *petros* (small rock) is used to translate *Kephas* and not the feminine form *petra* (large rock), is out of respect for Peter who is a man.[250]

Finally, it is reasonable to conclude that the context of this chapter of Matthew indicates that Jesus intended to give Peter papal primacy. In the following description of this passage from Matthew, interpretation C does not make sense in light of verses A, B and D whose interpretations are not in debate. Interpretation C of verse 18b is in contradiction with the praise and gifts Jesus gives to Peter before and after verse 18b.

A. Jesus praises Simon as blessed. "Blessed are you, Simon son of Jonah!" (Matthew 16:17 NRSV)

---

ordinary language. It was, though, occasionally used in ancient Greek poetry. Patrick Madrid, *Pope Fiction* (Dallas: Basilica Press, 1999), 42.

[250] Patrick Madrid, *Pope Fiction* (Dallas: Basilica Press, 1999), 37-50.

B. Jesus gives Simon the new name of Peter. "I tell you are Peter [*petros*]." (Matthew 16:18a NRSV)

C. Jesus sarcastically calls Peter a pebble, since the Church will be built upon a big rock and not the small pebble who is Peter. "and on this rock [*petra*] I will build my church..." (Matthew 16:18b NRSV)

D. Peter promises Peter the keys of the kingdom. "I will give you the keys of the kingdom of heaven...." (Matthew 16:19 NRSV)[251]

Objection 3 – That Jesus Called Peter "Satan" in Matthew 16:23 Indicates that Jesus Never Intended to Make Peter the First Pope

In Matthew chapter sixteen, Jesus did not institute Peter as the first Pope rather he promised he would do so later. Peter was given this role after Jesus rose from the dead, when Jesus told Peter to feed and tend His sheep. (John 21:15-17 NRSV) After this post-Resurrection appearance and commission, Peter gradually took on the duties of his office until at Pentecost he fully embraced his office.[252]

---

[251] Patrick Madrid, *Pope Fiction* (Dallas: Basilica Press, 1999), 54.
[252] Patrick Madrid, *Pope Fiction*, 51-53.

Objection 4 – Peter's False Teaching That Paul Rebuked Him for in Galatians 2:11-14 Indicate That Neither Peter Nor His Supposed Successors Are Infallible

Paul was only correcting Peter for his behavior and not for his teaching. Despite Peter's clearly teaching at the Council of Jerusalem that gentiles are not required to follow purity laws, such as not eating pork, in order not to offend Jewish-Christians Peter had stopped eating with gentiles. This apparent hypocrisy infuriated Paul. To be fair to Peter, though, Paul in his letter to the Romans actually in a way advocates a prudential practice similar to Peter's. In this letter Paul states:

> Let us therefore no longer pass judgment on one another, but resolve instead never to put a stumbling block or hindrance in the way of another. I know and am persuaded in the Lord Jesus that nothing is unclean in itself; but it is unclean for anyone who thinks it unclean. If your brother or sister is being injured by what you eat, you are no longer walking in love. Do not let what you eat cause the ruin of one for whom Christ died. So do not let your good be spoken of as evil. For the kingdom of God is not food and drink but righteousness and peace and joy in the Holy Spirit. (Romans 14: 13-17 NRSV)

Even if the above advice of Paul does not apply to

Peter's actions for which Paul criticized Peter, and presuming that Paul accurately pointed out hypocrisy within Peter, this does not necessarily mean that Paul was rejecting Peter's authority. For example, in more modern terms, if a citizen publicly criticizes his president this does not mean that the citizen, especially if he is a Christian, is necessarily rejecting the president's authority. Even when a ruler commits hypocritical actions, Christians citizens are called to follow the inspired teaching that Paul gives in his Letter to the Romans:

> Let every person be subject to the governing authorities; for there is no authority except from God, and those authorities that exist have been instituted by God. Therefore, whoever resists authority resists what God has appointed, and those who resist will incur judgment. For rulers are not a terror to good conduct, but to bad. Do you wish to have no fear of the authority? Then do what is good, and you will receive its approval; for it is God's servant for your good. But if you do what is wrong, you should be afraid, for the authority does not bear the sword in vain! It is the servant of God to execute wrath on the wrongdoer. Therefore, one must be subject, not only because of wrath but also because of conscience. For the same reason you also pay taxes, for the authorities are God's

servants, busy with this very thing. Pay to all what is due them—taxes to whom taxes are due, revenue to whom revenue is due, respect to whom respect is due, honor to whom honor is due." (Romans 13:1-7 NRSV)

Paul wrote these words when the brutal dictator Nero was in office. If Paul could in some way accept Nero's authority, all the more so could he accept Peter's authority. Through imperfect leaders God can reveal his perfect, infallible truth. Scripture indicates this with respect to the high priest Caiaphas:

Caiaphas, who was high priest that year, said to them, "You know nothing at all! You do not understand that it is better for you to have one man die for the people than to have the whole nation destroyed." He did not say this on his own, but being high priest that year he prophesied that Jesus was about to die for the nation, and not for the nation only, but to gather into one the dispersed children of God. (John 11: 49-52 NRSV)

As the above passage from Scripture indicates, at times God chooses to reveal his truth through sinful men. Other sinful leaders in Scripture whom God revealed truth through include Moses, who murdered an Egyptian (Exodus 2:12), Paul, who also was a murderer but as an accomplice (Acts

7:58), and King David, who was a murderer and an adulterer.[253]

Objection 5 – According to Scripture, Peter Did Not Pass Down His Authority to Anyone Else - Apostolic Succession, Therefore, Is a False Teaching

Scripture does explicitly describe apostolic authority being handed down. In Acts 1:15-26, Matthias is chosen to replace the Apostle Judas, who had committed suicide. In his letters to Timothy, Paul directly refers to his apostolic authority that he received from Christ. (2 Tim. 1:1) He also passes down this authority he received to Timothy (2 Tim. 1:6) and warns Timothy to be careful to whom apostolic authority is passed down to. [254] (2 Tim. 2:2)

In accordance with Scripture, the early Church Fathers affirmed the existence of apostolic succession. Pope St. Clement of Rome (r. 88-99 AD) does so in his *Epistle to the Corinthians*, also known as the *First Epistle of Clement*:

> Our apostles also knew, through our Lord Jesus Christ, that there would be strife on account of the office of the episcopate. For this reason, therefore, inasmuch as they had obtained a perfect fore-knowledge of this, they appointed those [ministers] already

---

[253] Patrick Madrid, *Pope Fiction*, 56-67.
[254] Patrick Madrid, *Pope Fiction*, 68-88.

mentioned, and afterwards gave instructtions, that when these should fall asleep, other approved men should succeed them in their ministry.[255]

St. Irenaeus refers to Apostolic Succession in his 180 AD letter *Against Heresies*. In his letter, St. Irenaeus rejects the Gnostic teaching that secret knowledge saves. He does so by appealing to apostolic succession. In referring to apostolic succession, Irenaeus affirms Rome's primacy that was providentially established so as to provide everyone with the opportunity to believe in the true faith without confusion:

> It is within the power of all, therefore, in every Church, who may wish to see the truth, to contemplate clearly the tradition of the apostles manifested throughout the whole world; and we are in a position to reckon up those who were by the apostles instituted bishops in the Churches, and [to demonstrate] the succession of these men to our own times; those who neither taught nor knew of anything like what these [heretics] rave about. For if the apostles had known hidden mysteries, which they were in the habit of imparting to the perfect apart and privily from the rest, they would have

---

[255] St. Clement, "Letter to the Corinthians," Chapter 44, newadvent.org, http://www.newadvent.org/fathers/1010.htm (accessed September 3, 2016).

delivered them especially to those to whom they were also committing the Churches themselves. ...

Since, however, it would be very tedious, in such a volume as this, to reckon up the successions of all the Churches, we do put to confusion all those who, in whatever manner, whether by an evil self-pleasing, by vainglory, or by blindness and perverse opinion, assemble in unauthorized meetings; [we do this, I say,] by indicating that tradition derived from the apostles, of the very great, the very ancient, and universally known Church founded and organized at Rome by the two most glorious apostles, Peter and Paul; as also [by pointing out] the faith preached to men, which comes down to our time by means of the successions of the bishops. For it is a matter of necessity that every Church should agree with this Church, on account of its preeminent authority, that is, the faithful everywhere, inasmuch as the tradition has been preserved continuously by those [faithful men] who exist everywhere.[256]

---

[256] St. Irenaeus, "Against Heresies (Book III, Chapter 3)," newadvent.org, http://www.newadvent.org/fathers/0103303. htm (accessed September 3, 2016).

Objection 6 Since the Roman Numerals of the Pope's Official Latin Title of *Vicarious Filii Dei* Adds Up to 666, the Pope Is the Anti-Christ

The title *Vicarious Filii Dei* has never been used as any official papal title. Instead, *Vicarius Christi* is an official title and, when the Roman letters are converted into numbers, only adds up to 214.[257] The reason for the confusion is that *Vicarious Filii Dei* was used in the forged document, the *Donation of Constantine* and mistakenly in *Our Sunday Visitor*'s 1915 issue which has since been corrected by this magazine. Finally, in Latin the name of Ellen Gould White who founded the Seventh-Day Adventist Church, which sometimes uses this objection, adds up to 666. Does this mean that she is the anti-Christ?[258]

Objection 7 According to Revelation 17:9 The Whore Of Babylon Is Situated on Seven Hills - Since Rome Has Seven Hills, The Catholic Church Is the Whore of Babylon

In Scripture, the Greek word *ore* (ὄρη) in Revelation 17:9 usually refers to mountains not hills, and the number seven is probably symbolic.

---

[257] In Latin letters are used for numbers. M is 1000. D is 500. C is 100 L is 50 X is 10 V is 5, and I is 1. When adding up Latin names it is important to remember that Latin does not have a letter u or w. Both of these letters are represented by v, v for v, and a double v for w.

[258] Patrick Madrid, *Pope Fiction*, 68-99.

Even if Revelation 17:9 is referring to the city of Rome, which is situated upon seven hills, Vatican City is on its own hill, Vatican Hill, which is not one of the seven Roman hills. Furthermore, although the Pope's cathedral, St. John Lateran, is outside of Vatican City and can be understood as residing, along with Rome, on the seven Roman hills, it is only a building and not a city.[259]

Objection 8 Since Scripture Does Not Ever State That Was Peter Ever in Rome He Could Not Have Been the First Bishop of Rome

Just because Scripture does not say Peter went to Rome does not mean that he didn't. Despite the lack of explicit Scriptural evidence, it is reasonable to maintain that Peter was in Rome since no other city has ever claimed to be the site of Peter's martyrdom. According to early Christian writings, Peter was crucified upside down in 65 AD during the persecution of Nero. Early Church Fathers repeatedly refer to Rome as the city where both Peter and Paul proclaimed the gospel and founded the Church. Church Fathers who identify Peter in relationship to Rome in this manner include: St. Irenaeus of Lyons's in his *Against Heresies*, St. Ignatius of Antioch's in his *Letter to the Romans*, St. Cyprian in his *Epistle 52*, St. Jerome in his *Epistle 15 to Pope Damascus* and Eusebius in his *Ecclesiastical History*, 2:25. Finally, modern day

---

[259] Patrick Madrid, *Pope Fiction*, 100-104.

archaeologists have provided convincing evidence that the bones of St. Peter are buried directly beneath the main altar of St. Peter's Basilica.[260]

Objection 9 The Modern Papacy is Invalid Since It Directly Contradicts the Simple Life of Peter

The Church has developed like a mustard seed. If we do not expect a mustard seed to look exactly the same after it has been planted and grown for a year, then why should we think the Church ought to look exactly the same in terms of defined faith and practice shortly after it was first established? (Mat. 13:31-32) An example of a teaching that all Christians accept which developed and became more explicit is the Trinity. Although Scripture does not record Jesus explicitly defining the Trinity, the Church relying on the Holy Spirit organically developed this doctrine.[261]

Objection 10 The Papacy was Invented During Medieval Times

The *Epistle of St. Clement* (c. 80 AD) by Pope St. Clement is a description of an early Bishop of Rome exercising his authority in another diocese. This was accepted since the Bishop of Rome was considered at the time as having authority over other bishops. In the following century, Pope Victor I (r.189-199) intervened in a dispute between

---

[260] Patrick Madrid, *Pope Fiction*, 105-110.
[261] Patrick Madrid, *Pope Fiction*, 111-118.

Eastern bishops and Western bishops over when to date the celebration of Easter. Pope Victor successfully settled this dispute since his authority was understood as entailing juridical power over other bishops.[262]

Objection 11 Early Christians Only Saw Rome as First Among Equals

Canon 6 of the Council of Nicaea establishes the jurisdiction of the Alexandrian see on the basis of the Roman see:

> The ancient customs of Egypt, Libya and Pentapolis shall be maintained, according to which the bishop of Alexandria has authority over all these places, since a similar custom exists with reference to the bishop of Rome. Similarly in Antioch and the other provinces the prerogatives of the churches are to be preserved.[263]

The above canon, along with the previously mentioned early Popes whose juridical authority outside their episcopal see was accepted by other bishops, indicates that according to the Council of Nicaea (325 AD) early Christians understood Rome as having juridical power over other bishops and

---

[262] Patrick Madrid, *Pope Fiction*, 119-125.
[263] Norman P. Tanner, *Decrees of the Ecumenical Councils: Volume One Nicaea I to Lateran V* (Washington: Georgetown University Press), 8-9.

their sees.[264] This primacy of juridical power is based on an even deeper primacy which is the Eucharist since Christ intends the Eucharist to unite us.[265]

Objection 12 The Numerous Bad Popes Is Proof that the Papacy was Never Intended by Christ

Christ chose the Apostles and yet they all acted cowardly when Jesus was undergoing his trial. In addition, the high priest Caiaphas who is not praised for his goodness in the gospels, spoke inspired prophecy. (John 11:49-52) These choices of God indicate that He does not only limit himself to choosing highly virtuous people to speak on his behalf. Since God is all powerful, He can reveal his truth without error through weak men.[266]

Objection 13 Papal Infallibility is False Since Not Only Did Popes Live Bad Lives but They Also Taught Falsehood

Infallibility, the inability to teach error, is not the same as sinlessness (impeccability). According to the doctrine of infallibility, in order for a pope to speak infallibly he must be a pope, his words must

---

[264] Patrick Madrid, *Pope Fiction*, 126-129.

[265] This is a theme within in Benedict XVI thought. Armin Schwibach, "Keeping Alive the 'Magnificent Theology' of Benedict XVI," *Inside the Vatican*, August-September (2016): 39.

[266] Patrick Madrid, *Pope Fiction*, 130-133.

pertain to faith and morals, and must do so officially, *ex cathedra*. This was defined at Vatican Council I (1870):

> Therefore, faithfully adhering to the tradition received from the beginning of the Christian faith, to the glory of God our savior, for the exaltation of the Catholic religion and for the salvation of the Christian people, with the approval of the Sacred Council, we teach and define as a divinely revealed dogma that when the Roman Pontiff speaks EX CATHEDRA, that is, when, in the exercise of his office as shepherd and teacher of all Christians, in virtue of his supreme apostolic authority, he defines a doctrine concerning faith or morals to be held by the whole Church, he possesses, by the divine assistance promised to him in blessed Peter, that infallibility which the divine Redeemer willed his Church to enjoy in defining doctrine concerning faith or morals. Therefore, such definitions of the Roman Pontiff are of themselves, and not by the consent of the Church, irreformable.[267]

---

[267] "First Vatican Council (1869-1870): Session 4: 18 July 1870 First Dogmatic Constitution on the Church of Christ, Chapter 4," ewtn.com, http://www.ewtn.com/library/COUNCILS/V1.HTM#6 (accessed September 5, 2016).

Another similar error people make is confusing infallibility with inspiration that provides additional public revelation to the faithful. As Madrid pithily explains, "While inspiration gives information, infallibility protects information."[268] The role of papal infallibility is to protect public revelation and not to add new public revelation, for as Vatican II's *Dei Verbum* clearly states, "The Christian dispensation, therefore, as the new and definitive covenant, will never pass away and we now await no further new public revelation before the glorious manifestation of our Lord Jesus Christ (see 1 Tim. 6:14 and Tit. 2:13)."[269]

---

[268] Patrick Madrid, *Pope Fiction*, 138.

[269] "Dogmatic Constitution on Divine Revelation, Dei Verbum," chapter 1, no. 4, vatican.va, http://www.vatican.va/archive/hist_councils/ii_vatican_council/documents/vat-ii_const_19651118_dei-verbum_en.html (accessed September 5, 2016). Cardinal Avery Dulles explains in his chapter titled "Faith and Revelation," "The modern mind, deeply impressed by the limitations imposed by the particularities of time and culture, has difficulty in admitting that there can be any absolute or unsurpassable disclosure within history. Even thinkers who reject the inevitability of progress and deny that 'later is better' consider that each age may be able to surpass its predecessors in some respects and to equate revelation with an ancient deposit would condemn the church to a continual loss of vitality and actuality. Vatican Council II, conscious of these concerns, avoided repeating the formula sometimes, used that revelation 'ceased with the death of the last apostle.' Instead, after describing Jesus as the perfecter and fulfillment of revelation, it stated: 'The Christian dispensation, therefore, as the new and definitive covenant, will never

Catholic Apologetics

Objection 14 The Action of Pope Liberius (352-366) Signing an Arian Creed Contradicts Papal Infallibility

It is unclear if Pope Liberius actually did this, but if he did documentary evidence indicates that he signed the creed under extreme physical duress, out of fear of being tortured and executed by orders of the Arian Emperor Constantius who had Pope Liberius arrested and then banished. Infallibility, though, requires that a pope exercise his free will

---

pass away, and we await no further public revelation before the glorious manifestation of our Lord Jesus Christ. (see 1 Tim. 6:14 and Tit. 2:13)' (DV 4). In the Constitution on the Church (*Lumen Gentium*) [hereafter LG]) Vatican II depicted the church as capable of showing forth 'in the world the mystery of the Lord in a faithful though shadowed way, until at the last it will be revealed in total splendor' (LG 8). These two statements avoid giving the impression that the church already possesses a total grasp of revelation in its fullness, but at the same time they emphasize the church's obligation to adhere faithfully to the 'mystery of the ord,' the 'Christian dispensation,' the 'new and definitive covenant.'" A footnote in this text included the following. "On at least two occasions the Theological Commission or its subcommissions rejected several *modi* requesting that *Dei Verbum*, no 4, be amended to state explicitly that revelation was closed (*clausam*) with the death of the apostles. See the *relationes* of July 3, 1964, and November 20, 1964. These are found respectively in the *Acta Synodalia Sacrosancti Concilii Oecumenic Vaticani II*, Periodus 3, vol. 3 (1974), and Periodus 4, vol. 1 (1976), p. 345. Francis Schussler Fiorenza and John P. Galvin, Systematic Theology Roman Catholic Perspectives Volume I (Minneapolis: Fortress Press,1991), 101-102.

free from external compulsion.[270]

Objection 15 The Action of Pope Vigilius (r. 537-555) Approving the Monophysite Heresy Directly Contradicts Papal Infallibility

Pope Vigilius never taught nor approved of heretical teaching. He was criticized by early Christians for his poor leadership skills and for approving, prior to becoming a Pope, three Monophysite heretics in order to gain favor from Empress Theodora, wife of Emperor Justinian I (r. 527-548).[271] Also, Vigilius's weak leadership as pope took place when he being harassed and even imprisoned by the emperor.[272]

---

[270] Patrick Madrid, *Pope Fiction*, 141-147.

[271] "Before he became pope Vigilius had promised to favor the Monophysites, ingratiated himself with the empress Theodora, and replaced the deposed pope, Silverius, who had been a Gothic choice. After Silverius' banishment the improperly reigning Vigilius [as an anti-pope] and his slaves took Silverius to the island of Palmaria, worked him over, and extorted a valid resignation. Vigilius did not keep all his promises to Theodora and was duly arrested in a church in Rome and carried off to Sicily for ten months. Although some obviously Monophysite letters are attributed to Vigilius, he did affirm the Chalcedonian principles but then vacillated, though not endlessly, for in 551 he refused to accept Justinian's edict." John Cumming, *Butler's Lives of the Saints: New Full Edition, August* (Collegeville: The Liturgical Press, 1998), 250.

[272] Patrick Madrid, *Pope Fiction*, 148-151.

Objection 16 Pope Gregory the Great's Rejection of the Title Universal Bishop is Proof that the Early Church Did Not Recognize the Papacy as Having Juridical Authority Over Other Bishops

The title Universal Bishop can be defined in two ways. According to one definition, the Pope as universal bishop has universal jurisdiction over the entire Church in such a way that he may legitimately interfere in the local authority of a brother bishop in order to settle a dispute. According to another definition of the term, the title Universal Pastor belongs to a bishop who is the only true bishop in whose office all other "bishops" participate.[273] Pope Gregory the Great rejected the

---

[273] The following is from one of my Church History lectures. "The *Decree On the Pastoral Office of Bishops* recognized that bishops have authority by virtue of their office. This means that their authority as bishops is not simply delegated to them by the pope. In the words of the Council, 'The bishops, by virtue of their sacramental consecration and their hierarchical communion with the head of the college and its other members, are constituted members of the episcopal body.' *Lumen Gentium* even more pointedly asserts that bishops are not 'to be regarded as vicars of the Roman Pontiff; for they exercise the power which they possess in their own right and are called in the truest sense of the term prelates of the people whom they govern.' As well described by O'Malley, it is incorrect to perceive the bishops relationship to the pope as equivalent to regional manager's relationship to their Corporate Executive Officers. Instead bishops as shepherds 'together with their head, the Supreme Pontiff, and never apart from him' participate individually and corporately in apostolic

second definition that was being applied by John the Faster, Archbishop of Constantinople to himself. Pope Gregory agreed with the first definition. This is evident in his interventions in diocese other than Rome in order to settle disputes.[274]

Objection 17 The Condemnation of Pope Honorius (r. 625-638) as a Heretic by the Third Council of Constantinople (680-681) Indicates that Popes are not Infallible

In reference to the Monothelite heresy, the Sixth Council of Constantinople did condemn Pope Honorius.[275] This condemnation, though, was done

---

succession and in the one priesthood of Jesus Christ." Second Vatican Council, Decree on the Pastoral Office of Bishops in the Church, *Christus Dominus,* no. 4 (28 October 1965), in Vatican Council II: The Conciliar and Post Conciliar Documents, ed. Austin Flannery (Boston: Daughters of St. Paul, 1980), 565-566; Second Vatican Council, Dogmatic Constitution on the Church, *Lumen Gentium,* no. 27 (21 November 1964), in Vatican Council II: The Conciliar and Post Conciliar Documents, ed. Austin Flannery (Boston: Daughters of St. Paul, 1980), 283; John W. O'Malley, *What Happened at Vatican II,* Kindle Edition (Cambridge: The Belknap Press of Harvard University Press, 2008), locations 6059-6069;

[274] Patrick Madrid, *Pope Fiction,* 152-157.

[275] "This pious and orthodox creed of the divine favor was enough for complete knowledge of the orthodox faith and a complete assurance therein. But since, from the first, the contriver of evil did not rest, finding an accomplice in the serpent and through him bringing upon human nature the poisoned dart of death, so toon

without the approval of Pope St. Agatho. Pope Agatho neither approved this condemnation nor confirmed the council's decrees because Pope Agatho died before these actions were delivered to Rome. The succeeding Pope, Leo II, confirmed the decrees of the council while clarifying that although Pope Honorius had not approved of Monothelitism he ought to have also condemned it. Pope Honorius' condemnation, therefore, was not for heresy but for inaction.[276]

Objection 18 If the Papacy was Instituted by Christ as a Principle of Ecclesial Unity, Then Why During the Middle Ages Did Three Men Claim to be Popes?

Just because three people claim to own a house does not mean one of the three is not the owner. Similarly, just because a number of people claim to

---

now he has found instruments suited to his own purpose – namely Theodore, who was bishop of Pharan, Sergius, Pyrrhus, Paul and Peter, who were bishops of this imperial city, and further Honorius, who was pope of elder Rome, Cyrus, who held the see of Alexandria, and Maracius, who was recently bishop of Antioch, and his disciple Stephen – and has not been idle in raising through them obstacles of error against the full body of the church, sowing with novel speech among the orthodox people the heresy of a single will and a single principle of action in the two natures of the one member of the hoy Trinity, Christ our true God, a heresy in harmony with the evil belief, ruinous to the mind...." Norman P. Tanner, *Decrees of the Ecumenical Councils: Volume One Nicaea I to Lateran V* (Washington, D.C: Georgetown University Press, 1990), 125-126

[276] Patrick Madrid, *Pope Fiction*, 158-162.

be pope does not necessarily mean that no one is pope. Throughout history there have been anti-popes. God, though, has consistently ensured that in the midst of these weeds the wheat of the true pope remains. In the Middle Ages, there were a number of powerful anti-popes, representing the weeds. During this confusing time, the only valid pope was the pope of the Roman line. Only the Roman line could trace its origins back to the Apostle Peter.[277]

Objection 19 Pope Joan, Who Gave Birth to a Child as Pope Before Being Killed by an Angry Mob Further Discredits the Papacy

Two early accounts of Pope Joan's life claim that she lived in different times. The 13th century Metz Dominica chronicler Jean Pierier de Mailly in his *Chronica Universalis Mettensis* claims that Pope Joan lived in 1099:

> Concerning a certain Pope or rather female Pope, who is not set down in the list of popes or Bishops of Rome, because she was a woman who disguised herself as a man and became, by her character and talents, a curial secretary, then a Cardinal and finally Pope. One day, while mounting a horse, she gave birth to a child. Immediately, by Roman justice, she was bound by the feet to

---

[277] Patrick Madrid, *Pope Fiction*, 163-166.

a horse's tail and dragged and stoned by the people for half a league, and, where she died, there she was buried, and at the place is written: 'Petre, Pater Patrum, Papisse Prodito Partum' [Oh Peter, Father of Fathers, Betray the childbearing of the woman Pope]. At the same time, the four-day fast called the "fast of the female Pope" was first established.[278]

However, according to other accounts Pope Joan supposedly lived around the 850s. According to highly verifiable, historical documentation, however, the following popes held office during the times it is claimed Pope Joan ruled.

Pope Saint Leo IV (reigned 847-855)

Pope Benedict III (reigned 855-858)

Pope Saint Nicholas I (reigned 858-867)

Pope Blessed Urban II (reigned 1088-1099)

Pascal II (reigned 1099 - 1118)

---

[278] Terry Breverton, *Breverton's Phantasmagoria: A Compendium of Monsters, Myths, and Legends* (New York: Quercus, 2014), https://books.google.com/books?id=yYoHBAAAQBAJ&pg=PT1&dq=Terry+Breverton%27s+Phantasmagoria:+A+Compendium+of+Monsters,+Myths+and+Legends&hl=en&sa=X&ei=P4UAVf__ObeJsQSz8oFY&ved=0CB4Q6AEwAA#v=onepage&q=copyright&f=false (accessed March 11, 2015).

Additional evidence even further discredits a woman named Joan from ruling as a pope, let alone existing. This includes the following. The earliest accounts of Pope Joan were written a couple hundred years after her supposed reign. Enemies of the papacy living during the time Pope Joan supposedly lived make no mention of a Pope Joan. For example, Photius I, Patriarch of Constantinople (r. 858-867 and 877-886) who wanted to discredit the papacy after he was deposed by Pope Nicholas I, never refers to a "Pope Joan" which he very likely would have if he had known of her. Photius could have used her reign as a way to discredit the papacy.[279]

Objection 20 The Papal Condemnation of Galileo Discredits the Infallibility of the Papacy

The pope's infallibility only extends to matters of faith and morals. The pope safeguards teaching on how to get to heaven not on how the heavens run, as Galileo taught.[280]

Objection 21 During the Crusades Popes Encouraged the Murder of Millions of Innocent, Peaceful Muslims

Ever since the fourth century, Christians have

---

[279] Patrick Madrid, *Pope Fiction*, 167-177.
[280] Christopher Baglow, *Faith, Science & Reason, Theology on the Cutting Edge* (Woodridge: Midwest Theological Forum, 2009), 80-81.

made pilgrimages to the Holy Land. Then, in 1009 AD these pilgrimages were placed in jeopardy when Al Hakim, the Muslim Caliph of Egypt commanded Catholics to leave Jerusalem and ordered the Church of the Holy Sepulcher to be demolished. In 1071, Jerusalem was forcefully overtaken by the Seljuk Turks. In response to this aggression, in 1095 Pope Urban II announced the first crusade. He did so in order to defend Catholics living in Constantinople and Catholics living in the Holy Land. Even though the First Crusade ended in a Catholic victory, subsequent Crusades did not and Jerusalem was taken back by its Muslim conquerors. Despite this apparent defeat, the crusades were effective in another way since they weakened the Muslim military power, thereby reducing the possibility of a successful invasion into Europe.[281]

Objection 22 Acting as a Mere Worldly Leader, in Pride Pope Alexander VI Divided up the New World Between Portugal and Spain

In 1493, Pope Alexander II issued the papal bull *Inter Caetera*. In this bull, the pope refers to a line of demarcation in the New World between Portugal and Spain. He did so in order to reduce the competitive element between Portuguese and Spanish missionaries and to encourage greater

---

[281] Patrick Madrid, *Pope Fiction*, 190-195. Madrid refers to Regine Pernoud, *The Crusades* (London: Secker & Warburg, 1960), 15-17, 208-212.

orderly cooperation between these missionaries. He did not intend this division to be interpreted as property boundaries.[282] In 1494, Spain and

---

[282] "Alexander, bishop, servant of the servants of God, to the illustrious sovereigns, our very dear son in Christ, Ferdinand, king, and our very dear daughter in Christ, Isabella, queen of Castile, Leon, Aragon, Sicily, and Granada, health and apostolic benediction. Among other works well pleasing to the Divine Majesty and cherished of our heart, this assuredly ranks highest, that in our times especially the Catholic faith and the Christian religion be exalted and be everywhere increased and spread, that the health of souls be cared for and that barbarous nations be overthrown and brought to the faith itself. ... In the islands and countries already discovered are found gold, spices, and very many other precious things of divers kinds and qualities. Wherefore, as becomes Catholic kings and princes, after earnest consideration of all matters, especially of the rise and spread of the Catholic faith, as was the fashion of your ancestors, kings of renowned memory, you have purposed with the favor of divine clemency to bring under your sway the said mainlands and islands with their residents and inhabitants and to bring them to the Catholic faith. ... And, in order that you may enter upon so great an undertaking with greater readiness and heartiness endowed with the benefit of our apostolic favor, we, of our own accord, not at your instance nor the request of anyone else in your regard, but of our own sole largess and certain knowledge and out of the fullness of our apostolic power, by the authority of Almighty God conferred upon us in blessed Peter and of the vicarship of Jesus Christ, which we hold on earth, do by tenor of these presents, should any of said islands have been found by your envoys and captains, give, grant, and assign to you and your heirs and successors, kings of Castile and Leon, forever, together with all their dominions, cities, camps, places, and villages, and all rights, jurisdictions, and appurtenances, all islands and

Catholic Apologetics

Portugal signed a treaty, the Treaty of Tordesillas, in which they established colonizing and trading rights. Then, in 1529, the two countries signed the Treaty of Saragossa that divided the known world at that time between Portugal and Spain. In time, as other European countries expanded into empires, this treaty was not followed.[283]

Objection 23 Proof of Papal Depravity is Their Long-Standing Support of Slavery

---

mainlands found and to be found, discovered and to be discovered towards the west and south, by drawing and establishing a line from the Arctic pole, namely the north, to the Antarctic pole, namely the south, no matter whether the said mainlands and islands are found and to be found in the direction of India or towards any other quarter, the said line to be distant one hundred leagues towards the west and south from any of the islands commonly known as the Azores and Cape Verde. With this proviso however that none of the islands and mainlands, found and to be found, discovered and to be discovered, beyond that said line towards the west and south, be in the actual possession of any Christian king or prince up to the birthday of our Lord Jesus Christ just past from which the present year one thousand four hundred and ninety-three begins. ...." "The Bull *Inter Caetera* (Alexander VI), May 4, 1493," Native Web, http://www.nativeweb.org/pages/legal/indig-inter-caetera.html (accessed December 24, 2015); Patrick Madrid, *Pope Fiction* (Dallas: Basilica Press, 1999), 196-198.

[283] Melvin E. Page, *Colonialism: An International Social, Cultural, and Political Encyclopedia*, Volume One: A-M (Santa Barbara: ABC CLIO, Inc., 2003), 585-586, 774.

The Catholic Church officially teaches that slavery is wrong. According to the *Catechism of the Catholic Church*:

> The seventh commandment forbids acts or enterprises that for any reason - selfish or ideological, commercial, or totalitarian - lead to the *enslavement of human beings*, to their being bought, sold and exchanged like merchandise, in disregard for their personal dignity. It is a sin against the dignity of persons and their fundamental rights to reduce them by violence to their productive value or to a source of profit. St. Paul directed a Christian master to treat his Christian slave "no longer as a slave but more than a slave, as a beloved brother, ... both in the flesh and in the Lord."[284]

Prior to the 1992 promulgation of the *Catechism of the Catholic Church* by St. John Paul II, the Catholic Church consistently condemned slavery. Pope Eugene IV in his papal bull *Sicut Dudum* (1435) condemned slavery. Pope Paul III in *Sublimis Deus* (1537)[285] condemned slavery. Pope

---

[284] "Catechism of the Catholic Church," no. 2414, vatican.va, http://www.vatican.va/archive/ccc_css/archive/catechism/p3s2c2a7.htm#2414 (accessed September 8, 2016).

[285] "We, who, though unworthy, exercise on earth the power of our Lord and seek with all our might to bring those sheep of His flock who are outside into the fold

Benedict XIV in *Immensa Pastorum* (1741) condemned slavery. Pope Gregory XVI in *In Supremo Apostolatus* (1839) condemned slavery. Pope Leo XIII in *Catholicae Ecclesiae* (1890) condemned slavery. Pope St. Pius X in *Lacrimabile Statu* (1912) condemned slavery.[286]

Objection 24 Pope Sixtus IV Began and Oversaw the Spanish Inquisition Under Which Thousands of Muslims and Jewish People Were Tortured and Murdered

The term inquisition comes from the Latin word *inquisitionem* meaning "a searching into...a

---

committed to our charge, consider, however, that the Indians are truly men and that they are not only capable of understanding the Catholic Faith but, according to our information, they desire exceedingly to receive it. Desiring to provide ample remedy for these evils, We define and declare by these Our letters, or by any translation thereof signed by any notary public and sealed with the seal of any ecclesiastical dignitary, to which the same credit shall be given as to the originals, that, notwithstanding whatever may have been or may be said to the contrary, the said Indians and all other people who may later be discovered by Christians, are by no means to be deprived of their liberty or the possession of their property, even though they be outside the faith of Jesus Christ; and that they may and should, freely and legitimately, enjoy their liberty and the possession of their property; nor should they be in any way enslaved; should the contrary happen, it shall be null and have no effect." Pope Paul III, "Sublimus Dei," May 29, 1537, papalencyclicals.net, http://papalencyclicals.net/Paulo3/p3subli.htm (accessed September 8, 2016).

[286] Patrick Madrid, *Pope Fiction*, 199-219.

legal examination."[287] The need for investigating worship and practices of followers of God is explicitly stated in Deuteronomy 17:2-7. In fulfillment with this ancient practice of the Jewish people, the Catholic Church has investigated the belief and practices of its people in order to preserve and defend the faith. During the late Medieval Era, these investigations were done more intensely than previously since heresies were considered not only a threat to Catholic belief but also as a threat to the political unity of Catholic kingdoms and empires. In order to ensure unity among its people, medieval Christian rulers approved the torture and sentencing to death of unrepentant convicted heretics.

The above mentioned Spanish Inquisition was, after obtaining permission from Pope Sixtus IV, begun by King Ferdinand and Queen Isabella who wanted to ensure Spain remained Catholic and would not revert back to an Islamic nation. The Church's role during the time of the inquisitions, both Spanish and non-Spanish, was not to sentence an individual to death since this was the role of the state. Rather, the Church's role was to determine after a trial if the accused was actually a heretic, and if so to then try to convince the confessed heretic to convert. Only if the accused refused to convert did the Church then hand over the accused to the state for punishment. While this role of the

---

[287] "Inquisition," etymonline.com, http://www.etymonline.com/index.php?term=inquisition (accessed September 8, 2016).

Church is jarring to our modern mindset it is important to remember that Protestants during the Protestant Reformation also tortured and killed heretics. For example, John Calvin approved of Michael Servetus's conviction and execution in the year 1553.[288]

Objection 25 Pope Sixtus V Ordered the Publication of an Error Filled Latin Vulgate Bible

Pope Sixtus V (r. 1585-1590) in 1590 planned on officially promulgating an error-filled revision of the Latin Vulgate. However, he died before he could fulfill this desire. Providentially, therefore, this version was never officially promulgated by the Church.[289]

Objection 26 Matthew 16 Neither Teaches Papal Succession nor Papal Infallibility and yet Vatican Council I (1870) Refers to This Passage When Defining Papal Infallibility

When defining papal infallibility, the council fathers never intended to issue, explains Madrid, "formal exegesis of Matthew 16."[290] Matthew 16 was referred to in order to provide reasons for papal infallibility.[291] With that said, the interpretation of this passage by Vatican I in which Peter is identified

---

[288] Patrick Madrid, *Pope Fiction*, 220-241.
[289] Patrick Madrid, *Pope Fiction*, 242-251.
[290] Patrick Madrid, *Pope Fiction*, 254.
[291] Patrick Madrid, *Pope Fiction*, 252-258.

as the rock upon which Christ built his Church is repeatedly taught by early Church Fathers including St. Hilary (c. 310-367),[292] St. John Chrysostom (347-407),[293] St. Augustine (354-

---

[292] "Matthew also, chosen to proclaim the whole mystery of the Gospel, first a publican, then an Apostle, and John, the Lord's familiar friend, and therefore worthy to reveal the deepest secrets of heaven, and blessed Simon, who after his confession of the mystery was set to be the foundation-stone of the Church, and received the keys of the kingdom of heaven, and all his companions who spoke by the Holy Ghost, and Paul, the chosen vessel, changed from persecutor into Apostle, who, as a living man abode under the deep sea 2 Corinthians 11:25 and ascended into the third heaven, who was in Paradise before his martyrdom, whose martyrdom was the perfect offering of a flawless faith; all have deceived me." Hilary of Poitiers, "On the Trinity," Book VI, Chapter 20, newadvent.org, http://www.newadvent.org/fathers/330206.htm (accessed September 9, 2016).

[293] "*Blessed are you Simon Bar Jonah, because flesh and blood did not reveal this to you, but my heavenly Father.*" This Peter, and when I say Peter I mean the solid rock, the tranquil foundation, the great apostle, the first disciple, the first one called by Christ, and the first one who obeyed." St. John Chrysostom, *The Fathers of the Church: St. John Chrysostom On Repentance and Almsgiving*, trans. Gus George Christo (Washington: The Catholic University of America Press, 1998), Homily 3, 39. "I would fain inquire then of those who desire to lessen the dignity of the Son, which manner of gifts were greater, those which the Father gave to Peter, or those which the Son gave him? For the Father gave to Peter the revelation of the Son; but the Son gave him to sow that of the Father and that of Himself in every part of the world; and to a mortal man He entrusted the authority over all things in Heaven, giving him the keys; who extended the

430),²⁹⁴ and St. Cyril of Alexandria (c. 376-444).²⁹⁵

---

church to every part of the world, and declared it to be stronger than heaven. "For heaven and earth shall pass away, but my word shall not pass away." Matthew 24:35 How then is He less, who has given such gifts, has effected such things? And these things I say, not dividing the works of Father and Son ("for all things are made by Him, and without Him was nothing made which was made"): but bridling the shameless tongue of them that dare so to speak. But see, throughout all, His authority: "I say unto you, you are Peter; I will build the Church; I will give you the keys of Heaven." John Chrysostom, *Homily 54 on Matthew* New Advent, http://www.newadvent.org/fathers/200154.htm (accessed January 1, 2015).

²⁹⁴ "2. For if the lineal succession of bishops is to be taken into account, with how much more certainty and benefit to the Church do we reckon back till we reach Peter himself, to whom, as bearing in a figure the whole Church, the Lord said: Upon this rock will I build my Church, and the gates of hell shall not prevail against it! Matthew 16:18 The successor of Peter was Linus, and his successors in unbroken continuity were these:— Clement, Anacletus, Evaristus, Alexander, Sixtus, Telesphorus, Iginus, Anicetus, Pius, Soter, Eleutherius, Victor, Zephirinus, Calixtus, Urbanus, Pontianus, Antherus, Fabianus, Cornelius, Lucius, Stephanus, Xystus, Dionysius, Felix, Eutychianus, Gaius, Marcellinus, Marcellus, Eusebius, Miltiades, Sylvester, Marcus, Julius, Liberius, Damasus, and Siricius, whose successor is the present Bishop Anastasius." St. Augustine, "Letter 53, To Generosus," chap. 1, no. 2, newadvent.org, http://www.newadvent.org/fathers/1102053.htm (accessed September 9, 2016).

²⁹⁵ "For not having needed a single word, nor even sought to learn who or whence the man came to Him; He says of what father he was born, and what was his own name, and permits him to be no more called Simon, already exercising lordship and power over him, as being

Objection 27 At Vatican Council I the Prominent Bishop Joseph Strossmayer Rejected Papal Infallibility

Bishop Joseph Strossmayer did not reject the reality of papal infallibility. Instead, he was opposed to defining papal infallibility because the early Fathers never formally taught papal infallibility, because previous councils never formally taught papal infallibility, and because of pastoral and ecumenical concerns.[296]

Objection 28 There Hasn't Been a Valid Pope Since Pope Pius XII

In Matthew 16:18, Jesus assures us that the "gates of Hell" will not prevail against the Church. Arguing that there has not been a valid pope for a significant amount of time, not counting the time it takes to elect another pope, is contrary this promise revealed to us in Sacred Scripture. [297]

His: but changes it to Peter from Petra 4: for upon him was He about to found His Church." St. Cyril of Alexandria, "Gospel According to John," Book II, tertullian.org, http://www.tertullian.org/fathers/cyril_on_john_02_book2.htm (accessed September 9, 2016). The source is the following. Cyril of Alexandria, Commentary on John, LFC 43, 48 (1874/1885). Book 2. pp. 130-284.

[296] Patrick Madrid, *Pope Fiction*, 259-271.
[297] Patrick Madrid, *Pope Fiction*, 272-279.

Objection 29 Appealing to Scripture and to the Fathers of the Church to Defend the Papacy is Anachronistic

Appealing to Scripture and to the Fathers of the Church when arguing in favor of the Papacy is not necessarily anachronistic if it can be demonstrated that both Scripture and the Fathers of the Church support belief in the papacy. This support is present as has been demonstrated in previous responses to other objections. Therefore, appealing in this manner to Scripture and the Fathers is not anachronistic.[298]

---

[298] Patrick Madrid, *Pope Fiction*, 280-284. Additional Scriptural indications of Peter's primacy include the following. **Before the Resurrection**: 1. Peter is named 195 times in the NT. The second most named Apostle is John coming in at 29 times. 2. Peter is always mentioned first, often with "Peter and the others". (Mat 10:2-5; Mark 3:16-19; Luke 6:14-17; Acts 1:13) 3. Only Peter's name was changed (from Simon – Mat. 16:18-19). Peter means rock. 4. He was chosen to receive "the keys of the kingdom." 5. Christ called Peter to leave the boat and walk on water. (Mat. 14:25-33) 6. Christ preached from Peter's boat. (Luke 5:3) **After the Resurrection**: 1. John waited for Peter to arrive at the tomb and enter first. (John 20:6) 2. Peter was the first Apostle that the risen Christ appeared to. 3. Christ gives to Peter the mission of "strengthening his brethren." (John 21) 4. Christ prays that Peter's faith may not fail. (John 21) 5. Christ appoints Peter shepherd of the flock and tells Peter three times to "feed my sheep." (Luke 22:31-32) **After the Ascension and Pentecost**: 1. Peter as the leading apostles helps to determine who will replace Judas. (Acts 1:13-26) 2. Peter both preaches the first homily after Pentecost and is the first to do a post-

Objection 30 Because Pope Pius XII Cowardly Refused to Denounce Hitler He is Responsible for the Murder of Millions

Since Pius XII (r. 1939-1958) lacked a military force capable of defeating Hitler, he chose to act diplomatically. In so doing, he was able to save thousands of lives that would not have been saved if he denounced the Nazi's openly. Very likely, the Nazis would have retaliated with great severity if he had.[299] As Pius XII once explained, "The Italians are certainly well aware of the terrible things taking place in Poland. We might have an obligation to utter fiery words against such things; yet all that is holding us back from doing so is the knowledge that if We should speak, We would simply worsen the predicament of these unfortunate people."[300]

Pentecost miracle. (Acts 3:1-10) 3. When before the Sanhedrin Peter represents the other apostles (Acts 4:1-12). 4. Peter officially teaches at the Council of Jerusalem that Gentiles are not required to observe Jewish dietary laws. (Acts 15) 5. Paul did not begin his mission to the Gentiles until he had gone to Jerusalem and spent time with Peter. (Galatians 1:18) Patrick Madrid, *Answer Me This*, loc. 1174-1207.

[299] Inside the Vatican Staff, "Pope Pius XII and the Vatican Archives," *Inside the Vatican* (November 2014), 44.

[300] Emilia Paola Pacelli, "Pius XII: The Martyrdom of Silence," EWTN Library, http://www.ewtn.com/library/ISSUES/PIUS12M.HTM (accessed December 6, 2014). Dr. Pacelli the following source. Audience with Italian Ambassador Dino Alfieri, 13 May 1940, in *Actes et Documents du Saint Siège relatifs à la Seconde Guerre*

Pius XII's fear was affirmed by the United States Central Intelligence Agency, which cautioned him against outwardly condemning Hitler since the probability, determined by precedent, was high that Hitler would retaliate violently.[301] However, despite being cautioned, Pius XII did choose to publicly denounce Nazi ethnic cleansing in his 1942 Christmas message. In this message he asserted:

> Should they not rather... vow not to rest until in all peoples and all nations of the earth a vast legion shall be formed of those handfuls of men who, bent on bringing back society to its center of gravity, which is the law of God, aspire to the service of the human person and of his common life ennobled in God. ... Mankind owes that vow to the hundreds of thousands of persons who, without any fault on their part, sometimes only because of their nationality or race, have been consigned to death or to a slow decline.[302]

---

mondiale, Libreria Editrice Vaticana, Vatican City, vol. 1, 1970, pp. 454-455.

[301] Inside the Vatican Staff, "Pope Pius XII and the Vatican Archives," *Inside the Vatican* (November 2014), 45. The source references are the papers of Allan Dulles, a former CIA director.

[302] Pius XII, "The Internal Order of States and People: Christmas Message of 1942," EWTN Library, http://www.ewtn.com/library/PAPALDOC/P12CH42.HTM (accessed December 6, 2014).

Prior to this message, the Nazis had suspected that Pius XII would defend the Jewish people and other people whom the Nazis intended to kill. This was evident even the day after Cardinal Eugenio Pacelli was elected Pope and assumed the name Pope Pius XII. On that day, the Nazi Berlin newspaper, *Morganpost* described his election as follows:

> The election of Cardinal Pacelli is not accepted with favor in Germany because he was always opposed to Nazism and practically determined the policies of the Vatican under his predecessor.[303]

After World War II ended in Nazi defeat, Pius XII's anti-Soviet, anti-communist position gained for him a new enemy in the Soviet Komitet Gosudarstvennoy Bezopasnosti (KGB, Committee for State Security). In order to discredit Pius XII's opposition, the KGB tried to systematically destroy his name. In admitting this character assassination campaign, the former KGB Ion Mihai Pacepa said:

> In my other life, when I was at the center of Moscow's foreign-intelligence wars, I myself was caught up in a deliberate Kremlin effort to smear the Vatican, by portraying Pope Pius XII as a coldhearted Nazi sympa-

---

[303] David G. Dalin, *The Myth of Hitler's Pope: Pope Pius XII and his Secret War against Nazi Germany* (Washington: Regnery Publishing, 2005), 64.

thizer... In February 1960, Nikita Khrushchev approved a super-secret plan for destroying the Vatican's moral authority in Western Europe... Pope Pius XII, was selected as the KGB's main target, its incarnation of evil, because he had departed this world in 1958. "Dead men cannot defend themselves" was the KGB's latest slogan. ...Because Pius XII had served as the papal nuncio in Munich and Berlin when the Nazis were beginning their bid for power, the KGB wanted to depict him as an anti-Semite who had encouraged Hitler's Holocaust. The hitch was that the operation was not to give the least hint of Soviet bloc involvement. The whole dirty job had to be carried out by Western hands....[304]

In order for the character assassination to be done by Western hands the Soviets promoted and funded a play written by the West German Rolf Hochhuth under the direction of a Communist producer Erwin Piscator. In the play, Pius XII is portrayed as supporting Hitler's goal to murder all the Jewish people. This play was first shown in 1963 and greatly helped in spreading a

---

[304] Ion Mihai Pacepa, "Moscow's Assault on the Vatican, January 25, 2007," The National Review, http://www.nationalreview.com/articles/219739/moscows-assault-vatican/ion-mihai-pacepa (accessed December 6, 2014).

misconception of Pius XII in relationship to the Nazis.[305]

---

[305] Inside the Vatican Staff, "Pope Pius XII and the Vatican Archives," *Inside the Vatican* (November 2014), 45; Ion Mihai Pacepa, "Moscow's Assault on the Vatican, January 25, 2007," The National Review, http://www.nationalreview.com/articles/219739/moscows-assault-vatican/ion-mihai-pacepa (accessed December 6, 2014). In his 1989 book *Hitler's Pope*, John Cornwell continued the character assassination campaign. Other evidence which reveal the character assassination campaign include the following. During WW II the New York Times repeatedly Pius XII. On Christmas Day, 1941, the New York Times claimed, "The voice of Pius XII is a lonely voice in the silence and darkness enveloping Europe this Christmas." Philip Jenkins, *The New Anti-Catholicism: The Last Acceptable Prejudice* (Oxford: Oxford University Press, 2003), 193. After the war Rome's chief rabbi, Israel Zolli (r. 1939-1945) converted to Catholicism and was baptized Eugenio in honor of Pius XII. Eugenio Zolli, *Before the Dawn: Autobiographical Reflections by Eugenio Zolli* (San Francisco: Ignatius Press, 2008), 11, 14, 18. Also, after the war Israel's Foreign Minister Golda Meir praised Pius XII with, "We share in the grief of humanity. When fearful martyrdom came to our people, the voice of the Pope was raised for its victims. The life of our times was enriched by a voice speaking out about great moral truths above the tumult of daily conflict. We mourn a great servant of peace." Margherita Marchione, "Pope Pius XII and the Jews," http://www.catholiceducation.org/en/culture/history/pope-pius-xii-and-the-jews.html (accessed December 5, 2014).

Quiz 9

1. Demonstrate in at least two ways per objection why the following are false.

   - Objection 1 – Peter Was Never a Pope
   - Objection 2 – The Original Greek New Testament Language Indicates that Jesus Did Not Build His Church on Peter as a Rock
   - Objection 3 – That Jesus Called Peter "Satan" in Matthew 16:23 Indicates that Jesus Never Intended to Make Peter the First Pope
   - Objection 4 – Peter's False Teaching That Paul Rebuked Him for in Galatians 2:11-14 Indicate That Neither Peter Nor His Supposed Successors Are Infallible
   - Objection 5 – According to Scripture, Peter Did Not Pass Down His Authority to Anyone Else - Apostolic Succession, Therefore, Is a False Teaching
   - Objection 6 Since the Roman Numerals of the Pope's Official Latin Title of Vicarious Filii Dei Adds Up to 666, the Pope Is the Anti-Christ
   - Objection 7 According to Revelations 17:9 The Whore Of Babylon Is Situated on Seven Hills - Since Rome Has Seven Hills, The Catholic Church Is the Whore of Babylon

- Objection 8 Since Scripture Does Not Ever State That Peter Ever in Rome He Could Not Have Been the First Bishop Of Rome
- Objection 9 The Modern Papacy is Invalid Since It Directly Contradicts the Simple Life of Peter Objection 10 The Papacy was Invented During Medieval Times
- Objection 11 Early Christians Only Saw Rome as First Among Equals
- Objection 12 The Numerous Bad Popes Is Proof that the Papacy was Never Intended by Christ
- Objection 13 Papal Infallibility is False Since Not Only Did Popes Live Bad Lives but They Also Taught Falsehood
- Objection 14 The Action of Pope Liberius (352-366) Signing an Arian Creed Directly Contradicts Papal Infallibility
- Objection 15 The Action of Pope Vigilius (r. 537-555) Approving the Monophysite Heresy Directly Contradicts Papal Infallibility
- Objection 16 Pope Gregory the Great's Rejection of the Title Universal Bishop is Proof that the Early Church Did Not See the Recognize the Papacy as Having Juridical Authority Over Other Bishops
- Objection 17 The Condemnation of Pope Honorius (r. 625-638) as a Heretic by the Third Council of Constantinople (680-681) Indicates that Popes are not Infallible

- Objection 18 If the Papacy was Instituted by Christ as a Principle of Ecclesial Unity, Then Why During the Middle Ages Did Three Men Claim to be Popes?
- Objection 19 Pope Joan, Who Gave Birth to a Child as Pope Before, Being Killed by an Angry Mob Further Discredits the Papacy
- Objection 20 The Papal Condemnation of Galileo Discredits the Infallibility of the Papacy
- Objection 21 During the Crusades Popes Encouraged the Murdered Millions of Innocent, Peaceful Muslims
- Objection 22 Acting as a Mere Worldly Leader, in Pride Pope Alexander VI Divided up the New World Between Portugal and Spain
- Objection 23 Proof of Papal Depravity is Their Long-Standing Support of Slavery
- Objection 24 Pope Sixtus IV Began and Oversaw the Spanish Inquisition Under Which Thousands of Muslims and Jewish People Were Tortured and Murdered
- Objection 25 Pope Sixtus V Ordered the Publication of an Error Filled Latin Vulgate Bible
- Objection 26 Matthew 16 Neither Teaches Papal Succession Nor Papal Infallibility and yet Vatican Council I (1870) Refers to This Passage When Defining Papal

Infallibility
- Objection 27 At Vatican Council I the Prominent Bishop Joseph Strossmayer Rejected Papal Infallibility
- Objection 28 There Hasn't Been a Valid Pope Since Pope Pius XII
- Objection 29 Appealing to Scripture and to the Fathers of the Church to Defend the Papacy is Anachronistic
- Objection 30 Because Pope Pius XII Cowardly Refused to Denounce Hitler He is Responsible for the Murder of Millions

Additional Activities and Resources

Respond to the above objections. Do so, though, according to the Socratic method of gathering, clarifying and challenging questions.

Readings

"The Papacy" in Madrid, Patrick. *Answer Me This*. Huntington: Our Sunday Visitor Publishing, 2003.

Madrid, Patrick. *Pope Fiction*. Dallas: Basilica Press, 1999.

Chapter Ten: The Communion of Saints and the Blessed Virgin Mary

Introduction

Catholic devotion to saints and, above all, to Mary as Queen of All Saints and as Queen of heaven is at times vigorously rejected. It is argued that praying to saints in heaven directly contradicts Scripture, which explicitly teaches in Exodus 20:5 to worship God alone. Catholics, on the other hand, believe devotion to saints is not form of a idolatry but only a form of respectful communication with heavenly friends. In presenting the debate, the Protestant objection will first be presented before delving into the Catholic response. Then, in light of the previous sections, we will carefully examine Catholic devotion to Mary, Queen of Saints.

Objections to the Communion of Saints

Representing a Protestant position, James White in a debate with Patrick Madrid argued that Scripture is self-sufficient for determining what is proper worship of God from what is not. This means that we are not to decide for ourselves what constitutes right worship. Exodus Chapter 20:4-6 explicitly forbids bowing down in worship to anyone or anything other than God:

> You shall not make for yourself an idol, whether in the form of anything that is in heaven above, or that is on the earth beneath, or that is in the water under the earth. You shall not bow down to them or worship them; for I the Lord your God am a jealous God, punishing children for the iniquity of parents, to the third and the fourth generation of those who reject me, but showing steadfast love to the thousandth generation of those who love me and keep my commandments. (Exodus NRSV 20:4-6)

Since, argues White, Catholics bow down in worship to the saints they are breaking this essential commandment of Scripture. Furthermore, the argument that Catholics are not breaking Scripture since they are only venerating saints and not worshipping them is invalid since it is based on a distinction that does not exist in the Old

Testament. The distinction Catholics make between *latria*, as worship, from *dulia*, as veneration, does not actually exist in Scripture. This is because these two terms come from Latin by way of a Greek translation of two Hebrew words that are consistently presented in Scripture as intertwined realities that cannot be separated from one another. Therefore, according to Scripture we are to bow down neither with *latria* nor with *dulia* to anyone or anything other than God.[306]

Finally, argues White, since those who are in heaven rest in Jesus Christ they are not aware of people's needs. If they were aware, then this awareness would disturb them and they would no longer be asleep in the Lord, but this is contrary to Scripture. Therefore, praying to the saints is not possible since they are asleep in the Lord. As Scripture states:

> But I do not want you to be ignorant, brethren, concerning those who have fallen asleep, lest you sorrow as others who have no hope. For if we believe that Jesus died and rose again, even so God will bring with Him those who sleep in Jesus. For this we say to you by the word of the Lord, that we who are alive *and* remain until the coming of the Lord will by no means precede those who are asleep. (1 Thessalonians 4:13-15 NKJV)

---

[306] Patrick Madrid, and James White, *Communion of Saints Debate MP3*.

Catholic Devotion to Saints Is Not Idolatrous

Madrid responded to White's objections in the following ways. First, it is important to acknowledge the context of a Scriptural passage in order to properly discern the message that God intends for us to receive through the inspired words. The context in which the Exodus condemnation of idolatry was written is different from today's context. We have a different, with some similarities, understanding of what is idolatry from what is not. Essentially, the reason for this difference is that Catholics interpret Exodus, which was written before the Incarnation, in light of Christ through whom, like an icon, we encounter God. In addition, although we share with people of the Old Testament context inclinations and temptations towards idolatry, how we express these inclinations differs. In the Old Testament times, idolatry was expressed by worshipping graven images, such as the golden calf. In contrast, it is very rare for people to worship graven images. Instead, when we fall into idolatry we often express it by worshipping other man made products such as cars, the latest technological gadget and military inventions.[307]

Second, Madrid brought to White's attention that Scripture teaches that the Church is Christ's

---

[307] Patrick Madrid, and James White, *Communion of Saints Debate MP3*.

Mystical Body.[308] In the mystical body, Christ, teaches St. Paul, "is the head of the body, the church." (Colossians 1:18 NRSV) Since Christ is one, the body that is united to him is one. This means that there are not multiple mystical bodies but one mystical body united to Him. The members of the mystical body who are in communion with one another include those on earth, in purgatory and in heaven.

For this reason, presuming we die in the state of grace, death does not separate us from Christ's mystical body. Instead, we are brought into another dimension of the mystical body, in purgatory or heaven. According to Paul's *Letter to Romans* nothing, other than mortal sin, can separate us from our corporate identity in Christ, even death:

---

[308] "For as in one body we have many members, and not all the members have the same function, so we, who are many, are one body in Christ, and individually we are members one of another." (Romans 12:4-5 NRSV); "For just as the body is one and has many members, and all the members of the body, though many, are one body, so it is with Christ. For in the one Spirit we were all baptized into one body—Jews or Greeks, slaves or free— and we were all made to drink of one Spirit." (1 Corinthians 12:12-13 NRSV); "For he is our peace; in his flesh he has made both groups into one and has broken down the dividing wall, that is, the hostility between us. He has abolished the law with its commandments and ordinances, that he might create in himself one new humanity in place of the two, thus making peace, and might reconcile both groups to God in one body through the cross, thus putting to death that hostility through it." (Ephesians 2:14-16 NRSV).

Who will separate us from the love of Christ? Will hardship, or distress, or persecution, or famine, or nakedness, or peril, or sword? As it is written, "For your sake we are being killed all day long; we are accounted as sheep to be slaughtered." No, in all these things we are more than conquerors through him who loved us. For I am convinced that neither death, nor life, nor angels, nor rulers, nor things present, nor things to come, nor powers, nor height, nor depth, nor anything else in all creation, will be able to separate us from the love of God in Christ Jesus our Lord.

As Paul teaches, what unites all members (militant, suffering and triumphant) in the one mystical body is supernatural charity. This divine gift of love moves us to pray and intercede, through the merits of Christ, for one another.[309] Since

---

[309] "Do not seek your own advantage, but that of the other." (1 Corinthians 10:24 NRSV); "Now concerning love of the brothers and sisters, you do not need to have anyone write to you, for you yourselves have been taught by God to love one another; and indeed you do love all the brothers and sisters throughout Macedonia. But we urge you, beloved, to do so more and more...." (1 Thessalonians 4:9-10 NRSV); "Therefore encourage one another and build up each other, as indeed you are doing." (1 Thessalonians 5:11 NRSV); "And we urge you, beloved, to admonish the idlers, encourage the fainthearted, help the weak, be patient with all of them. See that none of you repays evil for evil, but always seek

Scripture encourages us to imitate holy people on earth, which may be aided by pictures and statues, and ask them for their prayers, it is highly reasonable, by reasons of faith, that we are also to ask the holy people in heaven for their intercessory prayers. Their love for us after they have died and have been embraced by God has not decreased but has increased since charity increases the closer people are to the source of charity, who is God.[310]

The early Church Father St. Jerome (342-420 AD) essentially states this in his writing *Against Vigilantius*:

---

to do good to one another and to all." (1 Thessalonians 5:14-15 NRSV).

[310] "Brothers and sisters, join in imitating me, and observe those who live according to the example you have in us." (Philippians 3:17 NRSV); "I appeal to you, brothers and sisters, by our Lord Jesus Christ and by the love of the Spirit, to join me in earnest prayer to God on my behalf, that I may be rescued from the unbelievers in Judea, and that my ministry to Jerusalem may be acceptable to the saints, so that by God's will I may come to you with joy and be refreshed in your company." (Romans 15:30-32 NRSV); "And we urge you, beloved, to admonish the idlers, encourage the fainthearted, help the weak, be patient with all of them. See that none of you repays evil for evil, but always seek to do good to one another and to all." (1 Thessalonians 5:14-15 NRSV); "First of all, then, I urge that supplications, prayers, intercessions, and thanksgivings be made for everyone, for kings and all who are in high positions, so that we may lead a quiet and peaceable life in all godliness and dignity. This is right and is acceptable in the sight of God our Savior, who desires everyone to be saved and to come to the knowledge of the truth." (1 Timothy 2:1-4 NRSV).

If Apostles and martyrs while still in the body can pray for others, when they ought still to be anxious for themselves, how much more must they do so when once they have won their crowns, overcome, and triumphed? A single man, Moses, of wins pardon from God for six hundred thousand armed men; and Stephen, the follower of his Lord and the first Christian martyr, entreats pardon for his persecutors; and when once they have entered on their life with Christ, shall they have less power than before? The Apostle Paul says that two hundred and seventy-six souls were given to him in the ship; and when, after his dissolution, he has begun to be with Christ, must he shut his mouth, and be unable to say a word for those who throughout the whole world have believed in his Gospel? Shall Vigilantius the live dog be better than Paul the dead lion? I should be right in saying so after Ecclesiastes, if I admitted that Paul is dead in spirit. The truth is that the saints are not called dead, but are said to be asleep. Wherefore Lazarus, who was about to rise again, is said to have slept. And the Apostle forbids the Thessalonians to be sorry for those who were asleep. As for you, when wide awake you are asleep, and asleep when you write, and you bring before me an apocryphal book which, under the name of Esdras, is read by you and those of your feather, and in this book it is written that after death no one dares pray for others. I have never read the book: for what need is there to take up what the Church does not receive?[311]

In affirming that the calling upon for help and veneration of the saints has been passed down and practiced from the earliest days of Christianity, including St. Jerome's times, the Council of Trent solemnly declared:

> The holy council commands all bishops and others who hold the office of teaching and have charge of the <cura animarum>, that in accordance with the usage of the Catholic and Apostolic Church, received from the primitive times of the Christian religion, and with the unanimous teaching of the holy Fathers and the decrees of sacred councils, they above all instruct the faithful diligently in matters relating to intercession and invocation of the saints, the veneration of relics, and the legitimate use of images, teaching them that the saints who reign together with Christ offer up their prayers to

---

[311] Philip Schaff, *Nicene and Post-Nicene Fathers of the Christian Church*, vol. 6, St. Jerome, Against Vigilantius (Grand Rapids: Wm. B. Eerdmans Publishing Company, 1892), 419, Christian Classics Ethereal Library, http://www.ccel.org/ccel/schaff/npnf206.iii.html (accessed January 7, 2015).

God for men, that it is good and beneficial suppliantly to invoke them and to have recourse to their prayers, assistance and support in order to obtain favors from God through His Son, Jesus Christ our Lord, who alone is our redeemer and savior; and that they think impiously who deny that the saints who enjoy eternal happiness in heaven are to be invoked, or who assert that they do not pray for men, or that our invocation of them to pray for each of us individually is idolatry, or that it is opposed to the word of God and inconsistent with the honor of the one mediator of God and men, Jesus Christ, or that it is foolish to pray vocally or mentally to those who reign in heaven.[312]

With respect to the definition in Scripture of *dulia* and *latria*, the Greek words *dulia* and *latria* are a Greek translation of a Hebrew word which signifies reverence given to another. This reverence can be given to men (Genesis 37:7-9, Genesis 49:2-27, Exodus 18:7) or may be given to God but in a different sense. In order to clarify the implicit distinction between reverence given to men and

---

[312] "The Council of Trent, Session XXV - which is the ninth and last under the Supreme Pontiff, Pius IV, begun on the third and closed on the fourth day of December, 1563," EWTN, http://www.ewtn.com/library/COUNCILS/TRENT25.HTM#2 (accessed January 7, 2015).

reverence due to God alone, Catholic tradition distinguishes *dulia*, signifying reverence appropriate to creatures, from *latria*, worship due to God alone. A further distinction was made with the term *hyperdulia* to signify the highest reverence one may give to a creature. The one creature we may venerate with *hyperdulia* is Mary as Mother of God. Due to the implicit distinctions in the original Hebrew text of the bible passages in the Old Testament, the referred to distinctions are reasonable distinctions.[313] As St. Augustine explains, with reference to the Greek Septuagint:

> For this is the worship which is due to the Divinity, or, to speak more accurately, to the Deity; and, to express this worship in a single word as there does not occur to me any Latin term sufficiently exact, I shall avail myself, whenever necessary, of a Greek word. Λατρεία, whenever it occurs in Scripture, is rendered by the word service. But that service which is due to men, and in reference to which the apostle writes that servants must be subject to their own masters, Ephesians 6:5 is usually designated by another word in Greek, whereas the service which is paid to God alone by worship, is always, or almost always, called λατρεία in the usage of those who wrote

---

[313] "Saint Worship," catholic.com, http://www.catholic.com/tracts/saint-worship (accessed September 15, 2016).

from the divine oracles.[314]

Because Catholics believe that the saints in heaven are aware of us on earth and of our needs, we can respect them with *dulia* not in the sense of worship given to God alone but in a similar sense that people, whatever their religion, ask for prayers from one another. If we can ask for prayers from the living on earth then, presuming those in heaven are aware of our prayers, we can also ask for prayers from the saints in heaven. God wishes this communication between us to occur so that we become more closely knit together as a communion of people more and more reflective of the Trinitarian relations in whose image we are made in.

According to Hebrews 12:1, the saints in heaven are aware of our struggles and wish us to persevere.[315] Jesus' parable on Lazarus (Luke 16:19, 30) indicates that those who have died and are in purgatory are concerned about those who have not and want to intercede for them. Also, Revelation 6:9-10 describes martyred saints who are praying against those who murdered them, perhaps to protect other Christians from suffering at their

---

[314] Augustine, *City of God*, bk. 10, chap. 1. http://www.newadvent.org/fathers/120110.htm (accessed January 7, 2015).

[315] "Therefore, since we are surrounded by so great a cloud of witnesses, let us also lay aside every weight and the sin that clings so closely, and let us run with perseverance the race that is set before us...." (Hebrews 12:1 NRSV)

hands.[316] In the preceding chapter (Revelation 5:4-8) elders in heaven are depicted offering prayers to God on behalf of their brothers and sisters on earth. These inspired passages and others indicate that the saints are very aware of our needs.[317]

Since, in accordance with Scripture, Catholics believe that saints are aware of our needs, are delighted when we ask them for help, and through the one mediation of Christ[318] intercede for us, when Catholics venerate saints they are not intending to worship them. Instead, they are relating to the saints as heavenly friends in a similar way that we ask friends on earth for help and that Scripture depicts people interceding on other's behalf including Abraham, Moses and Paul. This means that if a Catholic is seen bowing his head before a statue of a saint the gesture does not automatically mean that the Catholic is worshipping the saint since the intention of the Catholic very likely is only to relate to the saints by

---

[316] "When he opened the fifth seal, I saw under the altar the souls of those who had been slaughtered for the word of God and for the testimony they had given; they cried out with a loud voice, 'Sovereign Lord, holy and true, how long will it be before you judge and avenge our blood on the inhabitants of the earth?'" (Revelation 6:9-10 NRSV)

[317] Patrick Madrid, "Any Friend of God is a Friend of Mine", Patrick Madrid.com (accessed 01/01/2015).

[318] "[T]here is also one mediator between God and humankind, Christ Jesus, himself human, who gave himself a ransom for all...." (1 Timothy 2:5-6 NRSV)

asking them for help through the merits of Christ.[319]

The objection that in order to answer our prayers saints needs to be, like God, all knowing and all powerful is unwarranted. Although many people may be asking a given saint at the same time that their requests be granted, the number of people asking will always be a finite number. The capacity the saints required in order to answer these finite prayers is likewise finite and not infinite.[320]

To the objection that since saints in heaven are dead, then praying to them is the same as trying to communicate with the dead through séances and magic, we may respond as follows. The intention of one attempting to communicate with the dead in a séance is essentially different from the intention of a devout Catholic praying to a saint. In a séance or magical ritual, those trying to communicate with the dead are doing so in order to control, harness and manipulate the power of the dead. However, the devout Catholic communication with the dead

---

[319] Madrid adds, that the local council of Elvira (305-306 AD) is the only case of a regional council issuing a canon (canon 36) that Christians are not to have icons or paint them on the walls of the Church. Catholic scholars remind us that at the time of this council Spain was fighting against paganism. Possibly, in order to discourage Christians from imitating the pagans this canon was stated. It could also be understood as a pastoral move in order not to scandalize the pagans who might think Catholics are doing the same thing they are forbidding the pagans to do.

[320] Patrick Madrid, "Any Friend of God is a Friend of Mine".

by praying to the saints is done not in order to control the dead but rather to ask help from a friend in heaven who is awake and due to charity wants to help us.[321]

Catholic Marian Doctrine

By focusing our attention on four Marian dogmas, we will now shift our attention to the Mary as the Queen of the Saints. These doctrines are frequently misunderstood and rejected. The four Marian doctrines are as follows: Mary's Immaculate Conception, Mary's Perpetual Virginity, Mary as Mother of God, and Mary's Assumption into heaven.

Immaculate Conception

Pope Pius IX in his apostolic constitution *Ineffabilis Deus* solemnly defined that at the moment of her conception Mary, through the merits of Jesus Christ, was conceived free from the "stain" of original sin.[322] This means that Mary was

---

[321] Patrick Madrid, "Any Friend of God is a Friend of Mine".

[322] "We declare, pronounce, and define that the doctrine which holds that the most Blessed Virgin Mary, in the first instance of her conception, by a singular grace and privilege granted by Almighty God, in view of the merits of Jesus Christ, the Savior of the human race, was preserved free from all stain of original sin, is a doctrine revealed by God and therefore to be believed firmly and constantly by all the faithful." Pius IX, "Ineffabilis Deus,"

redeemed by her son in an anticipatory manner by being preserved from sin. In contrast, we are redeemed by Jesus from sin in an antecedent manner. Since God is outside of time as its creator, He is not restricted from applying redemption to only those who lived after Christ was born. The former Evangelical and convert to Catholicism Matthew Leonard counters the objection that while this may be theoretically possible it did not actually occur since according to Scripture "all have sinned."[323] (Romans 3:23 NRSV)

Leonard points out that, as with any Scripture passage, in order for Romans 3:23 to be interpreted correctly its context needs to be taken in account. The context of Romans 3:23 is Paul's comparison of a Jewish group with a non-Jewish group. With the word "all" Paul is stating that both the Jewish group and the non-Jewish group are guilty of sin. He is not, though, claiming that everyone within these groups is guilty of sin, for this would mean that even Jesus is a sinner, which St. Paul does not teach. Because of Jesus's sinless nature, it is most fitting that He be born of a sinless woman as the Catholic Church teaches.[324]

December 8, 1854, ewtn.com, https://www.ewtn.com/faith/teachings/marye1.htm (accessed June 12, 2016).

[323] "For there is no distinction, since all have sinned and fall short of the glory of God...." (Romans 3:22-23 NRSV).

[324] Matthew Leonard, *The Bible and the Virgin Mary Journey Through Scripture*, 5 DVDs (Steubenville: St. Paul Center for Biblical Theology, 2014); Matthew Leonard, *The Bible and the Virgin Mary Journey*

Catholic Apologetics

Perpetual Virginity

Protestants object to the teaching that Mary was a Perpetual Virgin before, during and after the birth of Jesus Christ. A common objection is that this teaching is not taught by Scripture and even if what is taught by tradition is given some weight since the teaching on Mary's virginity is a late tradition it is a very doubtful tradition. Some go further to claim that the late tradition of Mary's virginity comes from outside of Christianity and is traceable to myths.

Benedict XVI prior to his election to the papacy responded to these objections. In response to the first objection, Ratzinger does not deny that the tradition on Mary's virginity is late. One of the earliest explicit teachings of this doctrine is found in an epistle by Pope St. Siricius (384-399) entitled *Accepi litteras vestras* of 392 AD.[325] The teaching

---

Through Scripture, Participant Workbook (Steubenville: St. Paul Center for Biblical Theology, 2014), 108.

[325] "Surely, we cannot deny that regarding the sons of Mary the statement is justly censured, and your holiness has rightly abhorred it, that from the same virginal womb, from which according to the flesh Christ was born, another offspring was brought forth. For neither would the Lord Jesus have chosen to be born of a virgin, if he had judged she would be so incontinent, that with the seed of human copulation she would pollute that generative chamber of the Lord's body, that palace of the eternal King. For he who imputes this, imputes nothing other than the falsehood of the Jews, who say that he could not have been born of a virgin, For, if they accept this authority from the priests, that Mary seems

was affirmed in a formal way at the Council of Constantinople II (553),[326] at the Lateran Council (649),[327] and at the Third Council of Constantinople (680-681).[328] While it is true that the teaching of Mary's perpetual virginity had a late public official reception in the Church, this does not necessarily mean that the tradition itself is late. Often, oral traditions are written down only when there is a need to clarify confusion over a teaching which was always believed as true.[329]

---

to have brought forth many children, they strive to sweep away the truth of faith with greater zeal." Henry Denzinger, *The Sources of Catholic Dogma*, Thirtieth Edition, trans. Roy J. Deferrari (St. Louis: B. Herder Book Co., 1957), 39.

[326] Henry Denzinger, *The Sources of Catholic Dogma*, 86. "Can. 3. If anyone does not confess that there are two generations of the Word of God, the one from the Father before the ages, without time and incorporeally, the other in the last days, when the same came down from heaven, and was incarnate of the holy and glorious Mother of God and ever Virgin Mary, and was born of her, let such a one be anathema."

[327] Henry Denzinger, *The Sources of Catholic Dogma*, 102. "Can. 3. If anyone does not properly and truly confess in accord with the holy Fathers, that the holy Mother of God and ever Virgin and immaculate Mary in the earliest of the ages conceived of the Holy Spirit without seed, namely, God the Word Himself specifically and truly, who was born of God the Father before all ages, and that she incorruptibly bore IHim?], her virginity remaining indestructible even after His birth, let him be condemned."

[328] Henry Denzinger, *The Sources of Catholic Dogma*, 114.

[329] "The literary form may be relatively late, but the tradition given in that form had already existed in

In response to the second objection, Ratzinger describes the myths of a Virgin Goddess as "only motifs which touch on the Christian assertion more or less closely. I see nothing negative in this: these may be the expression of a psychological archetype in whose confused longing, as in all authentic archetypes, a deep knowledge of reality is expressed. Be the reality ever so remote, the human heart with its intimations and anticipatory questions already awaits its fulfillment."[330]

Another objection claims that because the New Testament refers to brothers of Jesus Mary could not have had retained her virginity after giving birth to Jesus. This objection is based on a faulty translation of the term brother in Scripture since both in the Old Testament and in the New

---

another form; no historical critique can exclude the possibility that the simple nucleus of the account is significantly more ancient." Joseph Ratzinger, *Daughter Zion: Meditations on the Church's Marian Belief*, trans. McDermott (San Francisco: Ignatius Press, 1983), 54. He continues with, "Furthermore, the agreement with regard to the nucleus of the account from two mutually independent traditions which otherwise show considerable formal diversities in detail is a norm of some significance—and this is what we can ascertain through a study of the sources of Matthew and Luke."

[330] Joseph Ratzinger, *Daughter Zion: Meditations on the Church's Marian Belief*, trans. McDermott (San Francisco: Ignatius Press, 1983), 56. In his essay, *Myth Became Fact*, C.S. Lewis similarly defends Christianity from those who resorting to the fallacy "post hoc, ergo propter hoc" argue that Christianity is derived from myths. C.S. Lewis, *God in the Dock* (Grand Rapids: Wm. B. Eerdmans Publishing Co., 1970), 54-60.

Testament the term brother is used not only in reference to brothers who were born of the same mother but also to cousins.[331]

Similar to the above objection, another objection to Mary's virginity is also based on a faulty interpretation of Scripture. According to this objection, since Scripture states that Joseph "had no marital relations" with Mary "until she had born a son" this means that after she gave birth to Jesus, Joseph had marital relations with Mary. (Matthew 1:25 NRSV) When this logic is applied to Jesus' words to his apostles that "I am with you always, even unto the end of the world" (Matthew 28:20 KJV) then this would mean that when the world ends Jesus will cease being present to us, an interpretation that few if any Protestants would accept as valid. Similarly, if a Christian says, "May the Lord bless you until we meet again" he ordinarily does not intend his words to be interpreted as meaning that when they meet again he wants God's blessings to cease. In reference to these arguments and others, Leonard concludes that the use of the word until does not mean that a

---

[331] See Genesis 13:8, 14:12; Mark 6:3, Matthew 27:56, Mark 15:40. The Genesis citations use the term brother as a term that also includes cousins. The synoptic gospel citations call James and Joseph brothers of Jesus and while identifying them as sons of a Mary other than the mother of Jesus. Scott Hahn, *Hail, Holy Queen* (New York: Image Books, 2001), 104; Matt Fradd, "Jesus had Brothers?" September 17, 2013, catholic.com, http://www.catholic.com/blog/matt-fradd/ jesus-had-brothers (accessed June 12, 2016).

change in Mary's virginity occurred after Jesus was born.[332]

Mother of God

The third ecumenical Council of Ephesus (431) condemned the position that Mary gave birth to Jesus's human nature but not Jesus as God. According to the council:

1. If anyone does not confess that Emmanuel is God in truth, and therefore that the holy virgin is the mother of God (for she bore in a fleshly way the Word of God become flesh), let him be anathema.
2. If anyone does not confess that the Word from God the Father has been united by hypostasis with the flesh and is one Christ with his own flesh, and is therefore God and man together, let him be anathema.[333]

Twenty years later, the Council of Chalcedon (451) clarified why Mary is the mother of God. It did so by distinguishing two natures in Jesus (human and divine as sources of action) united in

---

[332] Matthew Leonard, *The Bible and the Virgin Mary Journey Through Scripture*, Participant Workbook (Steubenville: St. Paul Center for Biblical Theology, 2014), 69.

[333] Norman P. Tanner, *Decrees of the Ecumenical Councils*, Volume I (District of Columbia: Georgetown University Press, 1990), 59.

one divine person.[334] Because the two natures of Jesus are united in the one divine person while retaining their distinction, what is experienced by one nature is experienced by the divine person Jesus.[335] Therefore, since the human nature of Jesus was born of Mary, the divine person Jesus experienced being born of Mary through his human nature. In simpler language, Mary, as with all women, gave birth to a person and not only to a nature.[336]

Objections to Mary as the Mother of God often do not take into account the careful explanation by the early councils of how Mary is the Mother of God and the early councils' careful explanation of God's Triune nature. For example, the claim that if Mary is the Mother of God then this means she is the Mother of the Trinity is based on confusing Jesus as the Second Person of the Trinity with the Trinity as a whole.[337]

---

[334] "The property of both natures is preserved and comes together into a single person and a single subsistent being; he is not parted or divided into two persons, but is one and the same only-begotten Son, God, Word, Lord Jesus Christ...." Norman P. Tanner, *Decrees of the Ecumenical Councils*, Volume I (District of Columbia: Georgetown University Press, 1990), 86.

[335] In theology this reality is referred to as the communication of idioms.

[336] Scott Hahn, *Hail, Holy Queen* (New York: Image Books, 2001), 100.

[337] Tim Staples, *Behold Your Mother: A Biblical and Historical Defense of the Marian Doctrines* (El Cajon: Catholic Answers, 2014), 28.

Assumption

Pope Pius XII with his 1950, apostolic constitution *Munificentissimus Deus* solemnly proclaimed that Mary was assumed into heaven. In doing he wrote:

> 44. ... [B]y the authority of our Lord Jesus Christ, of the Blessed Apostles Peter and Paul, and by our own authority, we pronounce, declare, and define it to be a divinely revealed dogma: that the Immaculate Mother of God, the ever Virgin Mary, having completed the course of her earthly life, was assumed body and soul into heavenly glory.
>
> ...
>
> 47. It is forbidden to any man to change this, our declaration, pronouncement, and definition or, by rash attempt, to oppose and counter it. If any man should presume to make such an attempt, let him know that he will incur the wrath of Almighty God and of the Blessed Apostles Peter and Paul.[338]

Those who object to Mary's Assumption

---

[338] Pius XII, "Munificentissimus Deus," November 1, 1950, no. 44, 47, w2.vatican.va, http://w2.vatican.va/content/pius-xii/en/apost_constitutions/documents/hf_p-xii_apc_19501101_munificentissimus-deus.html (accessed June 13, 2016).

typically point out that the earliest historical reference to Mary's Assumption only comes from the fourth century. However, as pointed out earlier with reference to Ratzinger, simply because a belief shows up fairly late in documentary history does not mean that it was not present in an oral manner prior to being written down. In addition, Leonard points out, while we do not have documentary evidence prior to the fourth century that indicate belief in Mary's Assumption, we also do not have any documentary evidence from this same time period that such a belief was denied, nor is there any documentary evidence that describe her relics, which would have been highly valued and very likely attested to.[339] We may reasonably maintain, therefore, that Mary's Assumption was universally believed in the Church until the fourth century, and when there was a need to make this belief more explicit it was written down.

Quiz 10

1. Respond to the following in a Catholic manner. Is praying to saints in heaven and venerating images of them contrary to Exodus 20:5? Include the following in your answer: mystical body, death, saints as asleep with Christ, charity, imitation, intercession, praise.

---

[339] Matthew Leonard, *The Bible and the Virgin Mary Journey Through Scripture*, 5 DVDs (Steubenville: St. Paul Center for Biblical Theology, 2014).

2. Respond to the following in a Catholic manner. The distinction Catholics make between latria and dulia is not present in Scripture. Therefore, we may not bow down with latria or dulia to anyone or anything other than God.
3. Mary cannot have been born without sin since Romans 3:23 teaches that "all have sinned."
4. Since Scripture says Jesus had brothers, Mary did not remain a virgin during her birth to Jesus.
5. Since both the traditions that Mary was a Perpetual Virgin and she was assumed into heaven are late traditions they were invented and come from myths.
6. Mary only gave birth to Jesus' human nature. This means she is not the Mother of God.

Additional Activities and Resources

Respond to the following. Do so according to the Socratic method of gathering, clarifying and challenging questions.

- Praying to Saints is Opposed to Christ's One Mediation
- Pray Directly to God Instead of Praying to Saints
- Praying to Saints Implies that Saints are All Knowing and All Powerful

- Praying to Saints is Necromancy
- Since the Following Syllogism is Contrary to the Christian Faith, Mary is not the Mother of God

   > Major premise: Jesus is God
   > Minor premise: Mary is the Mother of Jesus
   > Conclusion: Mary is the Mother of God
   > Major premise: God is Trinity
   > Minor premise: Mary is the Mother of God
   > Conclusion: Mary is the Mother of the Trinity[340]

- Mary cannot have been born without sin since Romans 3:23 teaches that "all have sinned."
- Since Scripture says Jesus had brothers, Mary did not remain a virgin during her birth to Jesus.
- Since both the traditions that Mary was a Perpetual Virgin and she was assumed into heaven are late traditions they were invented and come from myths.
- Mary only gave birth to Jesus' human nature. This means she is not the Mother of God.

---

[340] Tim Staples, *Behold Your Mother: A Biblical and Historical Defense of the Marian Doctrines* (El Cajon: Catholic Answers, 2014), 28.

Readings

Paragraphs 963-972, 1192 of the *Catechism of the Catholic Church*

Madrid, Patrick. *Any Friend of God's is a Friend of Mine*. San Diego: Basilica Press, 1996.

Audio

Madrid, Patrick and James White. *Communion of Saints Debate*. Audio CDs.

Fr. Peter Samuel Kucer, MSA

Chapter Eleven: Mormonism

Introduction

Beginning with Mormonism, these last two chapters will focus on an inter-religious context. Catholic responses to the following Mormon teaching will be presented: The Great Apostasy, Eternal Progression, and extra-biblical public revelation. We will conclude with reflection on recent developments within Mormon theology that may be bringing Mormon doctrine closer to Catholic belief.

The Great Apostasy

According to the Mormon Elder Gary Coleman, from the time of Adam and Eve apostasies have been frequently occurring. After each apostasy, God responded by inspiring prophets to restore the true teaching that was completely lost in each apostasy. Even after the coming of Jesus Christ, apostasies continued to occur. This explains why in the New Testament there are no further Scripture passages after Revelation chapter 22. This absence of further inspired books after Revelation chapter 22 is due to God's decision to restrict further revelation and prophecy to His people at the time Revelation was written because yet another apostasy, called the Great Apostasy, had occurred.

During the nineteenth century, God inspired the prophet Joseph Smith to restore His true teaching that had been completely lost during the Great Apostasy. Through Joseph Smith, God revealed additional teaching intended for all people that are not contained in the New Testament. Joseph Smith was given these revelatory truths by God in a similar way as Abraham, Moses and Christ received revelation. Members of Joseph Smith's Church, the Church of the Latter Day Saints, continue God's mission of restoring truth and transmitting new revelatory truth.[341]

In a dialogue with Coleman, Madrid responded

---

[341] Patrick Madrid and Elder Gary Coleman, *The First Catholic – Mormon Dialogue*, 2 CDs (1990). In 1820, Joseph Smith claimed that he saw and was spoken to by God the Father and Jesus Christ. They two revealed to Joseph that in the first century after the birth of Christ, Christianity underwent a total apostasy from the true faith. Joseph was then given the mission to restore Christianity to its original purity. In being tasked with this mission, Joseph was given a book of revelation called the Book of Mormon that, claimed Joseph Smith, contains writings of Jewish prophets who once lived in America. Patrick Madrid, "Mormonism and the 'Great Apostasy' Theory" Patrick Madrid.com

to the Mormon doctrine of the Great Apostasy as follows. Both the Mormon Church and the Catholic Church claim to be the true Church. However, only one can be. Mormonism uses the bible to support its claim that Mormonism is the true Church. The passages they use come from a canon recognized by the Catholic Church. The passages they refer to are also situated in a Scriptural context which explicitly dismisses a central claim of Mormonism that a Great Apostasy occurred shortly after Jesus' life on earth.

Since Christ promised that His Church will not apostatize, by being completely overcome, and because Christ is not a liar, how could a Great Apostasy have occurred if we believe in Christ? In Matthew 16:18, Jesus promises Peter, "[Y]ou are Peter, and on this rock I will build my church, and the gates of Hades will not prevail against it." (NRSV) A number of chapters later in Matthew 28:20, Jesus promises that "I am with you always, to the end of the age." (NRSV) In the Gospel of John, Jesus assures His disciples that although He may be absent from them in his bodily presence He will be present spiritually since the Holy Spirit will "be with you forever." (John 14:15 NRSV) The Holy Spirit, explains Jesus, "will guide you into all the truth...." (John 16:13 NRSV)

Simply because Jesus promised that His presence and the Holy Spirit's will protect the Church in the truth does not mean that the Church will only be comprised of perfectly, truthful people. In accordance with Jesus' Parable of the Weeds

(Matthew 13:24-30), the Church does not deny that there were, are, and will be sinful, imperfect members in the Church. Rather, the Church teaches that because Christ is God and as God is true to His promises, the Church in her official beliefs will never stray from the truth into apostasy. A key means Jesus has used to preserve truth in the Church is apostolic succession, in particular the succession of the office of Peter. Acts 1:24-26 describes the first instance of apostolic succession:

> Then they prayed and said, "Lord, you know everyone's heart. Show us which one of these two you have chosen to take the place in this ministry and apostleship from which Judas turned aside to go to his own place." And they cast lots for them, and the lot fell on Matthias; and he was added to the eleven apostles. (NRSV)

As the Church continued her mission received by Christ of extending His presence through time, she began conferring apostolic succession upon others when they died. (1 Timothy 4:14; 1 Timothy 5:22) Since the Church is Christ's Mystical Body, it is not reasonable that Christ would allow his body to be subject to Satan by falling into a total apostasy. (Romans 12:1-5, 1 Corinthians 12:12-27; Ephesians 3:4-6; 5:21-32; Colossians 1:18). Being more powerful than Satan, Christ will not allow His Mystical Body to become completely divorced from its head by falling into a total apostasy. (1 John 4:4)

Scripture, though, does refer to partial apostasies of individuals and groups of individuals within the Church. Despite these partial apostasies, including some bishops but never a pope in an official way, there has never been a general apostasy of the entire Church.

As early as the first century of Christianity, references are made in Christian literature to both apostolic succession and the primacy of the Pope as head of the successors to the apostles. In the *Letter to the Church of Corinth*, Pope St. Clement I (r. 92-99), describes apostolic succession and settled a dispute within the Church of Corinth even though he was the bishop of Rome. Interestingly, although the Apostle John was alive (d. circa 100 AD), he was not asked to settle this dispute. Instead, the bishop of Rome was. The dispute within the Corinthian Church was addressed to Pope St. Clement because, although not one of the original Twelve Apostles, he was the Bishop of Rome and, consequently, was considered as having primacy over other sees.[342]

While documentary evidence of very early belief in apostolic succession and papal primary exists, no documentary evidence exists that a General Apostasy took place during these early days of Christianity. Finally, Madrid points out that the events that are to take place before the apostasy at

---

[342] Other early testimonies to Apostolic Succession include St. Ignatius of Antioch's letters (c. 110 AD) and a letter by St. Polycarp of Smyrna (80-167 AD) written to the Philippians.

the end of times, which 2 Thessalonians 2:1-12 refers to, have not yet occurred. Romans 11 identifies these as Gentiles coming into the Church in their "full number," which will be followed by the salvation of all of Israel.[343]

Eternal Progression

The Mormon doctrine of Eternal Progression is based on their henotheistic beliefs. Mormons believe that the Father and the Son and the Holy Spirit are separate, individual divine beings. This means that although Jesus is believed by Mormons to be God, he is understood by Mormons as literally a Son of God, meaning that he is distinct from the Father, and not one with the Father. Since Mormon belief entails believing in a plurality of Gods, they do not consider themselves polytheists but rather henotheists since they worship one supreme God while accepting the existence of other Gods.

The doctrine of Eternal Progression teaches that not only does Jesus have a God who precedes him

---

[343] Biblical verses that Mormons often cite to back their Great Apostasy doctrine only refer to a partial falling away from the faith and not to a complete apostasy. In addition, these passages locate this partial apostasy during end of times. Since the world has not yet come to an end, the end times are either coming soon or in far away in the future. These times definitely are not, according to Scripture, in the past, as Mormons claim. (Mat. 24:4-12; Mark 13:21-23; Luke 21:7-8; Acts 20:29-30; 2 Thessalonians 2:1-12; 2 Timothy 3:1-7, 4:1-4; 2 Peter 2:1-3; and Jude 17-19)

as his father, but also above his father is another God. This pattern of succession is traced back to infinity and continues in the present. It continues in the present since all men are called to become divine, to become Gods after the example of Jesus who once was a man and then became a God.[344]

In countering Mormon henotheistic belief and the Mormon doctrine of Eternal Progression, Madrid argues that the Catholic Church has rightly defined God as one in accordance with Scripture which teaches that there are not many Gods, but only one God. The relational dimension of the one God, called the Trinity, is implicitly and explicitly taught in the bible.[345]

---

[344] Patrick Madrid, "Mormonism's God(s)" Patrick Madrid.com. According to the Mormon foundational revelatory text, *The Pearl of Great Price*, prior to becoming a God, the Father of Jesus was born a human being on a planet orbiting the Kolob star. Similarly, his son Jesus was born a man on earth before he became a God. *The Pearl of Great Price*, Abraham 3.

[345] "In the beginning was the Word, and the Word was with God, and the Word was God. He was in the beginning with God." (John 1:1-2 NRSV); "Are you greater than our father Abraham, who died? The prophets also died. Who do you claim to be?" Jesus answered, "If I glorify myself, my glory is nothing. It is my Father who glorifies me, he of whom you say, 'He is our God,' though you do not know him. But I know him; if I would say that I do not know him, I would be a liar like you. But I do know him and I keep his word. Your ancestor Abraham rejoiced that he would see my day; he saw it and was glad." Then the Jews said to him, "You are not yet fifty years old, and have you seen Abraham?" Jesus said to them, "Very truly, I tell you, before Abraham was, I am." So they picked up stones to throw

Due to the rise of heresies, in the second century of Christian history the teaching of God as three in one was clarified with the term Trinity. The first record we have the word Trinity being used in a Christian context was by Bishop Theophilus of Antioch. In his *Apologia ad Autolycum* (181 AD), Theophilus used the Greek word for Trinity when referring to God the Father, God the Son, as Logos, and God the Holy Spirit, as Sophia.[346] Later, the Latin Father Tertullian (160-225 AD) used the Latin word *trinitas* when referring to the three divine persons.[347]

According to Catholic belief in God as Triune, God is being itself (*ipsum esse*) that by being itself, by being existence itself, is not caused. As existence

---

at him, but Jesus hid himself and went out of the temple." (John 8:53-59 NRSV). In identifying himself as "I am" Jesus is referring to the book of Exodus (3:14) when God tells Moses "'I am who I am.' He said further, 'Thus you shall say to the Israelites, 'I am has sent me to you.'" The Jewish listeners of Jesus' words would have understood that Jesus was identifying himself with God. This explains why in John 8:59 "they picked up stones to throw at him." (NRSV) With respect to the Holy Spirit as God see Acts 5:3-4 and 1 Corinthians 3:16. Scripture passages on the Triune nature of the one God include the following: Matthew 3:16-17, 28:19; 2 Corinthians 13:14. That God is one is clearly taught in Deuteronomy 6:4; 1 Corinthians 8:4; Galatians 3:20; and 1 Timothy 2:5.

[346] Theophilus of Antioch, "Apologia ad Autolycum Book 2, Chapter 15," http://www.earlychristianwritings.com/text/ theophilus-book2.html, Early Christian Writings (accessed March 30, 2015).

[347] Tertullian, "Adversus Praxean," Chapter 3, http://www.tertullian.org/works/adversus_praxean.htm, Tertullian.org (accessed March 31, 2015).

itself, as the ground and foundation of all contingent, dependent beings, God is the first cause of all beings. Contingent, dependent beings cannot rely on an endless line of other prior dependent contingent beings for existence since this would mean that all beings are receivers of existence. If all are only mere receivers of existence, then it is impossible for the reality of existence to be given. There must, therefore, be a necessary being itself that is the source of all being and did not receive its existence from anyone else. Simply the presence of people wanting to borrow books is not the necessary condition of a library. There first must be someone to lend books in order for people to receive and borrow the books. In this sense, God is like a divine librarian who loans us existence, which properly belongs to him alone. Catholics believe that the Triune God wants to lend, wants to share His existence since He is a communion of persons.

With respect to the idea that there could be two or more infinite Gods who give us existence, it is impossible for there to be two or more infinite grounds of all being of existence itself since these infinities would cancel each other out. If there were a number of infinite, distinct beings they would cancel each other out, since infinities cannot share infinity with one another without contradicting their infinite nature.[348]

---

[348] Patrick Madrid and Elder Gary Coleman, *The First Catholic – Mormon Dialogue*, 2 CDs (1990). According to the same logic, Madrid adds that proposing the actual existence of an infinite number of events leads

Fr. Peter Samuel Kucer, MSA

Extra-Biblical Public Revelation

According to the Mormon Elder Frank Bradshaw, there can be and have been additional public revelations to the New Testament. Mormons believe that revelation comes from the Father, through Jesus Christ, and through the prophets, some of whom were born after Jesus Christ.[349] One example of further public revelation that complements while not replacing the New Testament is, Mormons believe, *The Book of Mormon*. According to the introduction of The Book of Mormon:

> The Book of Mormon is a volume of holy scripture comparable to the Bible. It is a record of God's dealings with ancient inhabitants of the Americas and contains the fullness of the everlasting gospel. The book was written by many ancient prophets by the spirit of prophecy and revelation. Their words, written on gold plates, were quoted and abridged by a prophet-historian named Mormon. The record gives an account of two great civilizations. One came from Jerusalem in 600 B.C. and afterward separated into two nations, known as the

---

to contradictions, such as result of subtracting infinity from infinity. If the answer is zero than infinity does not actually exist.

[349] Patrick Madrid and Elder Frank Bradshaw, *The Second Catholic-Mormon Dialogue*, 2 CDs (1991).

Nephites and the Lamanites. The other came much earlier when the Lord confounded the tongues at the Tower of Babel. This group is known as the Jaredites. After thousands of years, all were destroyed except the Lamanites, and they are among the ancestors of the American Indians. The crowning event recorded in the Book of Mormon is the personal ministry of the Lord Jesus Christ among the Nephites soon after His resurrection. It puts forth the doctrines of the gospel, outlines the plan of salvation, and tells men what they must do to gain peace in this life and eternal salvation in the life to come. After Mormon completed his writings, he delivered the account to his son Moroni, who added a few words of his own and hid up the plates in the Hill Cumorah. On September 21, 1823, the same Moroni, then a glorified, resurrected being, appeared to the Prophet Joseph Smith and instructed him relative to the ancient record and its destined translation into the English language. In due course the plates were delivered to Joseph Smith, who translated them by the gift and power of God. The record is now published in many languages as a new and additional witness that Jesus Christ is the Son of the living God and that all who will come unto Him and obey the laws and ordinances of His gospel may be saved.

Concerning this record the Prophet Joseph Smith said: "I told the brethren that the Book of Mormon was the most correct of any book on earth, and the keystone of our religion, and a man would get nearer to God by abiding by its precepts, than by any other book." In addition to Joseph Smith, the Lord provided for eleven others to see the gold plates for themselves and to be special witnesses of the truth and divinity of the Book of Mormon. Their written testimonies are included herewith as "The Testimony of Three Witnesses" and "The Testimony of Eight Witnesses." We invite all men everywhere to read the Book of Mormon, to ponder in their hearts the message it contains, and then to ask God, the Eternal Father, in the name of Christ if the book is true. Those who pursue this course and ask in faith will gain a testimony of its truth and divinity by the power of the Holy Ghost. (See Moroni 10:3–5.) Those who gain this divine witness from the Holy Spirit will also come to know by the same power that Jesus Christ is the Savior of the world, that Joseph Smith is His revelator and prophet in these last days, and that The Church of Jesus Christ of Latter-day Saints is the Lord's kingdom once again established on the earth, preparatory to the Second Coming of the Messiah.[350]

In responding to Bradshaw, Madrid explained that we cannot teach a baby to tie his shoes, nor teach a baby proper table manners, since a baby does not yet have the capacity to understand our instructions. As the baby grows into a child and then into an adult his capacity to understand and learn from his parents also ordinarily grows. Similarly, after the Fall and expulsion from the Garden of Eden, humans underwent a process of development. Respecting this law of growth extended throughout history, God gradually imparted his teaching. Only at the fullness of time (Galatians 4:4), when the time was right, did God send His son as the fullness of revelation. After the coming of Jesus, there will be no further public revelation since no prophet can surpass the revelation give through Jesus who is the only Son of God.

The Mormon difficulty of accepting that there can be a fullness of disclosure during a particular time in history is reflective of a modern approach to reality. In describing this modern mindset, Cardinal Avery Dulles writes, "The modern mind, deeply impressed by the limitations imposed by the particularities of time and culture, has difficulty in admitting that there can be any absolute or unsurpassable disclosure within history. Even

---

[350] *The Book of Mormon: Another Testament of Jesus Christ* (Salt Lake City: The Church of Jesus Christ of Latter-day Saints, 2013), vii.

thinkers who reject the inevitability of progress and deny that 'later is better' consider that each age may be able to surpass its predecessors in some respects and to equate revelation with an ancient deposit would condemn the church to a continual loss of vitality and actuality."[351]

In countering this modern assumption, Vatican Council II pastorally, explains Dulles:

> avoided repeating the formula sometimes, used that revelation 'ceased with the death of the last apostle.' Instead, after describing Jesus as the perfecter and fulfillment of revelation, it stated: 'The Christian dispensation, therefore, as the new and definitive covenant, will never pass away, and we await no further public revelation before the glorious manifestation of our Lord Jesus Christ.[352] In the Constitution on the Church Vatican II depicted the church as capable of showing forth 'in the world the mystery of the Lord in a faithful though shadowed way, until at the last it will be revealed in total splendor'[353] These two statements avoid giving the impression that the church already possesses a total grasp of revelation in its fullness, but at the same

---

[351] Francis Schussler Fiorenza and John P. Galvin, *Systematic Theology Roman Catholic Perspectives Volume I* (Minneapolis: Fortress Press,1991), 101.

[352] 1 Tim. 6:14 and Tit. 2:13; *Dei Verbum* 4.

[353] *Lumen Gentium* 8.

Catholic Apologetics

time they emphasize the church's obligation to adhere faithfully to the 'mystery of the Lord,' the 'Christian dispensation,' the 'new and definitive covenant.'[354]

Catholics, consequently, agree with Mormons that we can grow in understanding revelation given in its fullness through Jesus Christ. However, due to our belief that as the Son of God Jesus "perfected revelation by fulfilling it,"[355] there will be no "further new public revelation before the manifestation of our Lord Jesus Christ."[356] Concretely, this means that The Book of Mormon is not an inspired text that contains further public revelation.

In arguing against the revelatory character of the Book of Mormon, Madrid points out that the

---

[354] "On at least two occasions the Theological Commission or its subcommissions rejected several *modi* requesting that *Dei Verbum*, no 4, be amended to state explicitly that revelation was closed (*clausam*) with the death of the apostles. See the *relationes* of July 3, 1964, and November 20, 1964. These are found respectively in the *Acta Synodalia Sacrosancti Concilii Oecumenic Vaticani II*, Periodus 3, vol. 3 (1974), and Periodus 4, vol. 1 (1976), p. 345." Francis Schussler Fiorenza and John P. Galvin, *Systematic Theology Roman Catholic Perspectives Volume I* (Minneapolis: Fortress Press,1991), 101-102.

[355] "Dogmatic Constitution on Divine Revelation: Dei Verbum," November 18, 1965, vatican.va, http://www.vatican.va/archive/hist_councils/ii_vatican_council/documents/vat-ii_const_19651118_dei-verbum_en.html (accessed September 29, 2016), 4.

[356] "Dogmatic Constitution on Divine Revelation: Dei Verbum," November 18, 1965, 4.

Mormon belief that Jewish prophets and tribes lived in South America is not supported by any archaeological evidence and even contradicts archaeological data. For example, there is no archaeological evidence of a 400 AD battle that the Book of Mormon describes taking place in America between the Nephites and Lamanites in which supposedly half a million of people died. It is highly reasonable to expect archaeologists would have discovered some evidence of this destructive battle, yet no such evidence exists.

Textual evidence obtained from the Book of Mormon tends to discredit its authenticity as an inspired document. For example, textual errors associated with the King James Bible from Joseph Smith's time are also present in the Book of Mormon. In addition, although the Book of Mormon describes horses in America before the Spanish arrived in the 1400s and 1500s, there is no evidence that horses existed prior to the arrival of the Spanish.[357]

Recent Developments in Mormonism

According to Joseph Smith's *Teachings* in Chapter Two, "God the Eternal Father":

---

[357] Patrick Madrid and Elder Frank Bradshaw, *The Second Catholic-Mormon Dialogue*, 2 CDs (1991); Crista Luis, Cristiane Bastos-Silveria, E. Gus Cothran and Maria do Mar Oom, "Iberian Origins of New World Horse Breeds," *Journal of Heredity*, December 21 (2005).

God Himself was once as we are now, and is an exalted man, and sits enthroned in yonder heavens! That is the great secret. If the veil were rent today, and the great God who holds this world in its orbit, and who upholds all worlds and all things by His power, was to make Himself visible,—I say, if you were to see Him today, you would see Him like a man in form—like yourselves in all the person, image, and very form as a man; for Adam was created in the very fashion, image and likeness of God, and received instruction from, and walked, talked and conversed with Him, as one man talks and communes with another.[358]

The close disciple of Joseph Smith, Lorenzo Snow and fifth president of the Mormons, summarized Joseph Smith's teaching on Eternal Progression with, "As man now is, God once was; as God now is, man may be."[359] According to the Mormon Teacher Support Consultant Gerald N. Lund that although, "To my knowledge there has been no 'official' pronouncement by the First

---

[358] Joseph Smith, "Chapter 2: God the Eternal Father," lds.org, https://www.lds.org/manual/teachings-joseph-smith/chapter-2?lang=eng (accessed October 2, 2016). The following is cited, *Teachings of Presidents of the Church: Joseph Smith* (2011), 36–44.

[359] Gerald N. Lund, "I Have a Question," lds.org, https://www.lds.org/ensign/1982/02/i-have-a-question?lang=eng (accessed October 2, 2016).

Presidency declaring that President Snow's couplet is to be accepted as doctrine. But that is not a valid criteria for determining whether or not it *is* doctrine."[360]

Lund then cites numerous official Mormon sources that teach the doctrine which this couplet of Snow captures. Afterwards, Lund concludes with, "It is clear that the teaching of President Lorenzo Snow is both acceptable and accepted doctrine in the Church today."[361] Lund's assertion appears to contradict the response of Gordon Hinckley who was the president of the Mormon Church in 1997. In April of 1997, when Hinckley was asked if Snow's couplet is official doctrine he responded with, "I wouldn't say that. There was a little couplet coined, 'As man is, God once was. As God is, man may become.' Now that's more of a couplet than anything else. That gets into some pretty deep theology that we don't know very much about."[362]

In interpreting Hinckley's statement and other similar statements issued by Mormons, Richard J. Mouw writes:

---

[360] Gerald N. Lund, "I Have a Question."

[361] Gerald N. Lund, "Is President Lorenzo Snow's oft-repeated statement-'As man now is, God once was; as God now is, man may be' – accepted as official doctrine by the Church?" lds.org, https://www.lds.org/ensign/1982/02/i-have-a-question?lang=eng (accessed October 2, 2016).

[362] Richard J. Mouw, "Mormons Approaching Orthodoxy," May 2016, *First Things*, http://www.firstthings.com/article/2016/05/mormons-approaching-orthodoxy (accessed May 14, 2016).

Hinckley was signaling a decision on the part of the Mormon leadership to downplay the Snow couplet within the corpus of Mormon teachings about the deity, not just to outsiders, but within their own community. This suggests that contemporary Mormonism is interested in joining the broad Jewish and Christian consensus that God is ontologically different from man—or at least that Mormons today don't want to directly contradict that consensus. Again, we're faced with a choice. Will we approach Mormonism under the assumption that its theology is heretical beyond repair? Or will we adopt the more optimistic assumption that Mormonism is capable of self-reformation?

The questions that Mouw raises are important ones when engaging with Mormons. It is possible that Mormons are increasingly being open to the Holy Spirit's desire to reform their doctrines in accordance with the truth of Jesus Christ and His Mystical Body the Catholic Church. When relating to Mormons may we keep this in mind and encourage further reformation by Mormons with the hope they will embrace Catholicism.

Quiz 11

1. Define the Mormon position of apostasy and restoration and then argue against it. Include the following in your response: Revelation 22, Joseph Smith, Church of Latter Day Saints, Matthew 16:18, Christ's promises, weed and wheat parable, apostolic succession, Pope St. Clement's *Letter to the Church of Corinth*.

2. Contrast the Mormon belief in Gods with the Catholic belief in the Trinity. Include the following in your response: the logical possibility of more than one infinite being, Sacred Scripture and Monotheism, Eternal Progression, Jesus, God the Father, and Kolob (see the footnotes).

3. Contrast the Catholic position on revelation and prophecy with the Mormon position. Include the following in your response: the bible, public revelation, prophets, apostasy, and false prophecy.

4. Contrast the Catholic position on the *Book of Mormon* with the Mormon position. Include the following in your response: bible, *Book of Mormon*, 400 AD battle between the Nephites and Lamanites, King James bible, textual errors, and anachronisms.

5. What are possible signs within recent development of Mormon theology of inner-reformative efforts that are bringing Mormonism closer to Catholicism? Include in your answer the following: Snow's couplet, Hinckley's statement, and self-reformation.

Additional Activities and Resources

Respond to the following. Do so according to the Socratic method of gathering, clarifying and challenging questions:

- In the first century of Christianity, the Church completely lost the faith.
- "As man now is, God once was; as God now is, man may be."
- There are an infinite number of infinite Gods.
- Public revelations are on ongoing reality.
- The Book of Mormon was revealed by God. It contains public revelation.

Readings

Deuteronomy 6:4, Isaiah 43-45
Paragraphs 198-327 of the *Catechism of the Catholic Church*
The Book of Mormon
The Pearl of Great Price
Teachings of Presidents of the Church: Joseph

Smith

Audio

Madrid, Patrick and Elder Gary Coleman. *The First Catholic – Mormon Dialogue*. 2 CDs (1990).
Madrid, Patrick and Elder Gary Coleman. *The Second Catholic-Mormon Dialogue*. 2 CDs (1991).

Chapter Twelve: Hinduism, Buddhism, Islam

Introduction

This final chapter will present Catholic doctrine that responds to teachings of Hinduism, Buddhism and Islam. We will begin with Hinduism. Especially when we engage in inter-religious dialogue may we remember the sage advice of Gustave Thibon: "Do you enter the match armed with powerful arguments, when your adversary expects a hug from you? Before proving him that you are right, tell him that you love him. After having hugged him, your poorest arguments will become irrefutable."[363]

Hinduism

Hinduism is not a word that originated from the

---

[363] Eusebe Menard, *Rule of Life* (1987), 224. Gustave Thibon (1903-2001) was a French Philosopher who convered to Catholicism.

land we associate with modern day India but rather is of Persian origin. The Persians live West of India in Iran, which is also known as Persia. The Persian based term "Hindu" means people from "the region of the Indus."[364] The Indus people developed a civilization around the Indus river that navigates through Pakistan and India. Currently, the term Hinduism is used as a catch term for many of the diverse religions of India. We will respond only to a dominant religious expression of "Hinduism," called Vedanta Hinduism.

The most sacred texts for Vedanta Hinduism, and other forms of Hinduism, are the Sanskrit written Vedas. The Vedas are divided into four books: Rigveda, Yajurveda, Samaveda and Atharvaveda. Each of these four books contain different types of writings. The text that we will focus on are the Upanishads.[365] The Upanishads (c. 900-500 BC) refer to the texts of the four books of the Vedas which focus on philosophy, prayer, spirituality and theology. The following quote from the Upanishads contains a central theological belief of Vedanta Hinduism:

> That self [Atman] is indeed Brahman.... Therefore the self is identified with desire alone....Thus does the man who desires (transmigrate). But the man who does not

---

[364] "Hindu," Online Etymology Dictionary, http://etymonline.com/index.php?term=Hindu&allowed_in_frame=0 (accessed July 10, 2015).

[365] Also called the Vedanta.

desire (never transmigrates). Of him who is without desires, who is free from desires, the objects of whose desire have been attained, and to whom all objects of desire are but the Self-the organs do not depart. Being but Brahman, he is merged in Brahman.[366]

According to the excerpt, as interpreted by the Vedanta Hindu Shankara (788-822), all souls are equivalent to the universal soul called the Brahman.[367] This means that it is an illusion to think individuals exist, since only Brahman, the universal soul, exists.

In contrast with Vedanta, Hindu monism, Catholicism teaches that there is a Creator, who as the foundation of all existence, as the ground of all being, created the world. This means that as we free ourselves of illusions about our identity we find our identity in the creator God by participating more deeply in His nature while at the same time retaining our fundamental difference from God as

---

[366] *The Brhadaranyaka Upanisad*, trans. Swami Madhavananda (Almora: Advaita Ashrama, 1950), 4.4.5-4.4.6, pp. 712- 717.

[367] Shankara wrote highly influential commentaries on the Upanishads. According to Shankara the four fundamental doctrines of the Upanishads, explains Jeanneane D. Fowler, are "1. Brahman is consciousness, 2. I am Brahman. 3. That you are. 4. This Atman is Brahman." Jeanneane D. Fowler, *Perspectives of Reality: An Introduction to the Philosophy of Hinduism* (Brighton: Sussex Academic Press, 2002), 239.

the creator, and from other creatures, each of which participates in God's being in diverse, complementary ways. In distinguishing God's absolute existence from our participated existence, Aquinas explains, "If, therefore, He [God] is not His own existence He will not be essential, but participated being. He will not therefore be the first being-which is absurd. Therefore God is His own existence, and not merely His own essence."[368] In other words, if we maintain along Vedanta Hinduism that there is no essential difference between God and creation, then we how can we explain the existence of anything? After all, out of nothing comes nothing. Only God is the non-dependent being, as being itself, who brought forth existence out of nothing.

Buddhism

Like Hinduism, Buddhism consists of many schools. Unlike Hinduism, Buddhism is traceable to one founder, Prince Siddhartha Gautama (563-483 BC). Gautama was born in modern day Nepal, situated by India's north eastern border. According to Gautama, also known as the Buddha, if people follow his way to enlightenment by practicing "contemplation," then they will be freed from being

---

[368] Thomas Aquinas, *Summa Theologica*, trans. Fathers of the Dominican Province (Allen: Christian Classics, 1981), I, q. 3, art. 4.

repeatedly reborn into this world of suffering.[369] Those who are not enlightened will continue to be reborn into this world of suffering. The way to be freed is contained in Buddha's teaching called the Four Noble Truths: suffering exists, the cause of suffering is desire, the remedy for suffering is to be freed from desire by following the eight-fold path:

~ The Four Noble Truths ~

[1] Suffering, as a noble truth, is this: Birth is suffering, aging is suffering, sickness is suffering, death is suffering, sorrow and lamentation, pain, grief and despair are suffering; association with the loathed is suffering, dissociation from the loved is suffering, not to get what one wants is suffering — in short, suffering is the five categories of clinging objects.

[2] The origin of suffering, as a noble truth, is this: It is the craving that produces renewal of being accompanied by enjoyment and lust, and enjoying this and that; in other words, craving for sensual desires, craving for being, craving for non-being.

---

[369] Asvaghosa, *The Buddha-Carita, or Life of the Buddha, or Acts of the Buddha*, ed. Edward B. Cowell supplemented by Anandajoti Bhikkhu with E.H. Johnson's translation of Asvaghosa's work, book XII, no. 103, http://ancient-buddhist-texts.net/Texts-and-Translations/Buddhacarita/Buddhacarita.pdf (accessed June 6, 22).

[3] Cessation of suffering, as a noble truth, is this: It is remainderless fading and ceasing, giving up, relinquishing, letting go and rejecting, of that same craving.

[4] The way leading to cessation of suffering, as a noble truth, is this: It is simply the noble eightfold path, that is to say, right view, right intention; right speech, right action, right livelihood; right effort, right mindfulness, right concentration.[370]

---

[370] "Dhammacakkappavattana Sutta: Setting Rolling the Wheel of Truth" (SN 56.11), translated from the Pali by Ñanamoli Thera. *Access to Insight (Legacy Edition)*, 13 June 2010, http://www.accesstoinsight.org/tipitaka/sn/sn56/ sn56.011.nymo.html. The means Buddha proposed to be released from suffering are called the Eight Fold Path. In listing these means Buddha taught, "It is the Noble Eightfold path, and nothing else, namely: right understanding, right thought, right speech, right action, right livelihood, right effort, right mindfulness and right concentration. This is the Middle Path realized by the Tathagata [the Buddha] which gives vision, which gives knowledge, and leads to calm, to insight, to enlightenment, and to Nibbana [Nirvana]." "Dhammacakkappavattana Sutta: Setting in Motion the Wheel of Truth" (SN 56.11), translated from the Pali by Piyadassi Thera. *Access to Insight (Legacy Edition)*, 30 November 2013, http://www.accesstoinsight.org/tipitaka/sn/sn56/sn56.011.piya.html. In chart form these means can be categorized in the following manner:

In contrasting the Buddhist method for salvation with Catholic belief, Pope St. John Paul II explained:

> The *Buddhist doctrine of salvation* constituted the central point, or rather the only point, of this system. Nevertheless, both the Buddhist tradition and the methods deriving from it have an almost exclusively *negative soteriology*.
>
> The "enlightenment" experience by Buddha comes down to the conviction that the world is bad, that it is the source of evil and of suffering for man. To liberate oneself from this evil, one must free oneself from this world, necessitating a break with the ties that join us to external reality—ties existing in our human nature, in our psyche, in our

Philosophy (or Wisdom)	Morality (or Ethics)	Spirituality
1. "Right View or Understanding"	3. "Right Speech"	6. "Right Effort"
2. "Right Thoughts or Intentions"	4. "Right Action"	7. "Right Mindfulness"
	5. " Right Livelihood"	8. "Right Concentration"

The direct quotes are within quotations. The schema is mine. Venerable Dr. Balangoda Ananda Maitreya Mahanayaka Thera Abhidhaja Maharatthaguru Aggamaha Pandita DLitt D Litt, Jayasili, *Introducing Buddhism* (Taipei: The Corporate Body of the Buddha Educational Foundation, 1993), 6.

bodies. The more we are liberated from these ties, the more we become indifferent to what is in the world, and the more we are freed from suffering, from the evil that has its source in the world.

Do we draw near to God in this way? This is not mentioned in the "enlightenment" conveyed by Buddha. Buddhism is in large measure an *"atheistic" system*. We do not free ourselves from evil through the good which comes from God; we liberate ourselves only through detachment from the world, which is bad. The fullness of such a detachment is not union with God, but what is called nirvana, a state of perfect indifference with regard to the world. *To save oneself* means, above all, to free oneself from evil by becoming indifferent to the world, *which is the source of evil*. This is the culmination of the spiritual process.[371]

The negative approach to the world and salvation that John Paul II identifies in Buddhism is particularly present in two forms of Buddhism, both of which emphasize nothingness: Theravada Buddhism and Zen Buddhism. Theravada Buddhism emphasizes nothingness with the doctrine of no-self. In explaining this doctrine, the Theravada

---

[371] John Paul II, *Crossing the Threshold of Hope*, trans. Jenny McPhee and Martha McPhee (New York: Alfred A. Knopf, 2005), 85-86

Buddhist monk Rahula states:

> Buddhism stands unique in the history of human thought in denying the existence of such a Soul, Self, or *Atman*. According to the teaching of the Buddha, the idea of self is an imaginary, false belief which has no corresponding reality, and it produces harmful thoughts of 'me' and 'mine', selfish desire, craving, attachment, hatred, ill-will, conceit, pride, egotism, and other defilements, impurities and problems. It is the source of all the troubles in the world from personal conflicts to wars between nations. In short, to this false view can be traced all the evil in the world.[372]

Zen Buddhism, predominant in Japan, also emphasizes nothingness. In teaching the Zen doctrine of nothingness, the prominent Zen Buddhist Dogen (1200-1253) wrote, "To study the Buddha way is to study the self. To study the self is to forget the self. To forget the self is to be actualized by myriad things. When actualized by myriad things, your body and mind as well as the bodies and minds of others drop away. No trace of realization remains, and this no-trace continues

---

[372] Steven Collins, *Selfless Persons: Imagery and Thought in Theravada Buddhism* (Cambridge: Cambridge University Press, 1982), 4.

endlessly."[373]

According to Catholic belief in creation, God, as existence itself, as that which is not dependent on anything, or anyone else, created something out of nothing (*creatio ex nihilo*). What is most fundamental in the Catholic mind to existence, therefore, is someone who is God. In contrast, what is most fundamental for Theravada and Zen Buddhism is not someone, or even something, but nothing. But since nothing comes from nothing, how is it possible to even have something, even illusions, since an illusion is still something? Furthermore, as pointed out by Malcolm David Eckel, the doctrine of no-self is irrational from the standpoint of the Buddhist doctrine of reincarnation. Eckel reveals this inner contradiction in the no-self doctrine with the doctrine of reincarnation by asking, "If there is no self, what is reborn?"[374]

Finally, the Theravada and Zen Buddhist emphasis on nothingness is based on the teaching of attaining nirvana that all Buddhists hold since Buddha clearly taught this. Often, nirvana is translated into enlightenment, but if the etymology of the Sanskrit word nirvana is carefully looked out

---

[373] "Actualizing the Fundamental Point, the Genjo-koan," trans. Robert Aitken and Kazuaki Tanahashi, The Zen Site, http://www.thezensite.com/ZenTeachings/Dogen_Teachings/GenjoKoan_Aitken.htm (accessed July 11, 2015).

[374] Malcolm David Eckel, *Great World Religions: Buddhism*, Course Guidebook (Chantilly: Great Courses, 2003), 14.

we see that nirvana literally means "a blowing out".[375] In other words, Buddhism stresses *despiration*,[376] while Catholicism stresses inspiration, since we, as followers of Christ, are to allow the Holy Spirit to fill us with His inspirations. Catholicism teaches that we are to seek to be breathed into by God and not blown out.

Islam

In 570 AD, the great promoter of Islam, Muhammad, was born in Mecca of modern day Saudi Arabia. Rather than perceiving Muhammad as the founder of Islam, Muslims believe that he was the prophet of the true religion of God which has been distorted in various religions. Christianity, it is claimed, distorted the true religion by its excessive emphasis on the next world, on mercy and with its Trinitarian doctrine. It is also believed by Muslims that Judaism distorted the true religion in the opposite direction with the Jewish emphasis on justice, law and this world. Muhammad believed he was specially chosen by God as God's greatest prophet to purify religions of these and other errors.[377]

---

[375] "Nirvana," Online Etymology Dictionary http://etymonline.com/index.php?allowed_in_frame=0&search=nirvana&searchmode=none (accessed July 5, 2015).

[376] "Nirvana," Online Etymology Dictionary.

[377] Gabriel Said Reynolds, "Jesus the Muslim Hippie," *First Things* December (2013), 23; *Koran*,

In time, after a succession of military victories, Muhammad amassed a large following of Arab clans. Under his leadership, in 630 they captured the city of Mecca, the city from which Muhammad had been banished in 622.[378] The following year, in 631, the majority of Arab tribes in awe of Muhammad's military skills allied themselves with Muhammad and his followers.[379] The peak of Muhammad's fame lasted very briefly since in June of 632 he died after he completed a pilgrimage to Mecca. The five essential practices of all followers of Muhammad's Islam are as follows:

1. The Creed
   The Creed is, "I bear witness that there is no god but God and Muhammad is the messenger of God."[380]
2. Daily Prayers
   Muslims are required to pray five prescribed times a day.[381]
3. Mandatory Almsgiving
4. Fasting

---

trans. Marmaduke Pickthall (New York: Alfred A. Knopf, 1992), xx-xxi.

[378] This banishment is called the Hijrah.

[379] Richard A. Gabriel, *Muhammad: Islam's First General* (Norman: University of Oklahoma Press, 2007), xviii-xix.

[380] Tamara Sonn, *Islam: A Brief History* Second Edition (Oxford: Blackwell Publishing Ltd., 2010), 29.

[381] Tamara Sonn, *Islam: A Brief History*, 29.

During the ninth Islamic month of Ramadan, Muslims who are physically capable are required to fast from sunrise to sunset.[382]

5. At Least One Pilgrimage to Mecca For Those Capable of Doing So[383]

Prominent Catholics around the time of Islam's rise to prominence viewed Islam not as a separate religion but rather as a Christian heresy. The reason was that according to early Muslim and early Christian records, Muhammad was instructed by a Christian Syrian heretic Bahira, also known as Sergius the Monk.[384] According to St. John of Damascus (c. 675-749):

> There is also the superstition of the Ishmaelites which to this day prevails and keeps people in error, being a forerunner of the Antichrist. They are descended from Ishmael, [who] was born to Abraham of Agar, and for this reason they are called both Agarenes and Ishmaelites. They are also called Saracens, which is derived from

---

[382] Tamara Sonn, *Islam: A Brief History* Second Edition (Oxford: Blackwell Publishing Ltd., 2010), 30.

[383] Tamara Sonn, *Islam: A Brief History*, 30.

[384] A. Abel "Bahira," *Enclyopedia of Islam, Second Edition*, Brill Online, 2013, http://referenceworks.brillonline.com/search?s.q=bahira&s.f.s2_parent=s.f.book.encyclopaedia-of-islam-2&search-go=Search (accessed April 28, 2015). Ibn Ishaq (died c. 770), Ibn Sa'd (784-845), Ibn Hisham (died c. 828) al-Tabari (839-923 AD) all refer in their writings to Muhammed's meeting with Bahira.

Sarras kenoi, or destitute of Sara, because of what Agar said to the angel: 'Sara hath sent me away destitute.' These used to be idolaters and worshiped the morning star and Aphrodite, whom in their own language they called Khabár, which means great. And so down to the time of Heraclius they were very great idolaters. From that time to the present a false prophet named Mohammed has appeared in their midst. This man, after having chanced upon the Old and New Testaments and likewise, it seems, having conversed with an Arian monk, devised his own heresy. Then, having insinuated himself into the good graces of the people by a show of seeming piety, he gave out that a certain book had been sent down to him from heaven. He had set down some ridiculous compositions in this book of his and he gave it to them as an object of veneration.[385]

The modern, British Catholic historian Hilaire Belloc also held that Islam is a heresy and not a new religion. In arguing this Belloc wrote:

---

[385] "St. John of Damascus's Critique of Islam," Orthodox Christian Information Center, http://orthodoxinfo.com/general/stjohn_islam.aspx (accessed April 30, 2015). The source is from the "*Writings*, by St John of Damascus, *The Fathers of the Church*, vol. 37 (Washington, DC: Catholic University of America Press, 1958), pp. 153-160. Posted 26 March, 2006."

Mohammedanism was a heresy: that is the essential point to grasp before going any further. It began as a heresy, not as a new religion. It was not a pagan contrast with the Church; it was not an alien enemy. It was a perversion of Christian doctrine. Its vitality and endurance soon gave it the appearance of a new religion, but those who were contemporary with its rise saw it for what it was not a denial, but an adaptation and a misuse, of the Christian thing. It differed from most (not from all) heresies in this, that it did not arise within the bounds of the Christian Church. The chief heresiarch, Mohammed himself, was not, like most heresiarchs, a man of Catholic birth and doctrine to begin with. He sprang from pagans. But that which he taught was in the main Catholic doctrine, oversimplified. It was the great Catholic world on the frontiers of which he lived, whose influence was all around him and whose territories he had known by travel which inspired his convictions. He came of, and mixed with, the degraded idolaters of the Arabian wilderness, the conquest of which had never seemed worth the Romans' while.

...

Mohammed preached with insistence that prime Catholic doctrine, on the human side the immortality of the soul and its responsibility for actions in this life, coupled with the consequent doctrine of punishment and reward after death. If anyone sets down those points that orthodox Catholicism has in common with Mohammedanism, and those points only, one might imagine if one went no further that there should have been no cause of quarrel. Mohammed would almost seem in this aspect to be a sort of missionary, preaching and spreading by the energy of his character the chief and fundamental doctrines of the Catholic Church among those who had hitherto been degraded pagans of the Desert. He gave to Our Lord the highest reverence, and to Our Lady also, or that matter. On the Day of Judgment (another Catholic idea which he taught) it was Our Lord, according to Mohammed, who would be the judge of mankind, not he, Mohammed. The Mother of Christ, Our Lady, "the Lady Miriam" was ever for him the first of womankind. His followers even got from the early fathers some vague hint of her Immaculate Conception.

But the central point where this new heresy struck home with a mortal blow against Catholic tradition was a full denial of the Incarnation. Mohammed did not merely take the first steps toward that denial, as the

Arians and their followers had done; he advanced a clear affirmation, full and complete, against the whole doctrine of an incarnate God. He taught that Our Lord was the greatest of all the prophets, but still only a prophet: a man like other men. He eliminated the Trinity altogether.

With that denial of the Incarnation went the whole sacramental structure. He refused to know anything of the Eucharist, with its Real Presence; he stopped the sacrifice of the Mass, and therefore the institution of a special priesthood. In other words, he, like so many other lesser heresiarchs, founded his heresy on simplification.

...

Mohammed's teaching never developed among the mass of his followers, or in his own mind, a detailed theology. He was content to accept all that appealed to him in the Catholic scheme and to reject all that seemed to him, and to so many others of his time, too complicated or mysterious to be true. Simplicity was the note of the whole affair; and since all heresies draw their strength from some true doctrine, Mohammedanism drew its strength from the true Catholic doctrines which it retained: the equality of all men before God

"All true believers are brothers." It zealously preached and throve on the paramount claims of justice, social and economic.[386]

In critiquing Islam, Benedict XVI in his September 12th, 2006, lecture at Germany's University of Regensburg chose to focus not on what Islam has in common with Christianity but rather how they essentially differ. He did so in reference to a written account of a 1391 conversation between the Christian Byzantine Emperor Manuel Palaeologus with an educated Persian Muslim. The dialogues reveal that, explains Benedict XVI, "for Muslim teaching, God is absolutely transcendent. His will is not bound up with any of our categories, even that of rationality."[387] In his modern edition of these dialogues, Fr. Theodore Khoury comments that influential Islamic, Spanish intellectual Ibn Hazm (994-1064) presented this Islamic understanding of God as pure will by going "so far as to state that God is not bound even by his own word, and that nothing would oblige him to reveal the truth to us.

---

[386] Hilaire Belloc, "The Great Heresies," EWTN, http://www.ewtn.com/library/doctrine/heresy.htm (accessed May, 1, 2015).

[387] Benedict XVI, "Faith, Reason, and the University: Memories and Reflections," Catholic Education Resource Center, http://www.catholiceducation.org/en/education/catholic-contributions/faith-reason-and-the-university-memories-and-reflections.html (accessed May 1, 2015).

Were it God's will, we would even have to practice idolatry."[388] In contrast, Catholicism believes that God is One but also Triune. As Triune, God has two inner processions, the eternal generation of His Word the Son as an act of the divine intellect, and the eternal spiration of the Holy Spirit as an act of divine will.[389] Since God is truth and love, He is

---

[388] Benedict XVI, "Faith, Reason, and the University: Memories and Reflections," Catholic Education Resource Center, http://www.catholiceducation.org/en/education/catholic-contributions/faith-reason-and-the-university-memories-and-reflections.html (accessed May 1, 2015).

[389] Thomas Aquinas, *Summa Theologica,* I, Q. 27, art. 5, newadvent.org, http://www.newadvent.org/summa/1027.htm (accessed October 9, 2016). "The divine processions can be derived only from the actions which remain within the agent. In a nature which is intellectual, and in the divine nature these actions are two, the acts of intelligence and of will. The act of sensation, which also appears to be an operation within the agent, takes place outside the intellectual nature, nor can it be reckoned as wholly removed from the sphere of external actions; for the act of sensation is perfected by the action of the sensible object upon sense. It follows that no other procession is possible in God but the procession of the Word, and of Love."

Frank Sheed distinguishes person from nature in the Trinity in the following way. Christians believe that in the Trinity there are three persons in one nature. Notice that the doctrine of the Trinity is not the same as teaching that there are "three persons in one person" or believing that there are "three natures in one nature". In order to understand why these are not equivalent the terms nature and person need to be defined. Nature indicates what something or someone is. Person indicates who someone is. For example, my nature or essence is a human being. I exist as a unique person who is a human being. With respect to action, nature is the source of my actions. The person is the one who does the action. As a human person I act in accordance with my nature out of which I act. In human beings the ratio of an existing human nature to a person is one to one. For every human nature that exists there is only one human person. There cannot be in fact one human nature with more than one human person even though in some mentally ill individuals suffering from Dissociative Identity Disorder they may think they have multiple personalities. person in it. You could not be a person unless you had a nature, yet it is not your nature that makes you a person...." Frank Sheed, *Theology and Sanctity* (No location given: Catholic Way Publishing, 2014), loc. 11101, 1336, 1376.

To maintain that God must, as man does, only have one nature per person is to make the error of anthropomorphism which means making God conform to man's image. Frank Sheed, *Theology and Sanctity* (No location given: Catholic Way Publishing, 2014), loc. 1041-1152. We, though, are made in God's image and not vice versa. As the Fourth Council of the Lateran defines, "There is one true God...Father Son and Holy Spirit, three persons but one absolutely simple essence, substance or nature." Norman P. Tanner, *Decrees of the Ecumenical Councils: Volume One Nicaea I to Lateran V* (Washington, D.C: Georgetown University Press, 1990), 230. The one divine nature is not shared, for this would indicate there are parts in God. Rather, the one divine nature is possessed in its entirety by each of the three persons. In possessing the divine nature, or Godhead, each person of the Trinity does so in their own unique manner. Frank Sheed, *Theology and Sanctity* (No location given: Catholic Way Publishing, 2014), loc.

bound by his own word since his own Word is God. Therefore, the notion of God contradicting himself signifies that nothingness for God is by his very nature truth, which as truth is not divided and in contradiction with itself. In questioning the Islamic understanding of God as only pure will, Benedict XVI asks:

> At this point, as far as understanding of God and thus the concrete practice of religion is concerned, we are faced with an unavoidable dilemma. Is the conviction that acting unreasonably contradicts God's nature merely a Greek idea, or is it always and intrinsically true? ... A profound encounter of faith and reason is taking place here, an encounter between genuine enlightenment and religion. From the very heart of Christian faith and, at the same time, the heart of Greek thought now joined to faith, Manuel II was able to say: Not to act "with logos" is contrary to God's nature.[390]

1382. In defense of the logical possibility that there could be more than one person in an infinite nature Sheed argues:

"[P]erson and nature are not so indistinguishably one that we can dismiss as unthinkable the idea that, if the nature were infinite, there might be more than one person in it. You could not be a person unless you had a nature, yet it is not your nature that makes you a person...." Frank Sheed, *Theology and Sanctity* (No location given: Catholic Way Publishing, 2014), loc. 1336.

[390] Benedict XVI, "Faith, Reason, and the University:

Quiz 12

1. Respond in a Catholic way to Shankara's absolute monism. Include the following in your response: individual soul, Brahman, Creator, being and participation.
2. Respond in a Catholic way to the Buddhist understanding of suffering. Include the following in your response: Desire, Four Noble Truths, Eight-Fold Path, positive and negative teachings on salvation.
3. Respond from both Catholic faith and from reason, without reference to Revelation, why the Theravada and Zen Buddhist teaching of no-self is problematic. Include the following in your response: individual soul, illusion, existence of evil, Creator and creation, inspiration and reincarnation.
4. According to Hilaire Belloc, why can Islam be understood as a Christian heresy? In your response prove at least four reasons.
5. How can God be three persons in one divine nature? (Read the footnotes before responding.)
6. Contrast the Christian Triune belief in God with the Muslim belief in God. Include the

---

Memories and Reflections," Catholic Education Resource Center, http://www.catholiceducation.org/en/education/catholic-contributions/faith-reason-and-the-university-memories-and-reflections.html (accessed May 1, 2015).

following in your answer: will, intellect, generation, spiration and contradiction in God.

Additional Activities and Resources

Respond to the following. Do so according to the Socratic method of gathering, clarifying and challenging questions:

- Desire is the cause of all suffering.
- Only God exists; all else is an illusion.
- We can be saved and freed by relying on ourselves in meditation.
- The belief in self is the cause of all evil.
- The self is an illusion. Those who are thus deluded are doomed to be reborn.
- In order to be saved, to experience nirvana, the self needs to be extinguished.
- Islam is the true religion that both Judaism and Christianity are a perversion of.
- God is pure will.

Readings

Belloc, Hilaire. "The Great Heresies." EWTN. http://www.ewtn.com/library/doctrine/heresy.htm
Schall, James V. *The Regensburg Lecture*. South Bend: St. Augustine's Press, 2007.

Chapters Six through Eight from Sheed, Frank. *Theology and Sanity*. Catholic Way Publishing, 2014.

www.ingramcontent.com/pod-product-compliance
Lightning Source LLC
Chambersburg PA
CBHW031313160426
43196CB00007B/512